Safety and Risk in Society

snova
New York

Safety and Risk in Society

Why Do (Some) Americans Love Their Guns? Questions and Answers from Both Sides
Michael R. Weisser (Editor)
2022. ISBN: 979-8-88697-202-3 (Softcover)
2022. ISBN: 979-8-88697-373-0 (eBook)

Gun Violence: An American Crisis
Gregory C. McGee (Editor)
2022. ISBN: 979-8-88697-168-2 (Hardcover)
2022. ISBN: 979-8-88697-209-2 (eBook)

An Essential Guide to Occupational Exposure
Marta Madalena Marques de Oliveira, PhD,
Simone Barreira Morais, PhD,
Francisca Pinto Lisboa Martins Rodrigues, PhD (Editors)
2022. ISBN: 978-1-68507-819-5 (Hardcover)
2022. ISBN: 978-1-68507-922-2 (eBook)

Sexual Harassment on Campus, at Work and in STEM Research
Jennifer Powell (Editor)
2021. ISBN: 978-1-53619-575-0 (Hardcover)
2021. ISBN: 978-1-53619-590-3 (eBook)

Sexual Harassment and Assault in Government Agencies
Margaret Brown (Editor)
2021. ISBN: 978-1-53619-576-7 (Hardcover)
2021. ISBN: 978-1-53619-591-0 (eBook)

More information about this series can be found at
https://novapublishers.com/product-category/series/safety-and-risk-in-society/

Joyce B. Dew
Editor

Keeping Our Children Safe Online

snova
New York

Library of Congress Cataloging-in-Publication Data

ISBN: 979-8-88697-659-5

Published by Nova Science Publishers, Inc. † New York

Contents

Preface

Increased internet usage presents many complicated risks such as children's online privacy. Growing bodies of research confirm the link between increased digital media use and depression and higher instances of addiction, anxiety, sleep deprivation, and obesity As discussed in Chapter 1, the Children's Online Privacy Protection Act (COPPA) must be updated to safeguard children online.

Chapter 2 surveys how selected countries from the European Union (EU), namely France, Denmark, Germany, Greece, Portugal, Romania, Spain, Sweden, the United Kingdom (UK) and the laws of the European Union (EU) itself, provide privacy rights for children online.

While social media has changed the way the world communicates, it has also created privacy and safety concerns. Chapter 3 discusses the benefits of social media for children and youth in foster care and provides tips for parents and caregivers who want to help them use social media safely.

Chapter 1

Kids Online during COVID: Child Safety in an Increasingly Digital Age*

Committee on Energy and Commerce

Thursday, March 11, 2021
House of Representatives, Subcommittee on Consumer Protection and Commerce, Committee on Energy and Commerce,
Washington, DC.

The subcommittee met, pursuant to notice, at 10:30 a.m., via Cisco Webex online video conferencing, Hon. Jan Schakowsky (chair of the subcommittee) presiding.

Members present: Representatives Schakowsky, Rush, Castor, Trahan, McNerney, Clarke, Cardenas, Dingell, Soto, Rice, Craig, Fletcher, Pallone, Bilirakis (subcommittee ranking member), Latta, Guthrie, Bucshon, Dunn, Pence, Lesko, Armstrong, and Rodgers.

Also present: Representatives Blunt Rochester and Walberg.

Staff present: Jeffrey C. Carroll, Staff Director; Lisa Goldman, Senior Counsel; Waverly Gordon, General Counsel; Daniel Greene, Professional Staff Member; Tiffany Guarascio, Deputy Staff Director; Perry Hamilton, Clerk; Alex Hoehn-Saric, Chief Counsel, Communications and Consumer Protection; Ed Kaczmarski, Policy Analyst; Zach Kahan, Deputy Director, Outreach and Member Services; Mackenzie Kuhl, Digital Assistant; David

* This is an edited, reformatted and augmented version of Virtual Hearing before the Subcommittee on Consumer Protection and Commerce, of the Committee on Energy and Commerce, House of Representatives, One Hundred Seventeenth Congress, First Session, Serial No. 117–11, dated March 11, 2021.

In: Keeping Our Children Safe Online
Editor: Joyce B. Dew
ISBN: 979-8-88697-659-5

Miller, Counsel; Elysa Montfort, Press Secretary; Kaitlyn Peel, Digital Director; Caroline Rinker, Press Assistant; Tim Robinson, Chief Counsel; Chloe Rodriguez, Clerk; Andrew Souvall, Director of Communications, Outreach and Member Services; Sydney Terry, Policy Coordinator; C.J. Young, Deputy Communications Director; Anna Yu, Professional Staff Member; Sarah Burke, Minority Deputy Staff Director; Michael Cameron, Minority Policy Analyst, Consumer Protection and Commerce, Energy, Environment; Nate Hodson, Minority Staff Director; Bijan Koohmaraie, Minority Chief Counsel; Tim Kurth, Minority Chief Counsel, Consumer Protection and Commerce; and Brannon Rains, Minority Professional Staff Member, Consumer Protection and Commerce.

Ms. SCHAKOWSKY. The Subcommittee on Consumer Protection and Commerce will now come to order. That is the gavel.

Today we will be holding a hearing entitled "Kids Online During COVID: Child Safety in an Increasingly Digital Age."

Due to the COVID–19 public health emergency, today's hearing is being held remotely. All Members and witnesses will be participating via video conference.

As part of our hearing, microphones will be set on mute for the purpose of eliminating inadvertent background noise. Members and witnesses, you will need to unmute yourselves each time that you wish to speak.

Additionally, Members will need to visibly be on screen in order to be recognized.

Documents for the record can be sent to Ed Kaczmarski, the staffer—sorry, Ed, for messing up your name—at the email address that we have provided to all staff.

All documents will be entered into the record at the end of the hearing.

I also wanted to mention that we do have votes that are being called right now, and people will have to go in and out. I will call on Tony Ca´rdenas, the vice chair of this committee, when I have to leave, but we can do it in segments. We are not going to recess for votes.

The Chair will now recognize herself for 5 minutes.

Statement of Hon. Jan Schakowsky, a Representative in Congress from the State of Illinois

Ms. SCHAKOWSKY. So, again, good morning, and welcome to our hearing on child safety online during the COVID–19 pandemic.

Children are spending twice as much time online as compared to before the pandemic. This time is increasingly spent on digital platforms not designed with children in mind.

Although we all hope—and in some cases, it is already happening—the kids will be able to safely return to schools, we should not be naive, however, and believe that in-person schooling will mean that companies stop targeting our children online.

Techniques honed by companies during the pandemic, and online habits developed by kids, will continue long after they are back in school. Many online platforms are addictive by design, grabbing attention and, of course, maximizing profits.

Children are especially vulnerable to addictive or manipulative techniques and technologies. They are more susceptible to coercive advertising and have trouble resisting attention-grabbing features.

The more time children spend online, the more likely they are to be subjected to harmful or age-inappropriate content.

There are few effective barriers that protect our children and teens, as well, from the harmful content and hate speech that plague our online discourse right now.

Nor are they shielded from the loss of privacy that has become a feature of online platforms. Platforms that are intended for general audiences are not required to protect the privacy of children, and many of the most popular platforms say they do not allow children that are under the age of 13 but do almost nothing to enforce their minimum age requirement.

The harms that children and teens experience online have very real and lasting side effects offline. More screen time has been associated with higher levels of anxiety, depression, sleep deprivation, obesity, and even suicide.

Children need tailored protections from privacy infringements and manipulative marketing practices. Children's privacy must be protected by updating COPPA, the current law, for our increasingly complex and connected digital word.

And thank you.

[The prepared statement of Ms. Schakowsky follows:]

Prepared Statement of Hon. Jan Schakowsky

Good morning, and welcome to our hearing on child safety online during the COVID–19 pandemic.

Children are spending twice as much time online compared to before the pandemic. This time is increasingly spent on digital platforms not designed with children in mind.

Although we all hope that kids will be able to safely return to school soon, we should not be naive and believe that in-person schooling will mean that companies stop targeting our children online.

Techniques honed by companies during the pandemic, and online habits developed by kids, will continue long after they are back in school.

Many online platforms are addictive by design, grabbing attention, and maximizing profits. Children are especially vulnerable to addictive or manipulative technologies. They are more susceptible to coercive advertising and have trouble resisting attention-grabbing features.

The more time children spend online, the more likely they are to be subjected to harmful or age-inappropriate content. There are few effective barriers protecting children and teens from the harmful content and hateful speech that plague our online discourse.

Nor are they shielded from the loss of privacy that has become a feature of online platforms. Platforms that are intended for general audiences aren't required to protect children's privacy.

Many of the most popular platforms say they do not allow children under the age of 13 but do almost nothing to enforce their minimum age requirement.

The harms that children and teens experience online have very real and lasting side effects offline. More screen time has been associated with higher levels of anxiety, depression, sleep deprivation, obesity and even suicide.

Children need tailored protections from privacy infringements and manipulative marketing practices. Children's privacy must be protected by updating COPPA, the current law, for our increasingly complex and connected digital word.

Thanks, and thank you to the witnesses for joining us today. I yield the remainder of my time to my colleague Ms. Castor.

Ms. SCHAKOWSKY. And at this time I want to yield to the author of this bill that we are going to be discussing today, Congresswoman Kathy Castor.

Ms. CASTOR. Well, thank you, Chair Schakowsky.

You are right. When Congress wrote the Children's Online Privacy Protection Act, COPPA, back in 1998, 23 years ago, the internet was in its infancy. The majority of households did not have a computer, and even less had the internet. There were no internet-connected cell phones or devices, and if a child wanted to get on the internet, they would have to go to the family desktop, usually in a shared space, and type in the Web address and wait for a dialup internet.

So, despite how antiquated this may seem to us in 2021, it was revolutionary in 1998, and at that time Congress acted to meet the moment, and they put in place safeguards to protect our children in this new online environment.

But, boy, have things changed since then. We are at another critical moment where technological innovations in our children are at the forefront. Their every move is being tracked and monetized by their phone, tablets, apps, and more.

Platforms are manipulating children to stay online longer and pushing them towards extreme content, infinite scrolling, and awards of badges for repeated interactions.

Big business is profiting, and our children are paying the price. And, as our witnesses point out, that price is the real-world harmful impact on our kids' safety, their development, and their mental health.

It has gotten worse during the pandemic. Children's screen time has gone up while parents' ability and time to monitor screen time has gone down. So parents are looking to Congress to make sure their kids are safe and that educational experiences work.

So we need to meet this moment. I intend to reintroduce my Kids PRIVCY Act and the KIDS Act to safeguard our kids, and I would like to invite Members from both sides of the aisle to work with me to update COPPA.

Thanks, and I yield back.

Ms. SCHAKOWSKY. The Chair now recognizes Mr. Bilirakis, the ranking member of the subcommittee, for his 5 minutes.

You are recognized, Mr. Bilirakis.

Statement of Hon. Gus Bilirakis, a Representative in Congress from the State of Florida

Mr. BILIRAKIS. Thank you, Madam Chair, and I want to thank you for holding this very important hearing.

I know we share a similar view that, while technology can be amazing in keeping us all connected, when it comes to substitution for interpersonal communications, we are all at a loss.

My father served on this committee, and back when he did serve, we could talk amongst the dais, write each other notes, communicate more directly on what is happening in our lives, both personally and professionally. Unfortunately, here we are all in a virtual hearing.

While we have gotten a bit better from the early days of virtual hearings, we are all human. I expect there will still be miscues today, like when someone is ready to talk or providing the kind of attention our witnesses deserve for their statements. And I appreciate them being here.

Now, think about what it is like for our kids. This is the new reality, and it is a sad one, in my opinion. The COVID–19 pandemic has caused so many Americans to become isolated in their homes, especially our kids.

Without the opportunity for children to interact in person with their friends directly, many turn to social media to fill the void. Sadly, this has led to a cascade of negative effects for me.

I believe this hearing can serve as an important alarm bell for safely reopening our schools and getting students and teachers back in the classroom and reverse this trend.

To be fair, at the beginning of the pandemic there was much unknown about the virus, and virtual school was seemingly viable. It is a viable bridge to educating students, and it is better than not having anything.

Distance learning can certainly be a positive tool for some students. But the facts now make clear that, as a primary means of instruction, it just does not work for advancing our kids' education, especially those children with disabilities.

There is good news, however. A number of schools have shown they can safely open up, including my great State of Florida, and so I hope we can find avenues for all students to have the same accessibility to educational opportunities.

The alternative is catastrophic, unfortunately. This was on full display in Clark County, Nevada, last year. In that case more than 3,000 alerts about students with suicidal thoughts flooded the inbox of district officials.

The school district since reopened to in-person schooling, but tragically too late. By December of last year, 18 students took their own lives. Eighteen families lost their children.

We all believe, like Clark County, history can repeat itself. That is why I was pleased that, earlier this year, President Biden pledged to reopen the schools by his 100th day in office, and the CDC Director Walinsky relayed that data indicated schools can begin to safely reopen—and more than one day a week, I'll add.

Still we are all alarmed by recent contradictory statements to the science behind these commitments. So it will be interesting to find out what changed. Hopefully, the panel will have some insight there.

I also want to know as privacy protection is on the agenda today that I want to be part of the real solution. Committee Republicans have been and remain committed to this.

And to speak more on this topic, I would like to yield to my good friend Congressman Tim Walberg for his efforts to reach a bipartisan deal on a bill to improve upon the Child Online Privacy Protection Act.

[The prepared statement of Mr. Bilirakis follows:]

Prepared Statement of Hon. Gus Bilirakis

Thank you Madame Chair for holding this important hearing.

I know we share a similar view that while technology can be amazing in keeping us all connected, when it becomes a substitution for interpersonal communications, we are all at a loss.

My dad served on this committee back when we could talk amongst the dais, write each other notes, communicate more directly on what's happening in our lives, both personally and professionally.

Unfortunately, here we all are, in a virtual hearing.

While we have gotten a bit better from the early days of virtual hearings, I expect there will still be missed cues today like when someone is ready to talk, or providing the kind of attention our witnesses deserve for their statements.

Now think about what it is like to be our kids. This is their new reality, and it is a sad one.

The COVID–19 pandemic has caused so many Americans to become isolated in their homes, especially our kids.

Without opportunities for children to interact in person with their friends directly, many turn to social media to fill the void.

Sadly, this has led to a cascade of negative effects for them.

I believe this hearing can serve as an important alarm bell for safely reopening our schools and getting students and teachers back in the classroom and reverse this trend.

To be fair, at the beginning of the pandemic there was much unknown about the virus, and virtual school was a seemingly viable bridge to educating students.

Distance learning can certainly be a positive tool for some students—but the facts now make clear that as a primary means of instruction, it just doesn't work for advancing our kids' education, especially those with disabilities.

There is good news. A number of schools have shown they can safely open up including in Florida, and so I hope we can find avenues for all students to have the same accessibility to educational opportunities.

The alternative is catastrophic. This was on full display in Clark County, Nevada last year.

In that case, more than 3,000 alerts about students with suicidal thoughts flooded the inbox of district officials.

The school district since re-opened to in person schooling, but tragically, too late.

By December of last year, 18 students took their own life. 18 families lost their children.

We all have a Clark County where history can repeat itself.

That's why I was pleased that earlier this year President Biden pledged to reopen schools by his 100th day in office and CDC Director Walensky relayed that data indicated schools can begin to safely reopen.

Still, we are all alarmed by recent contradictory statements to the science behind these commitments, so it will be interesting to find out what changed. Hopefully the panel will have some insight there.

I also want to note as privacy protections are on the agenda today that I want to be part of a real solution.

Committee Republicans have been and remain committed to this, and to speak more on this topic, I would like to yield to my good friend, Congressman Tim Walberg, for his efforts to reach a bipartisan deal on a bill to improve upon the Child Online Privacy Protection Act.

Thank you.

Mr. BILIRAKIS. I yield the rest of my time to Representative Walberg.

Thank you.

Mr. WALBERG. I thank my good friend.

When I first introduced the PROTECT Kids Act, there was a pressing need to modernize the Children's Online Privacy Protection Act to reflect the digital era.

In the midst of this global pandemic, with children and their parents challenged, there is an even more pressing need than ever. While the FTC made improvement to COPPA in 2013, they did not go far enough to protect children against new threats in the evolving digital ecosystem.

The internet has drastically changed since 2013, and while increased internet usage presents many complicated risks, children's online privacy is one area Congress established clear law.

But the law is outdated. It needs to be updated to ensure children are protected from troubling conduct of Big Tech. The PROTECT Kids Act represents a commonsense, bipartisan solution, and I appreciate my good friend Congressman Rush for joining me in this effort to put children's wellbeing at the top of Congress' priority list.

Together we are continuing to work with stakeholders to strengthen this bill. We welcome input from members of this subcommittee and look forward to working together to pass these much-needed reforms.

I thank you, and I yield back.

Ms. SCHAKOWSKY. The gentleman yields back.

And the Chair now recognizes Mr. Pallone, chair of the full committee, for 5 minutes for his opening statement.

Statement of Hon. Frank Pallone, Jr., a Representative in Congress from the State of New Jersey

Mr. PALLONE. Thank you, Chairwoman Schakowsky.

The COVID–19 pandemic is an unprecedented public health and economic crisis which has greatly disrupted our lives. The children, in particular, have had their world turned upside down. Visits with friends and extended family have been replaced by video conferencing and in-person activities replaced with video games, social media, video services, and other digital activities.

And as a result, kids' screen time has doubled during the pandemic, and you just told me that, Madam Chair, on the elevator and I did not realize it was that much, twice.

As this subcommittee has heard time and time again, consumers online face manipulative advertising, disinformation, harassment, dark pattern manipulation, and privacy intrusions. For adults, these dangers are extremely hard to manage, but for children, such practices are downright predatory.

Children do not possess the same levels of cognitive development to defend themselves and are often uniquely vulnerable to any negative effects. The online world can affect children's mental and physical health.

Growing bodies of research confirm the link between increased digital media use and depression and higher instances of addiction, anxiety, sleep deprivation, and obesity. And we also have seen harmful behaviors such as cyber bullying increase during the pandemic.

Unfortunately, many companies are well aware that children are spending more time online, and they are taking advantage of that by proactively targeting, manipulating, and monetizing our children. For example, some internet platforms, app developers, and content creators propagate addiction by design through sophisticated, thoroughly tested means to keep kids on their sites and extract money.

Common elements include pressuring in-app purchases without parental consent, so-called freemium apps that tease paid versions, and gamification marketing where gameplay elements themselves are used to promote purchases or products.

And then there is influencer advertising, Madam Chair. People on social media with lots of followers post photos and videos of themselves using a product, but kids, and sometimes adults, do not understand that those people are often paid for those posts.

And young children frequently have no idea that the video they are watching of someone opening a new toy is actually meant to sell the toy.

So online advertising spending is now the largest of any medium, and spending on digital ads specifically targeting children is expected to reach $1.7 billion this year.

Most apps directed to or used by children contain ads, including 95 percent of the apps aimed at kids under 5. Ads for toys or junk food are commonplace, but far too often kids are exposed to ads for tobacco products, alcohol, violent movies or video games, or other age-inappropriate content.

And it is deeply concerning that business models online continually seek to maximize engagement to increase revenue at the expense of children's health. Many parents try to balance the benefits of internet use, such as social connections and educational apps, while trying to limit the possible negative effects.

But many parents are overwhelmed, and even their best efforts are not enough to protect their kids against sophisticated predatory practices.

And the pandemic has made it painfully clear this problem is not going to fix itself, nor will the harmful activities targeting our kids stop when the pandemic is behind us.

Despite laws to protect children's privacy, data collection and tracking of children is disturbingly prevalent. Many apps for kids on mobile devices are notorious for collecting personal information, and their personal information is then bought and sold, resulting in targeted advertising designed to influence and manipulate children even more.

So Congress granted the FTC rulemaking authority under the Children's Online Privacy Protection Act, or COPPA, precisely so it could update the safeguards for children online as technology advanced, and the internet has experienced a sea change since the last updates to the COPPA rule.

I know that Ms. Castor mentioned this with her legislation, and it is clear those rules are out of date and no longer provide the intended protections for our kids.

So, while the FTC has started the process of updating its rules under COPPA, we also must examine whether the statute should be updated and whether other practices targeting children should be regulated. We cannot leave it all to parents.

The challenges children face online existed before the pandemic, but they have only gotten worse. And it is going to continue to increase after the pandemic is behind us, unless we do something about it.

So I just wanted to thank you, Madam Chair, and also Kathy Castor because of the fact that you are having this hearing drawing attention to this with the legislation.

I look forward to this expert panel on what is a very important topic.

Thank you.

[The prepared statement of Mr. Pallone follows:]

Prepared Statement of Hon. Frank Pallone, Jr.

The COVID–19 pandemic is an unprecedented public health and economic crisis, which has greatly disrupted our daily lives. Children, in particular, have had their worlds turned upside down. Visits with friends and extended family have been replaced by video conferencing. And in-person activities replaced with video games, social media, video services, and other digital activities. As a result, kids' screen time has doubled during the pandemic.

As this subcommittee has heard time and time again, consumers online face manipulative advertising, disinformation, harassment, dark pattern manipulation, and privacy intrusions. For adults, these dangers are extremely hard to manage, but for children such practices are downright predatory. Children do not possess the same levels of cognitive development to defend themselves and are often uniquely vulnerable to any negative effects.

The online world can affect children's mental and physical health. Growing bodies of research confirm the link between increased digital media use and depression and higher instances of addiction, anxiety, sleep deprivation, and obesity. We also have seen harmful behaviors such as cyber bullying increase during the pandemic.

Unfortunately, many companies are well aware that children are spending more time online and they are taking advantage of that by proactively targeting, manipulating, and monetizing our children.

For example, some internet platforms, app developers, and content creators propagate "addiction by design" through sophisticated, thoroughly tested means to keep kids on their sites and extract money. Common elements include pressuring in-app purchases without parental consent, so-called freemium apps that tease paid versions, and "gamification" marketing where gameplay elements themselves are used to promote purchases or products.

Influencer advertising to kids is also prominent. People on social media with lots of followers post photos and videos of themselves using a product, but kids, and sometimes adults, don't understand that those people are often paid for those posts. Young children frequently have no idea that the video they're watching of someone opening a new toy is actually meant to sell the toy.

Online advertising spending is now the largest of any medium, and spending on digital ads specifically targeting children is expected to reach $1.7 billion this year. Most apps directed to or used by children contain ads, including 95 percent of the apps aimed at kids under five. Ads for toys or junk food are commonplace but far too often kids are exposed to ads for tobacco products, alcohol, violent movies or video games, or other age inappropriate content.

It is deeply concerning that business models online continually seek to maximize engagement to increase revenue at the expense of children's health.

Many parents try to balance the benefits of internet use—such as social connections and educational apps—while trying to limit the possible negative effects. But many parents are overwhelmed and even their best efforts are not enough to protect their kids against sophisticated predatory practices. The pandemic has made it painfully clear this problem will not fix itself. Nor will the harmful activities targeting our kids stop when the pandemic is behind us.

Despite laws to protect children's privacy, data collection and tracking of children is disturbingly prevalent. Many apps for kids on mobile devices are notorious for collecting personal information from children. Their personal information is then bought and sold, resulting in targeted advertising designed to influence and manipulate children.

Congress granted the Federal Trade Commission (FTC) rulemaking authority under the Children's Online Privacy Protection Act, or COPPA, precisely so it could update the safeguards for children online as technology advanced. The internet has experienced a sea change since the last updates to the COPPA Rule in 2013, and it's clear those rules are out of date and no longer provide the intended protections for our kids.

While the FTC has started the process of updating its rules under COPPA, we also must examine whether the statute should be updated and whether other practices targeting children should be regulated. We can't leave it all to parents.

The challenges children face online existed before the pandemic, but it's only gotten worse. And it will continue to increase after the pandemic is behind us, unless we do something about it.

I look forward to hearing our expert panel on the challenges our children are facing online and how we can best protect them.

Ms. SCHAKOWSKY. The gentleman yields back.

And the Chair now recognizes Mrs. Rodgers, ranking member of the full committee, for 5 minutes for her opening statement.

Statement of Hon. Cathy McMorris Rodgers, a Representative in Congress from the State of Washington

Mrs. RODGERS. Good morning, Madam Chair. And, everyone, welcome.

Our discussion today is especially important to me not just as a Member of Congress but as a mom. We absolutely need to have a serious discussion about what is happening to our kids online, their mental health and safety, and what needs to happen to reopen schools immediately.

Yesterday we heard from four doctors who wrote in USA Today, quote, "Keeping schools closed, even partially closed, based on what we know now, is harming our children." They said the Biden administration misinterpreted their research and science when creating the CDC guidance, and it ultimately led to harmful policies that hamstrung States to reopen schools quickly.

The science is clear. Viral transmission is minimal in schools. Children are not at significant risk of poor outcomes from COVID–19. It is time to reopen immediately and listen to the experts who are saying loud and clear "follow the science."

School closures are harming children. It is more than just a homework gap. There are serious health and mental health risks associated with children spending more time online. And as we have heard today, it has doubled.

These are stories I am hearing from parents who are pleading for schools to reopen. I hear it every day. Our kids are not active. They are not engaged. They are falling asleep during remote school. They are isolated.

Suicide and overdose risks are going up. As our children spend more time online, they are more at risk to online predators.

This has all happened in my community, and I know we are not alone. The science tells us all these risks of despair far outweigh COVID–19 in schools.

In addition to the USA Today, I encourage everyone also to read a piece from the New York Times. It documents scientific insights from health professionals.

Here is what one pediatrician from San Francisco said, quote, "We are witnessing a significant public health crisis in our children who are experiencing unprecedented mental and physical illness during this time. This would be mitigated, if not completely alleviated, by in-person schooling," end quote.

I understand that our focus today is on child safety in an increasingly digital age. For the safety of our children, surely, we can all agree science, not fear, should dictate how we protect them and build a better future, a future with hope.

We can mitigate a lot of the harms and risks we are talking about today by not letting another day go by of school closures. That is what is going to give our children the best chance to succeed and thrive in life.

Now, specifically regarding the protection online, I am committed and convinced as to the importance of updating and modernizing our laws. I look forward to joining bipartisan work for data and privacy protections, especially children's privacy.

I sincerely hope these efforts resume soon and that this committee plows the hard ground necessary to legislate in a bipartisan way again.

As we look to the future of building a better world for the next generation, I want to be clear: America can lead a new era of technological innovation. We must lead with our values for freedom, human rights, and human dignity.

But we are failing with closed schools, and this yearlong experiment of remote learning, more screen time, and more isolation is failing our kids. Our kids are in crisis.

Technology should add to education. It is not a substitute for everyday learning. It is not a substitute, period. Reopening for in-person learning does not mean 2 days a week. It means 5 days, both with the teacher and the children in the classroom together.

Before the President's address tonight, we should all be asking why more is not being done to reopen. Just as the doctors wrote in USA Today, this is a human rights issue. Let's open the doors of our schools and let our kids learn and thrive again.

Thank you.

And, Ms. Chairman, I ask unanimous consent to include both articles I mentioned in the record.

[The prepared statement of Mrs. Rodgers follows:]

Prepared Statement of Hon. Cathy McMorris Rodgers

Good morning and welcome.

Our discussion today is one especially important to me, not just as a Member of Congress, but as a mom.

We need to leave politics at the door and have a serious discussion about what is happening to our kids online.

... their mental health and safety.

... and what needs to happen to reopen schools immediately.

Schools

Yesterday, we heard from four doctors who wrote in USA TODAY.

Quote: "keeping schools closed or even partially closed, based on what we know now, is harming our children."

They said the Biden administration misinterpreted their research and science when creating the CDC guidance.

... and it ultimately led to harmful policy that hamstrung States to reopen schools quickly.

Science

The science is clear.

Viral transmission is minimal in schools. Children are not a significant risk either of poor outcomes from COVID–19.

It's time to reopen immediately and listen to the experts who are saying loud and clear, follow the science… school closures are harming children.

It's more than just a homework gap. There are serious health and mental risks associated with our children spending more time online.

These are stories, I'm hearing from parents who are pleading for schools to reopen.

I hear this every day.

Our kids aren't active.

They are not engaged and falling asleep during remote school. They are isolated. suicide and overdose risks are going up.

And as children spend more time online, they are more at risk to online predators. This has all happened in my community and I know we aren't alone.

The science tells us all these risks of despair far outweigh COVID–19 in schools.

More Health Experts

In addition to USA Today, I encourage everyone to also read a piece from the New York Times.

It documents scientific insight from health professionals. Here's what one pediatrician from San Francisco said:

"We are witnessing a significant public health crisis in our children, who are experiencing unprecedented mental illness and physical ailments during this time.

"This would be mitigated, if not completely alleviated, by in-person schooling." End quote.

I understand that our focus today is child safety in an increasingly digital age.

For the safety of our children, surely we can all agree science—not fear—should dictate how we protect them and build a better future....

... A future with hope.

We can mitigate a lot of the harms and risks we are talking about today by not letting another day go by of school closures.

That's what will give our children the best chance to succeed and thrive in life.

Protecting Online

Now, specifically regarding their protection online...

I am always open to updating and modernizing our laws.

I'm committed to bipartisan work for data and privacy protections, especially children's privacy.

I sincerely hope those efforts resume soon....

... and this committee does the hard work of legislating in a bipartisan way again.

Win the Future

As we look to the future of building a better world for the next generation, I want to be clear.

America can lead a new era of technological innovation.

We must lead with our values for freedom, human rights, and human dignity.

But we are failing with closed schools and this year long experiment of remote learning, more screen time, and more isolation.

Technology should add to education. It's not a substitute for everyday learning.

It's not a substitute period. Reopening for in-person learning doesn't mean two days a week.

It means five days—with both the teacher and children in the classroom together.

Before the President's address tonight, we should all be asking why isn't more being done to reopen.

Just as the doctors wrote in USA Today, this is a human rights issue. Let's open the doors of our schools and let our kids learn and thrive again. Thank you.

Ms. Chairman, I ask unanimous consent to include both articles I mentioned in the record.

* * *

Ms. SCHAKOWSKY. All of those will be added at the end of the hearing, and she yields back.

Mrs. RODGERS. I yield back. Sorry, Madam Chair.

Ms. SCHAKOWSKY. Thank you.

And the Chair would like to remind Members that, pursuant to committee rules, all Members' written opening statements shall be made part of the record.

And now I will introduce the witnesses that we have and thank them so much for their participation today.

Dr. Nusheen Ameenuddin—did I get that?—Ameenuddin, chair of the Council on Communications and Media at the American Academy of Pediatrics.

We have Corey A. DeAngelis, Ph.D., Director of School Choice at the Reason Foundation, adjunct scholar at the Cato Institute, and executive director of the Educational Foundation Institute.

And Ariel Fox Johnson, who is the senior counsel of global policy at Common Sense Media.

And we want to thank all of you for joining us for this very important hearing today, which I am getting the feeling has a good deal of bipartisan support, and we look forward to your testimony.

So, Dr. Ameenuddin, you are recognized.

Statements of Nusheen Ameenuddin, M.D., Chair, Council on Communications and Media, American Academy of Pediatrics; Corey A. DeAngelis, Ph.D., Director of School Choice, Reason Foundation; and Ariel Fox Johnson, Senior Counsel, Global Policy, Common Sense Media

Statement of Nusheen Ameenuddin, M.D.

Dr. AMEENUDDIN. OK. Thank you.

Good morning, Chair Schakowsky, Ranking Member Bilirakis, Chair Pallone, and Ranking Member Rodgers, along with members of the subcommittee. Thank you so much for inviting me to discuss young people's digital media use during the pandemic.

I am Dr. Nusheen Ameenuddin, and I am a pediatrician at the Mayo Clinic in Rochester, Minnesota. I am here today representing the American Academy of Pediatrics, a nonprofit, professional medical organization of more than 67,000 pediatricians, where I serve as chair of the Council on Communications and Media.

Today's youths are growing up immersed in digital media. In 1970, kids began watching TV around 4 years of age, but today babies start interacting with digital media within the first few months of their lives.

Media's impact on children has been an issue for years, well before a global pandemic forced us all to move our lives online. The pandemic has laid bare this longstanding issue, creating an opportunity to address structural issues within the digital ecosystem.

As a pediatrician who has been caring for patients this entire pandemic, I have to acknowledge the unprecedented challenges that families are up against. It is no surprise that screen time has increased significantly under these circumstances.

As pediatricians, we also have to acknowledge the reality of the ubiquity of digital devices. We do not simply preach device abstinence. We encourage moderate, balanced, pro social use of devices as part of the media diet.

Technology can have important benefits for children and teens, like broadening horizons and as a learning tool. The internet provides space for community building among youth who are marginalized, including children with serious diseases. Children of color who face racism can build resilience by sharing those experiences and finding support online.

With these benefits in mind, we also need to focus on the real threats posed by technology. The bottom line is that parents need help, and technology companies must be held accountable for the products that they create.

Data collection and compromised privacy are among the most pervasive threats facing young people. Companies can contact, track, and influence users through digital trails that they leave behind. Users can unknowingly disclose location, activities, likes and dislikes, along with in-app behavior.

This intentionally opaque process is then used to make ads more effective and platforms more successful and profitable. Children using these products do not fully understand the ramifications of this data collection, which can also influence the information that reaches them.

Ad content is tailored to their interests and creates false norms that undermine healthy behaviors. Algorithms can accurately predict what a child will want to watch next. These elements make it so hard for young brains to resist.

Many products feature manipulative design that nudges users into specific behaviors. An example is the autoplay feature on platforms like Netflix and

YouTube, which places the onus entirely on young people to opt out of watching the next video, making increased screen time an almost foregone conclusion.

But that is not all. Gamified ads and in-app purchases that reward users for watching ads and buying products are very appealing to children.

During the pandemic, users of a supposedly free math game were shown 16 different ads and only four math problems over 19 minutes of game play.

Social media allows companies to reach young people with paid influence they are marketing through platforms like YouTube and TikTok. Young people are led to believe that posts reflect the genuine preferences of the poster when, in fact, they are actually being targeted by marketing campaigns.

Algorithms also drive young people to inaccurate, inappropriate, and even harmful content like misinformation about COVID–19 and vaccines, another issue that pediatricians experience firsthand and have for a while.

Youth of color face challenges accessing positive aspects of technology due to a longstanding digital divide, which includes disproportionate targeting for unhealthy ads that worsen health disparities and increase screen time stemming from structural issues.

In order to make real progress for children and families, we must preserve the positive aspects of technology while removing the pervasive threats it can pose. The AAP recommends that Congress strengthen the Children's Online Privacy Protection Act. An enhanced COPPA should protect all children under the age of 18 and cover the wide array of devices that collect data from children.

If data collection is even allowed for young people, it should be an opt in.

Congress must also ban targeted advertising to those under age 18.

And, finally, Congress should fund efforts to improve digital literacy, address digital equity, and expand research on how digital media impacts children.

The issues that young people and their families face in the digital world are not insurmountable. Through effective public policy, it is possible to build a better digital world for our children during and after this pandemic.

Thank you.

[The prepared statement of Dr. Ameenuddin follows:]

Prepared Statement of Nusheen Ameenuddin, MD

Good morning. Chair Schakowsky, Ranking Member Bilirakis, and members of the subcommittee, it is my pleasure to be here today to address young people's digital media use during the pandemic. Pediatricians have been raising concerns about the impact of media use on children for years, particularly digital and online media, and I look forward to sharing more about the opportunities and challenges presented to us by these technologies. It is in our power to create a digital ecosystem that works better for children and families, and I hope we will seize this opportunity to do that.

My name is Dr. Nusheen Ameenuddin, and I am the chair of the American Academy of Pediatrics Council on Communications and Media. I am also a pediatrician with extensive clinical experience in how communications and media impact children. I currently serve as an Assistant Professor of Pediatrics at the Mayo Clinic in Rochester, Minnesota, in the Division of Community Pediatric and Adolescent Medicine. During routine well-child visits, I invest significant time in conversations with children, teens, and their parents about the safe and appropriate use of digital media. I answer their questions and counsel them as they make difficult decisions about how to set boundaries with their devices. I am also passionate about advocating for underserved populations and immigrant populations who face systemic barriers to realizing optimal health and achieving their full potential. In our discussions about the challenges presented by the digital ecosystem, it is critical we not lose sight of the fact that structural racism and inequities compound and feed into the challenges young people of color are facing online.

I am here today representing the American Academy of Pediatrics (AAP), a non-profit professional medical organization of more than 67,000 pediatricians, pediatric medical subspecialists, and pediatric surgical specialists across the United States. The AAP is dedicated to the health, safety, and well-being of infants, children, adolescents, and young adults. In my role as chair of the Council on Communications and Media, I work to ensure that children, families, and pediatricians have the knowledge and tools to make informed choices about children's media use. The Council also develops the Academy's official evidence-based policy on issues ranging from children's screen time to digital advertising targeting children. Our policies include recommendations for pediatricians, families, and policymakers to create an optimal digital environment for young people.

Today's generation of children and adolescents is growing up immersed in media, using platforms that allow users to both consume and create content, including broadcast and streamed television and movies; sedentary and active video games; social and interactive media that can be creative and engaging for both individuals and groups; and even highly immersive virtual reality. In 1970, children began watching TV regularly at about 4 years of age, whereas today, children begin interacting with digital media as young as a few months of age. In 2015, according to research published in *Pediatrics*, most 2-year-olds used mobile devices on a daily basis and 92.2% of 1-year-olds had already used a mobile device.[1] Many preschoolers in this study were already media multitasking (using more than one form of media at a time). Data has also shown that three-quarters of teenagers own a smartphone, 24% of adolescents describe themselves as "constantly connected" to the internet, and 50% report feeling "addicted" to their phones.

All of this was the reality we faced long before a global pandemic forced all of us to migrate much of our lives online. It is therefore essential that we address not just the issues of the moment but also the broader structural issues with the digital ecosystem that the pandemic has simply laid bare.

Young People & Digital Technology in the Age of COVID-19

This is an unusual time for children and parents, and it is important that we acknowledge this reality from the outset. Parents and families have faced unprecedented challenges over the last year as children have experienced extended periods of virtual schooling, isolation from family, friends, and supportive networks, and increased emotional, financial, and other stressors. Millions of parents are working from home while managing their children's education and extracurricular activities, while countless others have lost jobs or seen their earnings reduced dramatically. Still others have faced the unique challenges of securing childcare for their children during a pandemic while they report to jobs that cannot be done virtually. In the face of these trying circumstances, families have shown enormous adaptability and resilience.

At a time when families are being strained more than any in recent memory, the pandemic has brought longstanding concerns about the digital ecosystem to the forefront, making normal screen time recommendations more challenging than ever to abide by and exacerbating concerns about exploitative industry practices that target young people. According to one survey-based study of Michigan school-aged children's media use during the pandemic, 35% of parents reported that their child had started using social media at a younger age than they had planned. The study also showed that 49% reported that their child has come across media content or videos that they consider creepy or not age-appropriate and 28% of parents report that their child is distracted during

[1] Yolanda (Linda) Reid Chassiakos, Jenny Radesky, Dimitri Christakis, Megan A. Moreno, Corinn Cross, American Academy of Pediatrics Council on Communications and Media. *Pediatrics*. Nov 2016, 138 (5) e20162593; DOI: 10.1542/peds.2016-2593.

virtual schooling with other websites or apps like YouTube on their learning device.[2] With advances in technology, the line between the online and offline world is increasingly blurred, making hard and fast rules about technology use challenging for parents to put into practice.

It has also become increasingly clear based on clinical experience and anecdotal reports that screen time has increased significantly since pandemic-related lockdowns and virtual schooling began. Initial data have shown children's screen time for both educational and entertainment purposes increasing in 2020.[3] One study of Indian school children found that children's screen media use increased during lockdown, particularly on weekdays. The study also found that children with higher screen media use had more sleep disruption, though the study was not able to establish causation.[4] Video game use among children also appears to have increased.[5] Though it will take time for a large body of rigorous, peer-reviewed studies to be published on this topic, we have seen enough to know that concerns about the impact of the pandemic on children's digital media use are justified.

As pediatricians, we recognize the need for moderation in device use, and we have adjusted the ways we counsel our patients to reflect our new reality. We are not simply preaching device abstinence or demanding families make unrealistic sacrifices that do not align with the modern world or the realities of the pandemic. Rather, we like to think of all the ways families use their devices on a daily basis in terms of a "media diet," recognizing that the myriad types of digital media out there are of varying quality and value from the educational, socioemotional, and developmental perspectives. We strive to help families achieve a balanced media diet.

When it comes to advising parents about their children's internet and digital device use, we recommend a collaborative approach that embraces open dialogue between parent and child and active monitoring of young people during their time on devices. Parents can talk with their children about age-appropriate content and ask children to share what they are doing on their

---

[2] Munzer T, Torres C, Domoff S, Levitt K, Weeks H, Schaller A, Radesky J. Media use practices of elementary-aged children during the COVID-19 pandemic. *In preparation.*

[3] Tuchow R. Kid device usage changing as a result of the pandemic. *Kidscreen.* Available at: https://kidscreen.com/2021/02/19/kid-device-usage-changing-as-a-result-of-the-pandemic/. Accessed March 8, 2021.

[4] Dutta, K., Mukherjee, R., Sen, D., & Sahu, S. (2020). Effect of COVID-19 lockdown on sleep behavior and screen exposure time: an observational study among Indian school children. *Biological Rhythm Research*, 1-12.

[5] BBC. Game maker Roblox's value rockets seven-fold during pandemic. *BBC.* 2021. Available at: https://www.bbc.com/news/business-55570009. Accessed March 8, 2021.

devices. Parents can also use parental controls to screen out inappropriate content when direct supervision is not possible.

Clear guidelines for when and how devices can be used are important to creating balance and moderation. We suggest families identify screen-free zones in the home, like bedrooms or family gathering areas, so that parents and children can connect with each other without distractions. Specifying times of the day when every member of the family should be fully offline and present, such as a screen-free dinner or active playtime, can also help families develop healthy media rituals. Though devices are ubiquitous in all aspects of children's lives, parents can place a firm limit on the amount of time screens are used for entertainment purposes, like streaming content or playing video games. We also encourage parents to disable apps and entertainment features on devices during the virtual school day, if possible, to minimize distractions.

There is no doubt that parents and pediatricians play an important role helping children and teens safely navigate the digital world. Ultimately, however, digital media and technology companies must be held to account for the products they create. While there is no substitute for parental supervision and guidance, families face huge headwinds using technology platforms designed to maximize profit and user engagement, goals at odds with a developmentally appropriate approach to technology. In short, parents need help, now more than ever.

The Promise of Technology for Young People

Despite the concerns that have brought us here today, it is important to remember that technology has important benefits for children and teens and even greater potential, should we as a society choose to capitalize on it.

For infants and toddlers still developing cognitive, language, sensorimotor, and socioemotional skills, screen time of any kind is typically discouraged, and adult interaction is crucial for toddlers to learn effectively from digital media. In this age range, co-viewing of media with parents in addition to teaching back after the fact may increase young children's engagement with media and understanding of content.[6] Interactive devices that allow apps to know whether a child is responding accurately and tailor responses, reinforcement, and next steps to the child's input may increase educational potential by providing scaffolding to build skills at the child's edge of competence. Additionally, young children can learn words from live

[6] Fidler AE, Zack E, Barr R. Television viewing patterns in 6-to 18-month-olds: the role of caregiver–infant interactional quality. *Infancy*. 2010;15(2):176–196.

video-chatting with a responsive adult or from carefully designed, interactive screen interfaces that prompt the child to tap on relevant learning items.[7,8] More broadly, video chats can provide an opportunity to connect with distant family and friends with the guidance of an adult, and therefore are appropriate for young children.[9]

Among school-aged children and teenagers, research studies as well as anecdotal reports have suggested benefits of media use, such as communication and engagement.[10] For children young and old, technology can help broaden horizons beyond their immediate surroundings and serve as a tool for learning. Cultural and educational institutions around the world, such as zoos and museums, have met this moment with new online offerings, allowing young people to see a live giraffe or tour the Louvre from their couch. Teenagers are able to share their art through online platforms or create their own digital content, allowing them to develop their creativity.

The internet has also created space for community-building among marginalized young people from a wide variety of backgrounds. For instance, young people with chronic illnesses or disabilities can connect with those dealing with similar conditions, and research suggests that these networks may be particularly helpful for patients with ongoing health issues.[11] Children of color can build resilience through digital community to help overcome lived experiences of racism and discrimination. Young people from religious minority backgrounds can come together for shared worship and cultural experiences that are reflective of their age and shared values.

Digital media platforms also allow young people to organize and advocate for issues that impact their generation. For instance, the post-Parkland movement to address gun violence, including the widely attended March for Our Lives, was youth-led and helped spur important changes in a dialogue that had stagnated for years. The potential for young people to demand change

---

[7] Roseberry S, Hirsh-Pasek K, Golinkoff RM. Skype me! Socially contingent interactions help toddlers learn language. *Child Dev*. 2014;85(3):956–970pmid:24112079.

[8] Kirkorian HL, Choi K, Pempek TA. Toddlers' word learning from contingent and noncontingent video on touch screens. *Child Dev*. 2016;87(2):405–413pmid:27018327.

[9] McClure ER, Chentsova-Dutton YE, Barr RF, Holochwost SJ, Parrott WG. "Facetime doesn't count": video chat as an exception to media restrictions for infants and toddlers. *Int J Child-Computer Interact*. 2015;6:1–6.

[10] Moreno MA, Gannon KE. Social media and health. In: Rosen D, Joffe A, eds. AM STARs Adolescent Medicine: State of the Art Reviews. *Young Adult Health*. 2013;24(3):538–552.

[11] Naslund JA, Aschbrenner KA, Marsch LA, Bartels SJ. The future of mental health care: peer-to-peer support and social media. *Epidemiol Psychiatr Sci*. 2016;25(2):113–122pmid: 26744309.

through collective action represents a real and meaningful bright spot from their exposure to the digital ecosystem.

Harms of Technology for Young People

With these benefits in mind, we must now turn to the real threats posed by the digital ecosystem to young people's health, well-being, and long-term trajectories. Technology companies and online platforms are not developed with child development in mind. Whether intended or not, they have incentives that harm children. It is therefore critical to understand the ways that common practices designed to benefit the goals of these companies impact young people.

Data Collection Practices and Children's Privacy Online

Data collection on a vast scale is a core characteristic of modern technology platforms. Nearly every connected platform, from social media to internet-connected virtual assistants, collects data from users in some form to inform commercial goals like product advertising. Despite limitations on the collection of data from young children enshrined in the Children's Online Privacy Protection Act (COPPA), this practice has accelerated largely unabated for children of all ages due to outdated statutory protections and insufficient enforcement. Enabled by an internet connection, companies can contact, track, and influence users, as guided by behavioral data collection, essentially a user's digital trail of location, activities, in-app behavior, likes, and dislikes.[12] These data contribute to a digital profile shared among many companies that can be used to make advertising messages more effective and technology platforms more successful.

A report examining this so-called "datafication" of children concluded that school-aged children up to teenagers do not comprehend the full complexity of how digital data are collected, analyzed, and used for commercial purposes.[13] For example, studies suggest that teenagers have a more interpersonal, and less technical, conceptualization of privacy, so they may not be as aware of the ramifications of sharing data with governments or corporations compared with sharing private information with friends or

---

[12] Jenny Radesky, Yolanda (Linda) Reid Chassiakos, Nusheen Ameenuddin, Dipesh Navsaria, American Academy of Pediatrics Council on Communications and Media. *Pediatrics*. Jul 2020, 146 (1) e20201681; DOI: 10.1542/peds.2020-1681.

[13] Livingstone S, Stoilova M, Nandagiri R. *Children's Data and Privacy Online: Growing up in a Digital Age*. An Evidence Review. London: London School of Economics and Political Science; 2019.

parents. Young children are more trusting of privacy-invasive technologies, such as location trackers, likely because of their convenience.[14]

In a recent report commissioned by the UK Information Commissioner's Office, children and parents reported not reading the terms and conditions or privacy notices in platforms, feeling pressured to accept cookies to use websites, and feeling uncomfortable with their data being used for targeted advertising.[15] In addition, preschool-aged children up to teenagers in this study believed they should have the right to erase or limit the use of their digital data. However, data-brokering services are highly complex, using evolving algorithms across multiple platforms, with business practices that are intentionally opaque, which even adults do not fully understand.[16]

Data collection also influences the information that reaches young people through the internet. Previous online behaviors shape what is delivered to users via news, notifications, and social media feeds, creating a filter bubble in which all input, unbeknownst to users, is tailored to their interests and creates false norms that can undermine healthy behaviors. When algorithms can accurately predict what a child will want to watch next, it is hard for young brains to resist social media feeds, or for parents to enforce limits.

In the United States, COPPA is meant to "place parents in control over what information is collected from their young children online" and limit the data that child-directed websites, apps, or other online services collect, use, or disclose to third parties in the absence of parental consent.[17] However, COPPA was originally enacted in 1998, making many of its protections better suited for the dial-up era than the complex digital ecosystem families inhabit today. COPPA leaves open many gaps in its protections. It generally does not protect children when they are using websites or apps that are considered targeted to a general audience, nor does it apply after a child is 13 years of age. In

---

[14] Gelman SA, Martinez M, Davidson NS, Noles NS. Developing digital privacy: children's moral judgments concerning mobile GPS devices. *Child Dev*. 2018;89(1):17–26.

[15] UK Information Commissioner's Office. Towards a better digital future: informing the age appropriate design code. 2019. Available at: https://ico.org.uk/media/about-the-ico/consultations/2614763/ico-rr-report-0703.pdf. Accessed March 5, 2021.

[16] Yao Y, Lo Re D, Wang Y. Folk models of online behavioral advertising. In: *Proceedings of the 2017 ACM Conference on Computer Supported Cooperative Work and Social Computing*; February 25–March 1, 2017; Portland, OR.

[17] US Federal Trade Commission. Complying with COPPA: frequently asked questions. Available at: https://www.ftc.gov/tips-advice/business-center/guidance/complying-coppa-frequently-asked-questions#General%20Questions. Accessed March 5, 2021.

addition, the law has not been enforced reliably.[18] For instance, research has found that two-thirds of Android apps played by 3- and 4-year-olds had data trackers and shared identifiers with third parties like Facebook graph and that children of parents with lower education were at higher risk for privacy violations.[19] In light of these considerations, widespread data collection and privacy concerns for children are among the most pervasive threats facing children and teens today, and the growing use of artificial intelligence and machine learning may further compromise young people's privacy through novel data collection and analysis processes that are not yet widely understood.

Manipulative Design Practices

The digital ecosystem is replete with features intended to influence user behavior while maximizing product use and engagement. Such design elements are intended to nudge users into specific behaviors by constraining choices, highlighting preferred buttons to click, or providing rewards for preferred behavior, and they are now a common part of digital design.[20] These design elements extend digital engagement in ways that increase product engagement and exposure to advertising, and children and teenagers may not be able to identify or resist. One very clear example of this type of design element is the auto-play feature found commonly on such platforms as Netflix and YouTube. With the clock rapidly counting down and the onus on young people to opt out of watching the next video, continued viewing becomes almost a forgone conclusion. Such practices are at odds with developmentally appropriate digital media use habits, which center moderation and active engagement from users.

Deceptive Marketing and Design Practices

Digital media also employ child-friendly tactics to extend engagement and sell products and services. Gamification of ads and in-app purchases rewards users for watching ads or buying products. The practice has evolved to include

---

[18] Binns R, Lyngs U, Van Kleek M, Zhao J, Libert T, Shadbolt N. Third party tracking in the mobile ecosystem. 2018. Available at: https://arxiv.org/pdf/1804.03603.pdf. Accessed March 5, 2021.

[19] Zhao F, Egelman S, Weeks HM, Kaciroti N, Miller AL, Radesky JS. Data collection practices of mobile applications played by preschool-aged children. *JAMA Pediatrics*. 2020 Dec 1;174(12):e203345-.

[20] Fogg BJ. *Persuasive Technology: Using Computers to Change What We Think and Do*. San Francisco, CA: Morgan Kaufmann Publishers; 2002.

advertising that is less evident to the child.[21] For example, an analysis of the most-downloaded free apps for children younger than 5 years on Google Play revealed that 96% contained commercial content, including hidden ads, interstitial ads that pop up automatically, and ads that, when viewed, provided incentives, such as more game tokens or making gameplay easier. App characters were noted to encourage in-app purchases in some games.[22]

During the pandemic, education technology companies have incorporated in-app purchases in school-sanctioned educational games assigned as part of the virtual curriculum. These games, advertised to schools as cost-free to use, encourage young people to upgrade to unlock additional game features or to advance in the game. In one instance, a math-oriented game was documented to have 16 unique advertisements for membership and only four math problems over 19 minutes of game play, according to a complaint filed with the Federal Trade Commission (FTC).[23] Students were told they could "have more fun" or get "better pets" in the game if they paid up. Such exploitative tactics prey on children.

User-created influencer marketing on platforms is another form of deceptive advertising targeting children. Such content appears regularly on social media platforms and video-streaming services such as TikTok and YouTube and involves commercial content and marketing messages. For instance, the highly popular unboxing and toy-play videos as well as influencers reviewing or using products with sponsorship from companies have become commonplace viewing among young people.

Tobacco companies are notorious for their use of youth-appealing product promotion to attract young people to experiment with and continue using their highly addictive products, and there is a correlation between exposure to tobacco product advertising and youth's desire to try tobacco products.[24,25] For

---

[21] Verhellen Y, Oates C, De Pelsmacker P, Dens N. Children's responses to traditional versus hybrid advertising formats: the moderating role of persuasion knowledge. *J Consum Policy*. 2014;37:235–255.

[22] Meyer M, Adkins V, Yuan N, Weeks HM, Chang YJ, Radesky J. Advertising in young children's apps: a content analysis. *J Dev Behav Pediatr*. 2019;40(1):32–39.

[23] Solon O. Child protection nonprofit alleges 'manipulative' upselling with math game Prodigy. *NBC News*. 2021. Available at: https://www.nbcnews.com/tech/tech-news/child-protection-nonprofit-alleges-manipulative-upselling-math-game-prodigy-n1258294. Accessed March 8, 2021.

[24] Agaku IT, Ayo-Yusuf OA. The effect of exposure to pro-tobacco advertising on experimentation with emerging tobacco products among US adolescents. *Health Educ Behav*. 2014;41(3):275–280.

[25] Mantey DS, Cooper MR, Clendennen SL, Pasch KE, Perry CL. E-cigarette marketing exposure is associated with e-cigarette use among US youth. *J Adolesc Health*. 2016;58(6):686–690.

instance, tobacco companies have been known to use paid social media influencers as a form of product promotion and have not always disclosed that the posts are ads.[26] In essence, young people are led to believe that the post is organic content that reflects the poster's genuine product preferences and habits, when in fact they are being targeted by a marketing campaign intended to influence their behavior.[27]

Child advocacy groups have highlighted the large amount of child-directed influencer marketing, often undisclosed, which is not allowed on children's television (i.e., "host selling," using stars of a television program in commercials airing during that program) because it is harder for children to identify or resist.[28]

Exposure to Extreme, Age-Inappropriate, or Inaccurate Content

Algorithms for digital platforms are designed to maximize user engagement by prioritizing sensational and outrageous content that draws users in over other content. This "click driven" mindset means that companies create platforms that often lead young people to videos that may be violent or adult in nature. Even a child who watches a child-oriented video will be served up content that is increasingly extreme, inappropriate, and even harmful. A report from Common Sense found that one in five videos viewed by children 8 and under on YouTube contained ads that were not age appropriate, including content that was violent or sexual in nature.[29] The same report found that nearly a quarter of videos that children under 8 watch on YouTube are intended for older audiences.

Pediatricians also have serious concerns about misleading health information that is shared online that makes our work with families more

---

[26] Campaign for Tobacco-Free Kids, American Academy of Family Physicians, American Academy of Pediatrics, et al. Request for Investigative and Enforcement Action to Stop Misleading Advertising Online. Available at https://www.takeapart.org/wheretheressmoke/wp-content/uploads/2018/08/FTC-Petition-Full.pdf. 2018. Accessed March 8, 2021.

[27] Maloney J. Juul's Marketing Practices Under Investigation by FTC. *Wall Street Journal.* 2019. Available at: https://www.wsj.com/articles/juuls-marketing-practices-under-investigation-by-ftc-11567096073. Accessed March 8, 2021.

[28] Campaign for a Commercial-Free Childhood, Center for Digital Democracy, and Public Citizen. Complaint, request for investigation, and request for policy guidance on the deceptive practice of influencer marketing directed to children. 2016. Available at: https://www.commercialfreechildhood.org/sites/default/files/FTCInfluencerComplaint.pdf. Accessed March 5, 2021.

[29] Radesky J, et al. *Young Kids and YouTube: How Ads, Toys, and Games Dominate Viewing.* Common Sense. 2020. Available at: https://d2e111jq13me73.cloudfront.net/sites/default/files/uploads/research/2020_youngkidsyoutube-report_final-release_forweb.pdf. Accessed on March 8, 2021.

challenging. Social media platforms are becoming an increasing source of news for most Americans; a recent study conducted by the Pew Research Center found 53% of U.S. adults get news from social media sites.[30] According to the same study, conducted in August-September of 2020, a majority of the people who get news on social media continue to question its accuracy. While technology companies have taken some strides to curtail misinformation and shore up accurate content in the wake of the pandemic, more needs to be done to ensure accurate information is reaching children, teens and adults who get their news from these platforms.[31]

In 2019, the AAP wrote to the heads of Google, Facebook and Pinterest urging them to take a more proactive role combating misinformation online related to vaccines.[32] While the outreach resulted in an effective partnership with Pinterest to do so, the other companies failed to make meaningful changes.[33] Misinformation around COVID-19 and the vaccines to stop its spread have only made the need to shore up scientific, accurate content while minimizing misleading content all the more urgent. Digital media offer anti-vaccine organizations a platform to spread misinformation about disproven harms claimed to be posed by vaccines or outright conspiracy theories. While the majority of families support vaccinations, conscientious vaccine-hesitant families need accurate information and guidance from a trusted health care provider, not exposure to inaccurate information.

Health and Developmental Risks of Media Use

A growing amount of evidence has established negative physical and mental health effects stemming from digital media use. Health concerns range from increased likelihood of obesity, poorer sleep quality, engagement in high-risk

---

[30] Shearer, E, Mitchell, A. *New Uses Across Social Media Platforms in 2020.* Pew Research Center. 2021. Available at: https://www.journalism.org/2021/01/12/news-use-across-social-media-platforms-in-2020/. Accessed March 8, 2021.

[31] Marr B. Coronavirus Fake News: How Facebook, Twitter, And Instagram Are Tackling The Problem. *Forbes.* 2020. Available at: https://www.forbes.com/sites/bernardmarr/2020/03/27/finding-the-truth-about-covid-19-how-facebook-twitter-and-instagram-are-tackling-fake-news/?sh=38db62751977. Accessed March 8, 2021.

[32] American Academy of Pediatrics. *AAP Urges Major Technology Companies to Combat Vaccine Misinformation Online.* 2019. Available at: https://services.aap.org/en/news-room/news-releases/aap/2019/aap-urges-major-technology-companies-to-combat-vaccine-misinformation-online/. Accessed March 8, 2021.

[33] Jenco M. AAP, Pinterest partner to fight vaccine misinformation. *AAP News.* 2019. Available at: https://www.aappublications.org/news/2019/08/28/pinterestvaccines082819. Accessed March 8, 2021.

behaviors among older children and teens, and higher incidence of mental health concerns like depression.

Screen media exposure may increase obesity risk through both decreasing young people's physical activity and exposing young people to sophisticated marketing campaigns for unhealthy foods. Over the course of decades, research has demonstrated that high levels of media use like television watching are linked to obesity and cardiovascular risk.[34] One study found that 5- to 10-year-olds who watched more than 5 hours of TV per day were 4.6 times more likely to be overweight than those who watched between 0 and 2 hours per day.[35] Another study found that screen media consumption is inversely correlated with fruit and vegetable intake and directly correlated with energy-dense, nutrient-poor snacks, drinks, and food.[36] Digital ads often promote high-calorie, low-nutrient food and beverages.

There is a growing body of evidence that suggests that media use negatively affects sleep.[37] Increased duration of media exposure and the presence of a TV, computer, or mobile device in the bedroom in early childhood have been associated with fewer minutes of sleep per night, especially among children of racial/ethnic minority groups.[38] Later bedtimes after evening media use and violent content in the media also may be contributing factors, and suppression of endogenous melatonin by blue light emitted from screens is another possible cause.[39],[40] Associations between media and sleep are seen in infants as well; 6- to 12-month-olds who were

---

[34] Bel-Serrat S, Mouratidou T, Santaliestra-Pasías AM, et al; IDEFICS consortium. Clustering of multiple lifestyle behaviours and its association to cardiovascular risk factors in children: the IDEFICS study. *Eur J Clin Nutr*. 2013;67(8):848– 854pmid:23632753.

[35] Gortmaker SL, Must A, Sobol AM, Peterson K, Colditz GA, Dietz WH. Television viewing as a cause of increasing obesity among children in the United States, 1986-1990. *Arch Pediatr Adolesc Med*. 1996;150(4):356–362pmid:8634729.

[36] Pearson N, Biddle SJ. Sedentary behavior and dietary intake in children, adolescents, and adults. A systematic review. *Am J Prev Med*. 2011;41(2):178–188.

[37] Bruni O, Sette S, Fontanesi L, Baiocco R, Laghi F, Baumgartner E. Technology use and sleep quality in preadolescence and adolescence. *J Clin Sleep Med*. 2015;11(12):1433–1441pmid: 26235161.

[38] Cespedes EM, Gillman MW, Kleinman K, Rifas-Shiman SL, Redline S, Taveras EM. Television viewing, bedroom television, and sleep duration from infancy to mid-childhood. *Pediatrics*. 2014;133(5). Available at: http://pediatrics.aappublications.org/content/133/5/e1163pmid:24733878.

[39] Garrison MM, Christakis DA. The impact of a healthy media use intervention on sleep in preschool children. *Pediatrics*. 2012;130(3):492–499pmid:22869826.

[40] Salti R, Tarquini R, Stagi S, et al. Age-dependent association of exposure to television screen with children's urinary melatonin excretion? *Neuroendocrinol Lett*. 2006;27(1-2):73–80pmid: 16648813.

exposed to screen media in the evening hours showed significantly shorter night-time sleep duration than those who had no evening screen exposure.[41]

The links between media and health behaviors among adolescents have been backed by decades of evidence in traditional media.[42],[43],[44],[45] For instance, studies have shown that exposure to alcohol or tobacco use or risky sexual behaviors in TV or movies is associated with initiation of these behaviors, leading some to describe TV as a "superpeer."[46],[47],[48] A growing body of evidence suggests that these influences also are strong in digital and social media.[49,50,51,52,53,54,55,56,57]

---

41 Vijakkhana N, Wilaisakditipakorn T, Ruedeekhajorn K, Pruksananonda C, Chonchaiya W. Evening media exposure reduces night-time sleep. Acta *Paediatr.* 2015;104(3):306–312pmid:25521612.

42 Gidwani PP, Sobol A, DeJong W, Perrin JM, Gortmaker SL. Television viewing and initiation of smoking among youth. *Pediatrics.* 2002;110(3):505–508pmid:12205251.

43 Dalton MA, Beach ML, Adachi-Mejia AM, et al. Early exposure to movie smoking predicts established smoking by older teens and young adults. *Pediatrics.* 2009;123(4). Available at: http://pediatrics.aappublications.org/content/123/4/e551pmid:19336346.

44 Dalton MA, Sargent JD, Beach ML, et al. Effect of viewing smoking in movies on adolescent smoking initiation: a cohort study. *Lancet.* 2003;362(9380):281–285pmid:12892958.

45 Titus-Ernstoff L, Dalton MA, Adachi-Mejia AM, Longacre MR, Beach ML. Longitudinal study of viewing smoking in movies and initiation of smoking by children. *Pediatrics.* 2008;121(1):15–21pmid:18166552.

46 Robinson TN, Chen HL, Killen JD. Television and music video exposure and risk of adolescent alcohol use. *Pediatrics.* 1998;102(5):E54pmid:9794984.

47 Klein JD, Brown JD, Childers KW, Oliveri J, Porter C, Dykers C. Adolescents' risky behavior and mass media use. *Pediatrics.* 1993;92(1):24–31pmid:8516081.

48 Strasburger VC, Wilson BJ, Jordan A. *Children, adolescents and the media.* Thousand Oaks, CA: Sage Publications; 2008.

49 Hinduja S, Patchin JW. Personal information of adolescents on the Internet: A quantitative content analysis of MySpace. *J Adolesc.* 2008;31(1):125–146pmid:17604833.

50 Moreno MA, Parks MR, Zimmerman FJ, Brito TE, Christakis DA. Display of health risk behaviors on MySpace by adolescents: prevalence and associations. *Arch Pediatr Adolesc Med.* 2009;163(1):27–34pmid:19124701.

51 Moreno MA, Parks M, Richardson LP. What are adolescents showing the world about their health risk behaviors on MySpace? *MedGenMed.* 2007;9(4):9pmid:18311359.

52 McGee JB, Begg M. What medical educators need to know about "Web 2.0." *Med Teach.* 2008;30(2):164– 169pmid:18464141.

53 Moreno MA, Ton A, Selkie E, Evans Y. Secret Society 123: understanding the language of self-harm on Instagram. *J Adolesc Health.* 2016;58(1):78–84pmid:26707231.

54 Moreno MA, Briner LR, Williams A, Walker L, Christakis DA. Real use or "real cool": adolescents speak out about displayed alcohol references on social networking websites. *J Adolesc Health.* 2009;45(4):420–422pmid:19766949.

55 Moreno MA, Kota R, Schoohs S, Whitehill JM. The Facebook influence model: a concept mapping approach. *Cyberpsychol Behav Soc Netw.* 2013;16(7):504–511pmid:23621717.

56 Litt DM, Stock ML. Adolescent alcohol-related risk cognitions: the roles of social norms and social networking sites. *Psychol Addict Behav.* 2011;25(4):708–713pmid:21644803.

57 Fogg BJ. Mass interpersonal persuasion: an early view of a new phenomenon. In: Oinas-Kukkonen H, Hasle P, Harjumaa M, Segerståhl K, Øhrstrøm P, eds. *Persuasive Technology,*

Health Equity

Youth of color encounter additional challenges from digital media and face barriers accessing the beneficial aspects of technology. Basic access to broadband internet and devices remains a major concern nationwide, and a year of virtual learning has only increased the stakes of this digital divide. Without access to an adequate internet connection or device, those left disconnected are missing out on critical opportunities for learning and socialization, with long-term implications for the achievement gap and developmental trajectories. A recent report found that 26% of Latinx, 30% of Black, and 35% of American Indian students lacked adequate connectivity to broadband and digital devices as compared to 18% of white students.[58]

Though recent data are limited, it appears that communities of color are disproportionately targeted ads for unhealthy products that worsen health. For instance, more fast food and sugar beverages are advertised in Black, Latinx, and low-income communities, as well as candy and cereals. Nearly 40% of ads on television targeted to Black and Latinx populations are for fast food and other restaurants.[59] Studies have also shown that Black, Latinx, and American Indian youth are exposed to alcohol content via social media, banner ads, and video ads at disparately high rates.[60,61,62] More broadly, the alcohol and tobacco industries have a long history of targeting communities of color with their harmful products. Targeted marketing also results in different products being advertised to different populations, which may accentuate existing disparities.

It is also clear that children from under-resourced communities tend to spend more time in front of a screen, which could be due to structural issues that limit access to safe spaces for them to play, parents who may work long hours or night shifts that do not allow them to actively supervise children,

---

Third International Conference, PERSUASIVE 2008, Oulu, Finland, June 4–6, 2008, Proceedings. Berlin, Germany: Springer-Verlag Berlin Heidelberg; 2008:23–34.

[58] 58Chandra S, et al. *Closing the K-12 Digital Divide in the Age of Distance Learning*. Common Sense. 2020. Available at: https://www.commonsensemedia.org/sites/default/files/uploads/pdfs/common_sense_media_report_final_7_1_3pm_w eb.pdf. Accessed March 8, 2021.

[59] Harris JL, Shehan C, Gross R, et al. *Food Advertising Targeted to Hispanic and Black Youth: Contributing to Health Disparities*. Hartford, CT: Rudd Center for Food Policy & Obesity; 2015.

[60] Jernigan DH, Rushman AE. Measuring youth exposure to alcohol marketing on social networking sites: challenges and prospects. *J Public Health Policy*. 2014;35(1):91–104.

[61] D'Amico EJ, Martino SC, Collins RL, et al. Factors associated with younger adolescents' exposure to online alcohol advertising. *Psychol Addict Behav*. 2017;31(2):212–219.

[62] Alaniz ML, Wilkes C. Pro-drinking messages and message environments for young adults: the case of alcohol industry advertising in African American, Latino, and Native American communities. *J Public Health Policy*. 1998;19(4):447–472.

limited affordable childcare options, and lack of access to high quality programs. For instance, Sesame Street recently moved from PBS to premium pay cable station HBO. We must be attentive to these specific considerations and others impacting communities of color as we craft solutions to these problems.

The Path Forward

In the face of this extraordinarily complex digital ecosystem, the question then becomes how we as a society move forward to make real progress for children and families. We must be bold in our thinking and ensure that government action on technology addresses the most pervasive and concerning industry practices that harm children and teens while preserving and enhancing the positive aspects of technology for young people.

It is critical that Congress act to improve and strengthen laws that are designed to protect children online. Updating the Children's Online Privacy Protection Act is a good place to start. An enhanced COPPA should, at a minimum, be expanded to protect all children under the age of 18 and cover the wide array of devices that collect data from children, including mobile devices, internet-connected toys, and others. Technology platforms should also be required to set the highest level of privacy protections as the default.

As a general rule, data collection should be considered an opt in practice for young people, if the practice is even allowed at all. In the event that data is collected, mandated disclosures with information on what data will be collected, how the data will be used, with whom data might be shared, and the risks and benefits to the consumer should be prominently provided at appropriate literacy and developmental levels. This must also include information about blocking this data collection and how young people can go about deleting their personal information permanently. Congress must also act to close the loophole that has allowed technology companies to evade COPPA regulations by claiming to be "general audience" rather than "child-directed" platforms.

We as pediatricians understand that young people are particularly vulnerable to deceptive or unfair marketing practices. We call on Congress to ban targeted (i.e., data-driven behavioral) advertising to all individuals under the age of 18. These invasive and extraordinarily effective ads have no place in our society targeting young people who may not fully understand that they are being sold a product or why. We further request that Congress ban all commercial advertising to children younger than 7 years, and limit advertising to older children and teenagers in light of developmental considerations.

Advertising for products with demonstrated health effects on young people, like unhealthy food, alcohol, and cannabis, need additional attention from Congress.

Congress should also fund digital literacy curricula in schools to ensure that children and teens are equipped with the skills they need to navigate an increasingly complex digital ecosystem. Congress can also fund efforts to promote digital equity by expanding access to broadband internet and devices, while also targeting digital media practices and marketing tactics that disproportionately impact youth of color. Lastly, we need more research to better understand how digital media impact children's health and development and ultimately how we can create a digital ecosystem that is most beneficial to young people.

The issues young people and their families face in the digital world are significant, but they are not insurmountable. It starts with holding digital platforms accountable for the real-world impacts on children of the products they create. Through effective public policy, it is possible to build a better digital world for our children.

Thank you for your attention to this critical issue.

Ms. SCHAKOWSKY. Thank you.

Now, I will recognize Dr. DeAngelis. You are recognized for 5 minutes.

Statement of Corey A. DeAngelis, Ph.D.

Dr. DEANGELIS. Thank you, Chair Schakowsky, Ranking Member Bilirakis, and distinguished Members of Congress. Thank you so much for the opportunity.

There have been substantial costs associated with keeping schools closed in terms of students losing ground academically, mentally, and physically, and many of these negative effects have disproportionately impacted less advantaged groups, leading to inequities.

Meanwhile, the evidence has generally indicated that schools can reopen safely for in-person instruction and that school reopenings are generally not associated with major increases in overall COVID–19 transmission or hospitalizations.

In addition to the science, actions by several teachers' unions and the stark contrast in the response to the pandemic from the private versus the public sectors suggest that reopening decisions have had more to do with political partisanship and power dynamics than safety and the needs of families.

Private schools have been open for the most part of the past year or have been fighting to reopen in that time. In fact, private schools in Kentucky took the fight to the Supreme Court in an attempt to provide in-person services, and private schools in States such as Ohio and Michigan took similar legal actions.

A private school in Sacramento even rebranded itself as a day care to try to get around the government's arbitrary school closure rules.

But many teachers' unions have been fighting to remain closed by shifting the reopening goalpost every step of the way. It is not because of a difference in intentions or benevolence on the part of the employees between the two sectors. The difference is one of incentives. One of these sectors gets children's education dollars regardless of whether they open their doors for business.

Several actions by teachers' unions also raise some eyebrows. Just as school closures hit in March 2020, union groups in States such as Oregon and Pennsylvania lobbied the governments to make it illegal for families to switch to virtual charter schools that have already been successfully providing students with remote instruction for years.

These actions aimed to protect a system at the expense of families at the worst time possible.

Then came the political demands. In their report on safely reopening schools, the Los Angeles Teachers' Union called for things unrelated to school reopening, such as defunding the police, Medicare for All, a wealth tax, and a ban on charter schools. At least 10 teachers' unions similarly joined the Democratic Socialists of America to hold a National Day of Resistance to demand safe schools, including political demands on two occasions in less than a year.

Other things just did not add up. Why was it safe enough for public school buildings to reopen for in-person child-care services but not for in-person learning?

Why was it safe enough for teachers' union officials to travel to Puerto Rico to vacation in person and to send their own children to in-person private schools but not safe enough for their members to return to work in person?

Why have four studies each found that school reopenings are more strongly related to political partisanship and teachers' union influence than COVID risk?

Why did the Congressional Budget Office estimate that only 5 percent of the $128 billion in relief funding would be spent this year, while up to 95 percent of the funding would be paid out after the pandemic if the goal is to reopen schools now?

Why did half of the Senate block an amendment that would have made a Federal funding conditional upon reopening schools in person if all teachers were vaccinated?

Why has Florida, a State that only spends about $10,700 per student, far below the national average, been able to essentially fully reopen its schools while California, a State that has much stronger teachers' unions and spends about 38 percent more per student, has kept its doors shut?

It might be because the school reopening debate has always been more about politics and power than safety and the needs of families.

The past year has put a spotlight on the main problem with K to 12 education in the U.S., a long existing, massive power imbalance between public school teachers' unions and individual families. And the only way that we are ever going to fix that messedup set of incentives that is baked into the public school system is to empower families by funding students directly.

Think about it this way. If a grocery store does not reopen, families can take their money elsewhere. If a school does not reopen, families should similarly be able to take their children's education dollars elsewhere.

After all, education funding is supposed to be meant for educating children, not for protecting a particular institution. Families have been getting a bad deal, and they are realizing that there is not any good reason to fund closed institutions when we can fund students directly instead.

The latest nationwide survey conducted by RealClear Opinion Research found that support for funding students directly surged by 10 percentage points between April and August of 2020.

And we already fund students directly in higher education with Pell Grants and the GI Bill and in pre-K with programs such as Head Start. The funding goes to individual students and families as opposed to buildings.

With all of these programs, in addition to food stamps, Section 8 housing vouchers, and Medicaid, we fund individuals instead of institutions. We should apply the same logic to K to 12 education and fund students, not systems.

Thank you so much.

[The prepared statement of Dr. DeAngelis follows:]

Prepared Statement of Corey DeAngelis, Ph.D.

Prepared for: United States House Subcommittee on Consumer Protection & Commerce

Date: March 11, 2021

Chairman Pallone, Chairwoman Schakowsky, Ranking Member Rodgers, Ranking Member Bilirakis, and Distinguished Members of Congress,

Thank you so much for the opportunity.

There have been substantial costs associated with keeping schools closed in terms of students losing ground academically, mentally, and physically – and many of these negative effects have disproportionately impacted less advantaged groups, leading to inequities. Meanwhile, the evidence has generally indicated that schools can safely reopen for in-person instruction and that school reopenings are not associated with major increases in overall Covid-19 transmission or hospitalizations.

In addition to the science, actions by several teachers' unions – and the stark contrast in the response to the pandemic from the private versus public sectors – suggest that reopening decisions have had more to do with political partisanship and power dynamics than safety and the needs of families.

Private schools have been open for most of the past year – or have been fighting to reopen in that time. In fact, private schools in Kentucky[63] took the fight to the Supreme Court in an attempt to provide in-person services, and private schools in states such as Ohio[64] and Michigan[65] took similar legal actions. A private school in Sacramento even rebranded itself as a daycare to try to get around the government's arbitrary closure rules.[66] But many teachers' unions have been fighting to remain closed by shifting the reopening

---

[63] Danville Christian Academy, Inc., et al. v. Andy Beshear, Governor of Kentucky. Supreme Court of the United States. Retrieved from https://www.supremecourt.gov/opinions/20pdf/20a96_e29g.pdf.

[64] Monclova Christian Academy; St. John's Jesuit High School & Academy; Emmanuel Christian School; Citizens for Community Values dba Ohio Christian Education Network v. Toledo-Lucas County Health Department. United States Court of Appeals for the Sixth Circuit. Retrieved from https://www.opn.ca6.uscourts.gov/opinions.pdf/20a0392p-06.pdf.

[65] Justice Department backs Michigan private schools in virus challenge. *U.S. News & World Report*. Retrieved from https://www.usnews.com/news/best-states/michigan/articles/2020-12-11/justice-department-backs-private-schools-in-virus-challenge.

[66] Sacramento County must stop Capital Christian School's coronavirus 'day care' stunt. *The Sacramento Bee*. Retrieved from https://www.sacbee.com/opinion/editorials/article245037380.html.

goalposts every step of the way.[67] That's not because of a difference in intentions or benevolence on the part of the employees between the two sectors. The difference is one of incentives. One of these sectors receives children's education dollars regardless of whether they open their doors for business.

Several actions by teachers' unions also raised some eyebrows. Just as school closures hit in March 2020, union groups in states such as Oregon[68] and Pennsylvania[69] lobbied the government to make it illegal for families to switch to virtual charter schools that have already been successfully providing students with remote instruction for years. These actions aimed to protect a system at the expense of families at the worst time possible.

Then came the political demands. In their report[70] on safely reopening schools, the Los Angeles teachers' union called for things unrelated to reopening schools, such as defunding the police, Medicare-for-All, a wealth tax, and a ban on charter schools. At least ten teachers' unions similarly joined with the Democratic Socialists of America to hold a "National Day of Resistance" to "Demand Safe Schools" including political demands on two occasions in less than a year.[71]

Other things just didn't add up: why was it safe enough for public school buildings to reopen for in-person childcare services, but not for in-person learning? Why was it safe enough for teachers' union officials to travel to Puerto Rico to vacation[72] in person, and to send their own children[73] to in-person private schools, but not safe enough for their members to return to work

---

[67] Teachers' Unions Make the Case for School Choice. *National Review*. Retrieved from https://www.nationalreview.com/2021/02/teachers-unions-make-the-case-for-school-choice/.

[68] Oregon's Coronavirus Education Lockdown. *The Wall Street Journal*. Retrieved from https://www.wsj.com/articles/oregons-coronavirus-education-lockdown-11585697080.

[69] Cyber charters in Pa. keep teaching amid confusion in coronavirus shutdown order. *WHYY*. Retrieved from https://whyy.org/articles/cyber-charters-in-pa-keep-teaching-amid-confusion-in-coronavirus-shutdown-order/.

[70] The Same Storm, but Different Boats: The Safe and Equitable Conditions for Starting LAUSD in 2020-21. *United Teachers Los Angeles*. Retrieved from https://www.utla.net/sites/default/files/samestormdiffboats_final.pdf.

[71] National Day of Resistance. *Demand Safe Schools*. Retrieved from https://www.demandsafeschools.org/demands/.

[72] CTU board member facing criticism for vacationing in Caribbean while pushing remote learning. *WGN*. Retrieved from https://wgntv.com/news/wgn-investigates/ctu-board-member-facing-criticism-for-vacationing-in-caribbean-while-pushing-remote-learning/.

[73] After Leading School Closures, Berkeley Teachers Union President Spotted Dropping Daughter Off at In-Person Preschool. *KQED*. Retrieved from https://www.kqed.org/news/11862469/after-leading-school-closures-berkeley-teachers-union-president-spotted-dropping-daughter-off-at-in-person-preschool.

in person? Why have four studies each found that school reopenings are more strongly related to political partisanship and teachers' union influence than Covid risk?

Why did the Congressional Budget Office estimate[74] that only 5 percent of the $129 billion in relief funding would be spent this year, while up to 95 percent of the funding would be paid out after the pandemic, if the goal is to reopen schools now? Why did half of the Senate block an amendment that would have made federal relief funding conditional on reopening schools in person if all teachers were vaccinated?

Why has Florida – a state that only spends about $10,700 per student[75] – been able to essentially fully reopen[76] its schools, while California – a state that has much stronger teachers' unions and spends about 38 percent more per student – has kept their doors closed?

It might be because the school reopening debate has always been more about politics and power than safety and the needs of families. The past year has put a spotlight on the main problem with K-12 education in the U.S.: a long-existing massive power imbalance between public school teachers' unions and individual families.

The only way that we're ever going to fix that messed-up set of incentives that's baked into the public school system is to empower families by funding students directly. Think about it this way: if a grocery store doesn't reopen, families can take their money elsewhere. If a school doesn't reopen, families should similarly be able to take their children's education dollars elsewhere. After all, education funding is supposed to be meant for educating children, not for protecting a particular institution.

Families have been getting a bad deal and they're realizing that there isn't any good reason to fund closed institutions when we can fund students directly instead. The latest nationwide survey conducted by RealClear Opinion Research found that support for funding students directly surged by 10 percentage points between April and August 2020.[77]

---

[74] Congressional Budget Office Cost Estimate. Retrieved from https://www.cbo.gov/system/files/2021-02/hEdandLaborreconciliationestimate.pdf.

[75] Table 11. Summary Tables. 2018 Public Elementary-Secondary Education Finance Data. *United States Census Bureau*. Retrieved from https://www.census.gov/data/tables/2018/econ/school-finances/secondary-education-finance.html.

[76] Burbio's K-12 School Opening Tracker. *Burbio*. Retrieved from https://cai.burbio.com/school-opening-tracker/.

[77] Support for School Choice Surges as Schools Start. *RealClear Opinion Research*. Retrieved from https://www.federationforchildren.org/support-for-school-choice-surges-as-schools-start/.

We already fund students directly in higher education with Pell Grants and the GI Bill and in pre-K with programs such as Head Start. The funding goes to individual students and families as opposed to buildings. With all of these programs – in addition to food stamps, Section 8, and Medicaid – we fund individuals instead of institutions. We should apply the same logic to K-12 education and fund students, not systems.

Students Are Losing Ground Academically, Mentally, and Physically

The negative effects on student learning have disproportionately harmed less advantaged groups, meaning school closures have exacerbated deep, already-existing, inequities in our school system and society. A nationwide analysis by McKinsey and Company (2020b) found that students lost about three months of learning in reading and math from school closures in 2020, and the researchers predicted that the learning losses would continue to escalate. In fact, the researchers predicted that the learning losses would actually increase to nearly 7 months overall, and to about 12 months for students from low-income families, even if schools had reopened for full-time in-person instruction back in January 2021 (see Figure 1 in Appendix) (McKinsey & Company, 2020a).

McKinsey and Company (2020a) further estimated that these negative effects on academic outcomes associated with keeping schools closed for in-person instruction would worsen existing achievement gaps by race by 15 to 20 percent. They also estimated that the learning losses associated with school closures could increase high school dropout rates by 2 to 9 percentage points, which would translate to about 232 thousand to 1.1 million additional ninth to eleventh graders dropping out of high school. They further estimated that the average K-12 student in the U.S. could lose $61,000 to $82,000 in lifetime earnings – with larger earnings reductions for Black and Hispanic students – solely as a result of COVID-19-related learning losses.

An analysis conducted by Stanford University's Eric Hanushek and the University of Munich's Ludger Woessmann, published by the Organisation for Economic Co-operation and Development (OECD) in Fall 2020, estimated that learning losses from school closures for students in grades 1 through 12 could reduce their lifetime earnings by around 3 percent. They additionally estimated that the learning losses that had already accrued by the Fall of 2020 could reduce long-run economic output in the U.S. by $14.2 trillion (Hanushek & Woessmann, 2020).

Christakis, Van Cleve, and Zimmerman (2020) similarly found that missed instruction during 2020 could be associated with an estimated 13.8

million years of life lost associated with reductions in educational attainment based on U.S. studies.

The nationwide analysis by McKinsey and Company (2020a) additionally found that students of color fell further behind academically than White students in the spring of 2020. The same study indicated that student engagement with online math coursework dropped 16 percent among low-income students, whereas the drop was about 2 percent for high-income students, suggesting more evidence of widening disparities in learning. A study of over 5 million students in grades 1 through 8 from all 50 states, conducted by *Renaissance Learning*, found evidence to suggest that students in some grades were performing as far as 7 weeks behind in reading and that students in all grades were performing 12 or more weeks behind in math.[78]

The same national analysis found that the negative effects were larger for students identified as Black, Hispanic, and American Indian, students who attended schools serving low-income families, and students in public schools as opposed to private schools. Another study of nearly 4.4 million studies in grades 3 through 8, conducted by Northwest Evaluation Association (NWEA), found that student achievement in Fall 2020 was 5 to 10 percentile points lower in math relative to the previous year (Kuhfeld et al., 2020). The same evaluation found that overall reading achievement in Fall 2020 was similar to Fall 2019, on average, but the researchers noted that there was evidence of reading declines that were disproportionately concentrated among students identified as Black and Hispanic. Agostinelli et al. (2020) found that "school closures have a large and persistent effect on educational outcomes that is highly unequal" and that "high school students from poor neighborhoods suffer a learning loss of 0.4 standard deviations, whereas children from rich neighborhoods remain unscathed."

Harvard University's Opportunity Insights Economic Tracker further highlights these disparities. Student progress on math achievement, as measured by data provided by Zearn Math, was relatively similar across income groups before the schools started to close after the pandemic emergency was declared on March 13th, 2019. Ever since then, through mid-February of 2021, the data have consistently indicated stark disparities in rates of math achievement progress by income levels (see Figure 2 in Appendix).[79]

[78] How Kids Are Performing. Tracking the Impact of COVID-19 on Reading and Mathematics Achievement. Special Report Series. Fall 2020 Edition. *Renaissance Learning, Inc*. Retrieved from https://renaissance.widen.net/s/wmjtlxkhbm.

[79] Percent Change in Student Math Progress. Opportunity Insights Economic Tracker. Harvard University. Retrieved from https://tracktherecovery.org/.

Several individual school districts have also reported surges in the percentages of students failing their courses in 2020. Fairfax County Public Schools, for example, reported that the percentage of middle and high school students failing two or more courses in 2020 increased by 83 percent overall since the same time in the previous school year.[80] That rate of failing grades increased even more, by 111 percent, for students with special needs. The percentage of students failing classes in St. Paul, Minnesota in 2020 increased by 127 percent for high school students and increased by 222 percent for middle school students since the same time in the previous school year.[81] At the same time, data reported by the Houston Chronicle indicated that nearly 4 in 10 students failed two or more classes in Houston Independent School District in Texas.[82]

Data from Arlington Public Schools in Virginia revealed that failing grades in 2020 increased by 91 percent since the previous year for middle school students with disabilities and by 81 percent for high school students with disabilities.[83] Data from Montgomery County Public Schools in Maryland revealed that failing grades skyrocketed, with 36 percent of ninth-grade students from low-income families failing the first marking period in English, representing about a 500 percent increase in the rate of failure from the same group of students during the previous year.[84]

Learning losses are just the tip of the iceberg. Significant evidence suggests school closures are also contributing to negative effects on children's mental health (Lee, 2020; Varas, Menon, & Bellafiore, 2021). A national survey of parents with school-aged children conducted by Gallup in May 2020

---

[80] Study of Teaching and Learning During the Covid 19 Pandemic. Analyses of Q1 Secondary Marks. *Fairfax County Public Schools*. Retrieved from https://go.boarddocs.com/vsba/fairfax/Board.nsf/files/BVJV847F7247/$file/Q1%20Marks%20Rpt%20-%20v6%20lzh.pdf.

[81] Retrieved from https://www.twincities.com/2020/12/08/st-paul-district-offers-second-chance-after-hs-students-fail-34-of-classes/.

[82] Failing grades spike in Virginia's largest school system as online learning gap emerges nationwide. *Washington Post*. Retrieved from https://www.washingtonpost.com/local/education/fairfax-schools-more-failing-grades/2020/11/24/1ac2412e-2e34-11eb-96c2-aac3f162215d_story.html.

[83] Secondary First Quarter 2020-21 Grade Report. *Arlington Public Schools*. Retrieved from https://go.boarddocs.com/vsba/arlington/Board.nsf/files/BWDQHQ696B9C/$file/D-1%20SY%2020-21%20Update%20-%20Secondary%201st%20Quarter%20Grades%20Rept.pdf.

[84] Failing grades double and triple — some rising sixfold — amid pandemic learning. *Washington Post*. Retrieved from https://www.washingtonpost.com/local/education/montgomery-county-failing-grades/2020/12/03/913affd0-34fb-11eb-8d38-6aea1adb3839_story.html.

found that 29 percent of respondents reported that their child was "already experiencing harm" to their emotional or mental health because of social distancing and school closures.[85] An additional 14 percent indicated that they believed their children could only continue distancing for "a few more weeks" until their mental health would suffer. Gallup additionally found[86] that 86 percent of parents said "being separated from classmates and teachers" was a challenge for their children, with 45 percent responding that the separation was a "major challenge."

A poll conducted by Pew Research Center in October 2020 found that 59 percent of parents were more concerned than before the pandemic about the emotional well-being of their children, with higher levels of concern among parents with children in remote learning environments relative to parents with children who had access to in-person instruction.[87] A national survey published in *Pediatrics* found that 14 percent of parents with children reported worsening behavioral health for their children between March and June of 2020 (Patrick et al., 2020).

A study published in The Journal of the American Medical Association Network Open compared reports of student mental health problems in China, before and after the pandemic started, and found that school closures were associated with an increase in depression, self-injury, and suicidal thoughts, plans, and attempts (Zhang et al., 2020). Viner et al. (2021) performed a systematic review of 72 studies on the topic and concluded that school closures are "associated with considerable harms to CYP [children and young people] health and wellbeing." Clark County Public Schools, the nation's fifth-largest school district, reopened their schools after 18 student suicides occurred over nine months, which was twice the amount from the previous year (Green, 2021).

Some pediatricians have also warned that school closures have led to weight gain among children. A pediatrician from Brooklyn, New York, for example, recently said[88] that they were "seeing a lot of elementary school-

---

[85] U.S. Parents Say COVID-19 Harming Child's Mental Health. *Gallup*. Retrieved from https://news.gallup.com/poll/312605/parents-say-covid-harming-child-mental-health.aspx.

[86] Social Factors Most Challenging in COVID-19 Distance Learning. *Gallup*. Retrieved from https://news.gallup.com/poll/312566/social-factors-challenging-covid-distance-learning.aspx.

[87] Most Parents of K-12 Students Learning Online Worry About Them Falling Behind. *Pew Research Center*. Retrieved from https://www.pewresearch.org/social-trends/2020/10/29/most-parents-of-k-12-students-learning-online-worry-about-them-falling-behind/.

[88] Remote Learning During Covid-19 Is Causing Children to Gain Weight, Doctors Warn. *The Wall Street Journal*. Retrieved from https://www.wsj.com/articles/remote-learning-during-covid-19-is-causing-children-to-gain-weight-doctors-warn-11613298602.

aged kids who are gaining 20 to 30 pounds in a year." Rundle et al. (2020) also reported that Covid-induced school closures "may exacerbate the epidemic of childhood obesity and increase disparities in obesity risk."

There are other unintended consequences of preventing families from having the option of in-person instruction. For example, recent studies have found that closures have disrupted the childcare market (Ali, Herbst, & Makridis, 2021) and that women have disproportionately dropped out of the labor market to school their children.[89] Economists from the Federal Reserve Bank of San Francisco found "significant differences between men and women conditional on their parental status several months into the pandemic recession as schools failed to re-open for the start of the new school year" (p.3) and that "prime aged women with a child at home experienced significant job loss and a weaker labor market recovery" (Lofton, Petrosky-Nadeau, & Seitelman, 2021, p.15). Another study by economists from the Federal Reserve Bank of Minneapolis reported that "school closures and child care issues have placed an added burden on parents" and that "mothers have increasingly left the labor force because of care responsibilities" (Boesch et al., 2021).

Some families might have privacy concerns associated with remote learning, particularly if they do not have access to an in-person alternative. Parents might also feel uncomfortable with having their children on virtual classrooms or might have concerns regarding screen time or data collection by third-party apps or other software that could be used to facilitate remote instruction.[90]

Schools Are Not Major Contributors of Community Spread and Can Reopen Safely

Substantial evidence suggests that schools can reopen in person safely and that schools are generally not major contributors of overall community transmission or COVID-19 hospitalizations (Christakis, Van Cleve, & Zimmerman, 2020; Harris, Ziedan, & Hassig, 2021; Honein, Barrios, & Brooks, 2021; Oster, 2020; UNICEF, 2020). A study published in *The Journal of the American Medical Association Network Open* by researchers from the

---

[89] How Covid-19 triggered America's first female recession in 50 years. *The Economist*. Retrieved from https://www.economist.com/graphic-detail/2021/03/08/how-covid-19-triggered-americas-first-female-recession-in-50-years.

[90] Massive Shift to Remote Learning Prompts Big Data Privacy Concerns. *Education Week*. Retrieved from https://www.edweek.org/technology/massive-shift-to-remote-learning-prompts-big-data-privacy-concerns/2020/03.

Centers for Disease Control and Prevention (CDC) concluded that "the preponderance of available evidence from the fall school semester has been reassuring insofar as the type of rapid spread that was frequently observed in congregate living facilities or high-density worksites has not been reported in education settings in schools" and that "there has been little evidence that schools have contributed meaningfully to increased community transmission" (Honein, Barrios, & Brooks, 2021, p. E1).

Data from Brown University's COVID-19 School Response Dashboard has consistently found that positivity rates in the schools are generally lower than the positivity rates in their overall communities (Oster, 2020). Harris, Ziedan, and Hassig (2021, p.26) concluded that their "results suggest that school reopenings have not increased COVID-19 hospitalizations, especially for the 75 percent of counties that had the lowest baseline hospitalizations." For the counties with the highest COVID-19 hospitalizations at baseline, Harris, Ziedan, and Hassig (2021, p.1) found that the "estimates are inconsistent across methods and are therefore inconclusive." *The Journal of the American Academy of Pediatrics* published a study of 11 school districts in North Carolina and found that "no instances of child-to-adult transmission of SARS-CoV-2 were reported within schools" (Zimmerman et al., 2021). Goldhaber et al. (2020) examined data from Michigan and Washington state and found that in-person schooling does not contribute to community transmission of the virus in locations with low levels of pre-existing COVID-19 cases.

Oster (2020) reported that "in-person schooling does not appear to increase the risk of Covid-19 transmission for staff and students, according to data from New York state." In New York City, the 7-day average of the citywide Covid-19 positivity rate was 6.35 percent[91] as of March 3rd, 2021, whereas the positivity rate in their schools was only 0.57 percent through March 4th, 2021.[92] New York Governor, Andrew Cuomo, noted[93] this fact as well, stating that New York is "not seeing spread in the schools. You see a very low percentage of positivity in the schools." At the end of November, 2020, Dr. Anthony Fauci said on ABC that "If you look at the data, the spread

---

[91] Daily Cases, Hospitalizations and Deaths. COVID-19: Data. *New York City Department of Health and Mental Hygiene*. Retrieved from https://www1.nyc.gov/site/doh/covid/covid-19-data.page.

[92] School Based Testing Report. *New York City Department of Education*. Retrieved from https://testingresults.schools.nyc/.

[93] Audio & Rush Transcript: Governor Cuomo Calls into MSNBC Live with Katy Tur. Governor Andrew M. Cuomo. *New York State*. Retrieved from https://www.governor.ny.gov/news/audio-rush-transcript-governor-cuomo-calls-msnbc-live-katy-tur.

among children and from children is not really very big at all" and that we should "close the bars and keep the schools open."

UNICEF (2020, p. 5) reported that "data from 191 counties collected from February to September 2020 show no consistent association between school reopening status and COVID-19 infection rates." *The New England Journal of Medicine* published a 2021 analysis of data from Sweden, a country that largely kept schools open in person in 2020, which found that 0.90 children between the ages of 7 and 16 per 100,000 were admitted to an ICU for Covid-19 and that "no child with Covid-19 died" (Ludvigsson et al., 2021) Ludvigsson et al. (2021) also found that the sex- and age-adjusted risk ratio of intensive care among schoolteachers was 0.43 relative to other occupations excluding healthcare workers. Another study from Sweden, published by Stockholm University, noted that "one other finding worth discussing on its own is the low Covid-19 mortality risk of children's and adolescents' teachers" (Billingsley et al., 2020).

Politics and Power Dynamics Influence School Reopening Decisions

Private schools have been substantially more likely to reopen for in-person instruction than public schools in the U.S., suggesting that incentives might have something to do with reopening decisions.[94]

In the private sector, school leaders understand that families can take their children's education dollars elsewhere if they are not sufficiently satisfied with the provided services (Chubb & Moe, 1988; Friedman, 1955; DeAngelis & Holmes Erickson, 2018). In the public sector, in general, the school district continues to receive children's K-12 education dollars despite the desires of individual families, and regardless of whether they open their doors for in-person instruction, because there are large transaction costs associated with switching out of residentially assigned schools – families would have to move residences to access a different public school, pay out of pocket for private school tuition and fees, or pay to cover the costs of home-based private education (Hanushek et al., 2007).

[94] Private schools pull students away from public schools. *Axios*. Retrieved from https://www.axios.com/private-schools-coronavirus-public-schools-d6aaf803-d458-4301-a3a7-71364b00a5b0.html; School reopenings more common in rural areas and in private schools, state data shows. Cal Matters. Retrieved from https://calmatters.org/education/2021/02/california-school-reopening-divide-public-private/; In the Same Towns, Private Schools Are Reopening While Public Schools Are Not. The New York Times. Retrieved from https://www.nytimes.com/2020/07/16/upshot/coronavirus-school-reopening-private-public-gap.html.

In fact, Hartney and Finger (2020) found evidence to suggest that private school competition was associated with a higher likelihood of nearby public school districts reopening for in-person instruction in 2020.

Some people have theorized that private schools have been more likely to reopen because they believe private schools are more well-funded than public schools, which would support the theory that reopening decisions are explained by resources.[95] However, there is no conclusive evidence that private schools, on average, are more well-funded than public schools on a per-student basis. On the contrary, Garet, Chan, and Sherman (1995) estimated that public K-12 schools spent an average of 43 to 52 percent more per student than private schools in the 1991-92 school year. A more recent analysis estimated that public K-12 school funding per student was about 80 percent higher than private school funding per student in the 2016-17 school year.[96] Another analysis similarly estimated that, on average, per-student funding was about 89 percent higher in public schools than private schools in 2018 (Van Kipnis, 2020). Moreover, K-12 private schools in the U.S. generally report tuition levels that are, on average, substantially lower than total public school revenues per student.[97]

An analysis by researchers at the Edunomics Lab at Georgetown University found that public school districts that decided to reopen fully or mostly remote in the 2020-21 school year generally demonstrated financial surpluses, suggesting that resources were not the primary reason that their schools did not reopen mostly in person.[98] For example, the researchers estimated that Los Angeles public schools, which opted to reopen remotely, had over a half of a billion dollar – or about a $1,100 per student – funding surplus in the 2020-21 school year.

DeGrow and Rigterink (2021) noted that the school districts receiving more federal CARES Act funding were less likely to reopen than districts receiving less funding. My latest analysis with MIT's Christos A. Makridis examined nationwide data from over 12,000 school districts, covering the vast

---

[95] Private schools pull students away from public schools. *Axios*. Retrieved from https://www.axios.com/private-schools-coronavirus-public-schools-d6aaf803-d458-4301-a3a7-71364b00a5b0.html.

[96] Public School Funding Per Student Averages 80% More Than Private Schools. *Just Facts*. Retrieved from https://www.justfactsdaily.com/public-school-funding-per-student-averages-80-more-than-private-schools.

[97] U.S. K-12 Education Spending Comparisons. *Educational Freedom Institute*. Retrieved from http://efinstitute.org/education-spending-comparisons/.

[98] Financial Turmoil: Open or Remote? What it Means for School District Budgets. *Edunomics Lab at Georgetown University*. Retrieved from https://edunomicslab.org/wp-content/uploads/2021/03/Financial-Turmoil-Webinar-Mar3.pdf.

majority of school-aged children, and did not find any evidence to suggest that higher levels of revenues or expenditures per student are associated with a higher probability of reopening schools in person (DeAngelis & Makridis, 2021b). Instead, we consistently found that public school funding is either uncorrelated, or even negatively correlated, with the decision to reopen in person.[99]

As found in a few other studies, we did not find a consistent relationship between Covid-19 risk in the community and the probability of reopening in person – but that school reopenings were instead strongly related to political partisanship in the surrounding area (DeAngelis, 2020; DeAngelis & Makridis, 2021a; 2021b; Flanders, 2020; Hartney & Finger, Valant, 2020). In a peer-reviewed study, accepted for publication at *Social Science Quarterly*, we found substantial evidence to suggest that public school districts with stronger teachers' unions were much less likely to reopen for in person instruction (DeAngelis & Makridis, 2021a).

These results were robust to various analytic techniques, four measures of union influence, and empirical specifications which included controls for district size and several county-level demographics including political partisanship, Covid risk, educational attainment, household income, marital status, gender, age, and race.

In the same study, we found that political partisanship strongly predicted reopening decisions, but that reopenings were not generally related to Covid-19 risk as measured by cases or deaths per capita. In a Brown University working paper, Hartney and Finger (2020) separately found that public school districts with stronger teachers' unions were less likely to reopen in person. Tulane University researchers also observed that public school districts with more teachers' union influence were less likely to reopen in person (Harris, Ziedan, & Hassig, 2021).

The stark contrast between Florida and California is a prime example of our overall findings (DeAngelis & Makridis, 2021a; 2021b). The latest data from Burbio[100] this month indicates that in Florida, a state that spends about $10,700 per student per year according to the latest data[101] from the U.S.

---

[99] School Isn't Closed for Lack of Money. *The Wall Street Journal*. Retrieved from https://www.wsj.com/articles/school-isnt-closed-for-lack-of-money-11615332385.

[100] Burbio's K-12 School Opening Tracker. *Burbio*. Retrieved from https://cai.burbio.com/school-opening-tracker/.

[101] 2018 Public Elementary-Secondary Education Finance Data. *United States Census Bureau*. Retrieved from https://www.census.gov/data/tables/2018/econ/school-finances/secondary-education-finance.html.

Census Bureau, nearly all public schools offer full-time in-person instruction. In California, which spends about 38 percent more per student and has much stronger teachers' unions, most public school students still don't have access to in-person options.

Several actions by public school teachers' unions also raised some eyebrows and suggested that the school reopening debate was more about politics and power than safety. Just as school closures hit in March 2020, union groups in states such as Oregon[102] and Pennsylvania[103] lobbied the government to make it illegal for families-in-need to switch to virtual public charter schools that have already been successfully providing students with remote instruction for years.

In their report[104] on safely reopening schools, the Los Angeles teachers' union called for things unrelated to reopening schools, such as defunding the police, Medicare-for-All, a wealth tax, and a ban on charter schools. At least ten teachers' unions joined with the Democratic Socialists of America to hold a "National Day of Resistance" to "Demand Safe Schools" on two occasions in less than a year. Included in their list of demands, in addition to more funding and staffing, were police-free schools, rent cancelation, unemployment benefits for all, and a ban on standardized tests and new charter schools.[105]

Other things just didn't add up: why was it safe enough for public school buildings to reopen for in-person childcare services, but not for in-person learning? Why was it safe enough for teachers' union officials to travel to Puerto Rico to vacation[106] in person, and to send their own children[107] to in-person private schools, but not safe enough for their members to return to work

---

[102] Oregon's Coronavirus Education Lockdown. *The Wall Street Journal.* Retrieved from https://www.wsj.com/articles/oregons-coronavirus-education-lockdown-11585697080.

[103] Cyber charters in Pa. keep teaching amid confusion in coronavirus shutdown order. *WHYY.* Retrieved from https://whyy.org/articles/cyber-charters-in-pa-keep-teaching-amid-confusion-in-coronavirus-shutdown-order/.

[104] The Same Storm, but Different Boats: The Safe and Equitable Conditions for Starting LAUSD in 2020-21. *United Teachers Los Angeles.* Retrieved from https://www.utla.net/sites/default/files/samestormdiffboats_final.pdf.

[105] National Day of Resistance. *Demand Safe Schools.* Retrieved from https://www.demandsafeschools.org/demands/.

[106] CTU board member facing criticism for vacationing in Caribbean while pushing remote learning. *WGN.* Retrieved from https://wgntv.com/news/wgn-investigates/ctu-board-member-facing-criticism-for-vacationing-in-caribbean-while-pushing-remote-learning/.

[107] After Leading School Closures, Berkeley Teachers Union President Spotted Dropping Daughter Off at In-Person Preschool. *KQED.* Retrieved from https://www.kqed.org/news/11862469/after-leading-school-closures-berkeley-teachers-union-president-spotted-dropping-daughter-off-at-in-person-preschool.

in person? Why have four studies each found that school reopenings are more strongly related to political partisanship and teachers' union influence than Covid risk?

Why did the Congressional Budget Office estimate[108] that only 5 percent of the $129 billion in relief funding would be spent this year, while up to 95 percent of the funding would be paid out after the pandemic, if the goal is to reopen schools now? Why did half of the Senate block an amendment that would have made federal relief funding conditional on reopening schools in person if all teachers were vaccinated?

It might be because the school reopening debate has always been more about politics and power than safety and the needs of students and their families. The past year has put a spotlight on the main problem with K-12 education in the United States: a long-existing massive power imbalance between public school teachers' unions and individual families.

The only way that we're ever going to fix that messed-up set of incentives that's baked into the public school system is to empower families by funding students directly. If a grocery store doesn't reopen, families can take their money elsewhere. If a school doesn't reopen, families should similarly be able to take their children's education dollars elsewhere. As a matter of fact, families should be able to take their children's education dollars elsewhere regardless of the reopening decision. Education funding is supposed to be meant for educating children, not for protecting a particular institution.

We already fund students directly in higher education with Pell Grants and the GI Bill and in pre-K with programs such as Head Start. The funding goes to individual students and families as opposed to buildings. With all of these programs – in addition to food stamps, Section 8, and Medicaid – we fund individuals instead of institutions. We should apply the same logic to K-12 education and fund students, not systems.

References

Agostinelli, F., Doepke, M., Sorrenti, G., & Zilibotti, F. (2020). When the Great Equalizer Shuts Down: Schools, Peers, and Parents in Pandemic Times (No. w28264). National Bureau of Economic Research.

Ali, U., Herbst, C. and Makridis, C. A. (2021). The Impact of Covid-19 on the U.S. Child Care Market: Evidence from Stay-at-Home Orders. *Economics of Education Review*, 82.

[108] Congressional Budget Office Cost Estimate. Retrieved from https://www.cbo.gov/system/files/2021-02/hEdandLaborreconciliationestimate.pdf.

Billingsley, S., Brandén, M., Aradhya, S., Drefahl, S., Andersson, G., & Mussino, E. (2020). Deaths in the frontline: Occupation-specific COVID-19 mortality risks in Sweden. *Stockholm Research Reports in Demography* no. 2020:36. Stockholm University.

Boesch, T., Grunewald, R., Nunn, R., & Palmer, V. (2021). Pandemic pushes mothers of young children out of the labor force. *Federal Reserve Bank of Minneapolis*. Retrieved from https://www.minneapolisfed.org/article/2021/pandemic-pushes-mothers-of-young-children-out-of-the-labor-force.

Christakis, D. A., Van Cleve, W., & Zimmerman, F. J. (2020). Estimation of US children's educational attainment and years of life lost associated with primary school closures during the coronavirus disease 2019 pandemic. *JAMA Network Open*, *3*(11), e2028786-e2028786.

Chubb, J. E., & Moe, T. M. (1988). Politics, markets, and the organization of schools. *American Political Science Review*, *82*(4), 1065-1087.

DeAngelis, C. A. (2020). School Reopenings Linked to Union Influence and Politics, Not Safety. *Reason Magazine*. Retrieved from https://reason.com/2020/08/19/school-reopenings-linked-to-union-influence-and-politics-not-safety/.

DeAngelis, C. A., & Holmes Erickson, H. (2018). What leads to successful school choice programs? A review of the theories and evidence. *Cato Journal*, *38*(1), 247-263.

DeAngelis, C. A., & Makridis, C. A. (2021a). Are School Reopening Decisions Related to Union Influence? *Social Science Quarterly*, DOI: 10.1111/ssqu.12955.

DeAngelis, C. A., & Makridis, C. A. (2021b). Are School Reopening Decisions Related to Funding? Evidence from Over 12,000 Districts During the Covid-19 Pandemic. *Social Science Research Network*. Retrieved from https://ssrn.com/abstract=3799694.

DeGrow, B., & Rigterink, A. (2021). Money for Nothing: Most Federal COVID Relief Went to Closed Classrooms. *Mackinac Center for Public Policy*. Retrieved from https://www.mackinac.org/money-for-nothing-most-federal-covid-relief-went-to-closed-classrooms.

Flanders, W. (2020). Politics in the Pandemic: The Role of Unions in School Reopening Decisions. *Wisconsin Institute for Law & Liberty*. Retrieved from https://www.will-law.org/wp-content/uploads/2020/12/reopening-brief.pdf.

Friedman, M. (1955). The role of government in education. In R. A. Solo (Ed.), *Economics and the Public Interest* (pp. 123-144). New Brunswick, NJ: Rutgers University Press.

Garet, M., Chan, T. H., & Sherman, J. D. (1995). Estimates of Expenditures for Private K-12 Schools. National Center for Education Statistics Working Paper Series. U.S. Department of Education.

Goldhaber, D., Imberman, S. A., Strunk, K. O., Hoptkins, B., Brown, N., Harbatkin, E., & Kilbride, T. (2020). To What Extent Does In-Person Schooling Contribute to the Spread of COVID-19? *Evidence from Michigan and Washington* (No. 247-1220). CALDER Working Paper.

Green, E. (2021). Surge of Student Suicides Pushes Las Vegas Schools to Reopen. *New York Times*. Retrieved from https://www.nytimes.com/2021/01/24/us/politics/student-suicides-nevada-coronavirus.html.

Hanushek, E. A., & Woessmann, L. (2020). The Economic Impacts of Learning Losses. *Organisation for Economic Co-operation and Development*. Retrieved from https://

www.oecd.org/education/The-economic-impacts-of-coronavirus-covid-19-learning-losses.pdf.

Hanushek, E. A., Kain, J. F., Rivkin, S. G., & Branch, G. F. (2007). Charter school quality and parental decision making with school choice. *Journal of Public Economics*, *91*(5-6), 823-848.

Harris, D., Ziedan, E., & Hassig, S. (2021). The Effects of School Reopenings on COVID-19 Hospitalizations. *National Center on Education Access and Choice*. Retrieved from https://www.reachcentered.org/uploads/technicalreport/The-Effects-of-School-Reopenings-on-COVID-19-Hospitalizations-REACH-January-2021.pdf.

Hartney, M. T., & Finger, L. K. (2020). *Politics, Markets, and Pandemics: Public Education's Response to COVID-19*. EdWorkingPaper No. 20-304. Annenberg Institute at Brown University. Retrieved from https://edworkingpapers.com/sites/default/files/ai20-304.pdf.

Honein, M. A., Barrios, L. C., & Brooks, J. T. (2021). Data and policy to guide opening schools safely to limit the spread of SARS-CoV-2 infection. *JAMA*. DOI: 10. 1001/jama.2021.0374.

Kuhfeld, M., Tarasawa, B., Johnson, A., Ruzek, E., & Lewis, K. (2020). Learning during COVID-19: Initial findings on students' reading and math achievement and growth. *NWEA*. Retrieved from https://www.nwea.org/content/uploads/2020/11/Collaborative-brief-Learning-during-COVID-19.NOV2020.pdf.

Lee, J. (2020). Mental health effects of school closures during COVID-19. *The Lancet Child & Adolescent Health*, *4*(6), 421.

Lofton, O., Petrosky-Nadeau, N., & Seitelman, L. (2021, February). Parents in a Pandemic Labor Market. *Federal Reserve Bank of San Francisco*. Retrieved from https://www.frbsf.org/economic-research/files/wp2021-04.pdf.

Ludvigsson, J. F., Engerström, L., Nordenhäll, C., & Larsson, E. (2021). Open Schools, Covid-19, and Child and Teacher Morbidity in Sweden. *New England Journal of Medicine*.

McKinsey & Company (2020a). COVID-19 and student learning in the United States: The hurt could last a lifetime. Retrieved from https://www.mckinsey.com/industries/public-and-social-sector/our-insights/covid-19-and-student-learning-in-the-united-states-the-hurt-could-last-a-lifetime.

McKinsey & Company (2020b). COVID-19 and learning loss—disparities grow and students need help. Retrieved from https://www.mckinsey.com/industries/public-and-social-sector/our-insights/covid-19-and-learning-loss-disparities-grow-and-students-need-help.

Oster, E. (2020). Schools are not spreading covid-19. This new data makes the case. *Washington Post*. Retrieved from https://www.washingtonpost.com/opinions/2020/11/20/covid-19-schools-data-reopening-safety/.

Patrick, S. W., Henkhaus, L. E., Zickafoose, J. S., Lovell, K., Halvorson, A., Loch, S., ... & Davis, M. M. (2020). Well-being of parents and children during the COVID-19 pandemic: a national survey. *Pediatrics*, *146*(4).

Rundle, A. G., Park, Y., Herbstman, J. B., Kinsey, E. W., & Wang, Y. C. (2020). COVID-19–related school closings and risk of weight gain among children. *Obesity*, *28*(6), 1008-1009.

UNICEF (2020). Averting a lost COVID generation. Retrieved from https://www.unicef.org/reports/averting-lost-generation-covid19-world-childrens-day-2020-brief.

Valant, J. (2020). School reopening plans linked to politics rather than public health. *Brookings Institution*. Retrieved from https://www.brookings.edu/blog/brown-center-chalkboard/2020/07/29/school-reopening-plans-linked-to-politics-rather-than-public-health/.

Van Kipnis, G. (2020). Reform the K-12 Government-School Monopoly: Economics and Facts. *American Institute for Economic Research*. Retrieved from https://www.aier.org/article/reform-the-k-12-government-school-monopoly-economics-and-facts/.

Varas, J., Menon, V., & Bellafiore, R. (2021). What's Next for Schools: Balancing the Costs of School Closures Against COVID-19 Health Risks. *United States Congress Joint Economic Committee*. Retrieved from https://www.jec.senate.gov/public/index.cfm/republicans/2021/2/what-s-next-for-schools-balancing-the-costs-of-school-closures-against-covid-19-health-risks.

Viner, R. M., Russell, S., Saulle, R., Croker, H., Stansfield, C., Packer, J., ... & Minozzi, S. (2021). Impacts of school closures on physical and mental health of children and young people: a systematic review. *MedRxiv*.

Zhang, L., Zhang, D., Fang, J., Wan, Y., Tao, F., & Sun, Y. (2020). Assessment of mental health of Chinese primary school students before and after school closing and opening during the COVID-19 pandemic. *JAMA Network Open*, *3*(9), e2021482-e2021482.

Zimmerman, K. O., Akinboyo, I. C., Brookhart, M. A., Boutzoukas, A. E., McGann, K., Smith, M. J., ... & Benjamin, D. K. (2021). Incidence and secondary transmission of SARS-CoV-2 infections in schools. *Pediatrics*.

Appendix

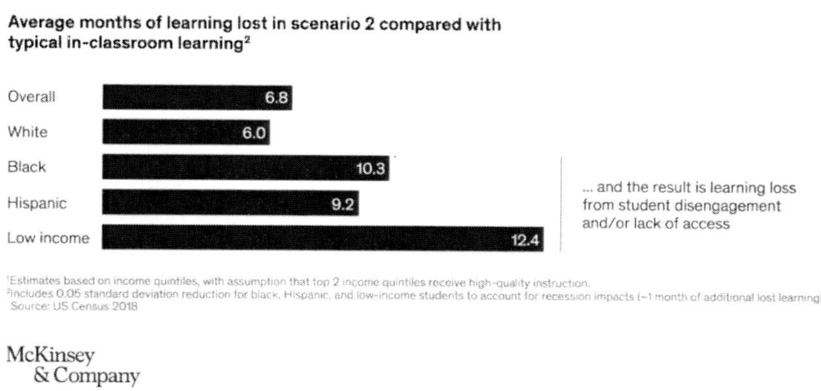

Notes. – Source: COVID-19 and student learning in the United States: The hurt could last a lifetime. *McKinsey & Company*. Retrieved from https://www.mckinsey.com/industries/public-and-social-sector/our-insights/covid-19-and-student-learning-in-the-united-states-the-hurt-could-last-a-lifetime.

Figure 1. Estimated months of learning lost overall and by subgroup.

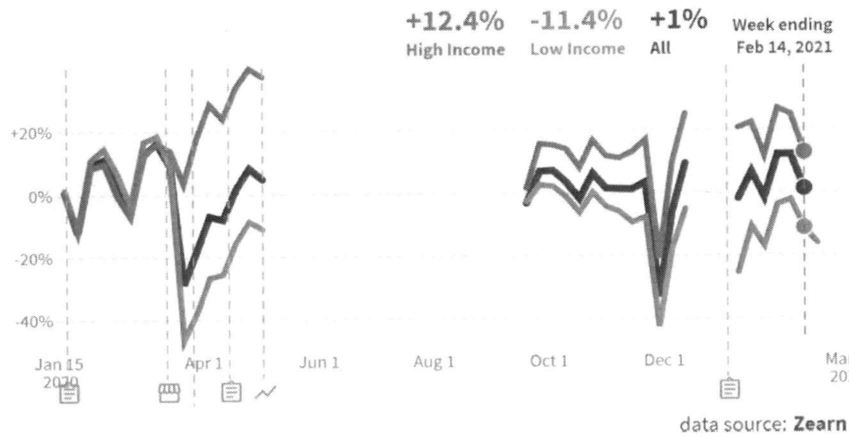

Notes. – Source: Percent Change in Student Math Progress. Opportunity Insights *Economic Tracker*. Harvard University. Retrieved from https://tracktherecovery.org/.

Figure 2. Percent change in student math progress before and after school closures.

Ms. SCHAKOWSKY. Ms. Johnson, you are recognized for 5 minutes.

Statement of Ariel Fox Johnson

Ms. FOX JOHNSON. Thank you. Ms. SCHAKOWSKY. OK. Go ahead.

Ms. FOX JOHNSON. Good morning. Good morning, Chair Pallone, Chair Schakowsky, Ranking Member McMorris Rodgers, Ranking Member Bilirakis, and members of the subcommittee.

Thank you for the invitation to appear before you and for recognizing that the digital world, for all of its opportunities, poses unique risks and harms to children and teens.

The pandemic has certainly exacerbated these risks and harms, but they existed before, and unless Congress acts, they will persist after.

I am Ariel Fox Johnson, Senior Counsel for Global Policy at Common Sense Media.

Common Sense is the leading organization dedicated to helping kids and families thrive in a rapidly changing digital world.

My testimony emphasizes three main points.

First, children and teens are on the front lines of our online world, and they are uniquely vulnerable to digital harm.

Second, the status quo is failing young people.

And, third, solutions to these challenges are the responsibility of Congress and tech leaders themselves.

We need a healthy internet, especially now. In my house, with limited to no childcare, our screen time rules have gone out the window. Just this weekend I told my children to go watch a movie or play on their tablet so that I could prepare this testimony.

While it was once debatable whether you could choose to be online, it is now clear that there is no choice. It is necessary to connect with family, to learn, and to play.

Our research shows that device ownership was already the norm for young children and that screen time had multiplied in recent years, with children in lower-income houses spending nearly 2 hours more daily with screens.

The pandemic has turbocharged this. Distance learning is a big driver for older kids, yes, but screen time is up for all kids. As of this fall, children ages 2 to 15 watch television, including streaming, a full day each week. YouTube and gaming consoles have seen spikes in usage, some with 82 percent more daily users.

Social media and mobile use is up, and one study found that kids were sending and receiving three times more messages than the year before.

Parents are worried. Parents' top child health concerns in 2020 were overuse of social media, bullying and cyber bullying, and internet safety.

Young people are impulsive, and they are prone to overshare. They do not understand that data shared on an app does not remain on their device, let alone grasp complex online data and advertising ecosystems. They are more susceptible to ads and other forms of online persuasion.

Kids are no match for tech companies who have grown unchecked and remain unaccountable. Too many are manipulating children, misusing their personal information, and exposing kids to harm. And this is not something that will magically stop when the pandemic ends.

Kids are surveilled everywhere. We talk about a digital footprint, but at this point it is more accurately a full body scan. Manipulative design pressures teens to click and scroll constantly and to tie their self-worth to numbers of likes.

Elementary students can drain their parents' credit cards with in-app purchases and get shamed by beloved characters to spend more money.

More than 9 in 10 teens report seeing violent content online. Our own forthcoming research details how the number of teens who have seen racist content online has nearly doubled in the past 2 years. Meanwhile, kids' mental health is taking a hit.

So what should Congress do? Madam Chair, you and others on this committee have been leaders here, and as we have seen from the statements in the committee and the witnesses today, there is clear agreement that there is a problem.

The challenge is ensuring that when Congress does act, it makes a real difference. There is a risk that Congress may act but not do enough.

We believe, as do many of you, that COPPA is outdated. It must be updated in a meaningful way.

Congress should pass a strong, comprehensive privacy law with special protections for vulnerable children and teens. The PRIVCY Act, introduced by Representative Castor along with Representative Dingell and other Members, would address many of COPPA's shortcomings, would force States to acknowledge kids, protect and empower teens, and prohibit behavioral marketing to kids.

Congress should also pass Representatives Castor, Clarke, and Wexton's KIDS Act, which would create rules around online marketing to kids and encourage kid-healthy content and design, banning autoplay and amplification of harmful content.

We support other steps to hold tech companies accountable as well, but we believe that there is much that industry can do right now. They do not need to wait for Congress to minimize information collection and design healthier products for kids. And their reluctance to act is inexcusable.

Technology and media offer enormous benefits, but kids deserve better online. They needed it before, and they will need it after the pandemic.

Thank you, and I look forward to questions.

[The prepared statement of Ms. Fox Johnson follows:]

Prepared Statement of Ariel Fox Johnson

Introduction

Good morning Chair Schakowsky, Ranking Member Bilirakis, and members of the Subcommittee, thank you for the opportunity to appear before you and for recognizing that the digital world, for all of its opportunities, poses unique risks and harms to children. The pandemic has exacerbated these risks and harms.

My name is Ariel Fox Johnson and I am the Senior Counsel for Global Policy at Common Sense Media. Common Sense, which was founded in 2003 by CEO James P. Steyer, is the leading organization dedicated to helping kids and families thrive in a rapidly changing digital world. We help parents, teachers, and policymakers by providing unbiased information, trusted advice, and innovative tools to help them harness the power of media and technology as a positive force in all kids' lives. Common Sense has helped millions of families and kids think critically and make smart, responsible choices about the media they create and consume.

Common Sense reaches 125 million households with its age-appropriate media ratings and reviews and our award winning Digital Citizenship Curriculum is the most comprehensive K-12 offering of its kind in the education field; we have over 1 million registered educators using our resources in over half of U.S. schools. Our Research Program offers reliable, independent data on children's use of media and technology and the impact it has on their physical, emotional, social, and intellectual development. Our Privacy program evaluates popular ed-tech products for homes and classrooms, and we actively support the unique needs of low-income families and families of color, empowering them to navigate the digital world with confidence.

We have long advocated for rules and policies that protect individuals' privacy, improve connectivity for students and families, and hold tech companies accountable to ensure a healthy internet for all. We've supported efforts to update the Children's Online Privacy Protection Act (COPPA) and the Federal Trade Commission's COPPA Rule. We were a sponsor of California's precedent-setting consumer privacy law, the California Consumer Privacy Act (CCPA). We have also sponsored and supported privacy and technology laws across the country and at the federal level, including California's landmark Student Online Privacy Information Protection Act and Delaware's Online Privacy and Protection Act. We have also advocated for more independent research to better understand the relationships between digital media use and early and adolescent development, such as the Children and Media Research Advancement Act (CAMRA). We have pushed to better connect students and families through E-Rate and Lifeline, and laid the groundwork for the American Rescue Plan's over $7 billion for connecting students and teachers. And we have supported innovative state and federal proposals to address manipulative design, curb harmful advertising, and create an online environment that lifts up children and families.

My testimony is divided into three sections that identify specific online threats and harms to children and offer policy solutions to those serious challenges. First, I will discuss how children and teens are on the front lines of our online world, uniquely vulnerable to digital harms. Kids spend an increasing and inordinate amount of time on devices, and at the same time their brains are still developing so they are particularly exposed. Second, I will discuss how the status quo is failing young people. Our youngest children are the most surveilled generation ever. Technology today manipulates kids to be 'always on' and drives them to more outrageous content. Companies and influencers commercialize childhood to a degree not seen in traditional media. Children and teens face a toxic online environment that they are ill-equipped to defend against, and it is hurting their mental well-being. Finally, I will discuss solutions to these challenges that can be taken by Congress and by tech leaders themselves. Updated privacy rules, a Children's Television Act for the digital world, and safeguards against digital manipulation will go a long way towards holding technology companies accountable. And in the meantime, there is much that companies can do on their own as well.

Children and Teens Are on the Front Lines Online

Kids Spend an Increasing Amount of Time on Devices

Even pre-pandemic, young people were spending increasing amounts of time on devices and online. And in the past year, it has felt like all of life has moved online: virtual playdates, ballet and soccer class, music lessons, and storytimes; video calls and online games with grandparents; remote school. While it was always debatable whether young people could "choose" to be online, given that so many of their peers were, it is now crystal clear that this is not a choice. In order to connect with friends and family, receive an education, and participate in cultural and community events, children had to be online this past year.

According to Common Sense research, by 2019, device ownership was the norm for even young children, and screen time had multiplied in recent years. Nearly half of 2- to 4-year-olds and more than two-thirds of 5- to 8-year-olds have their own tablet or smartphone. By age 11, a majority of kids have their own smartphone, and by 12 more than two-thirds do. Prior to the pandemic, children from birth to age 8 use about two and a half hours of screen media a day (almost 40 minutes a day watching online videos on platforms like Youtube and Tiktok), 8- to 12-year-olds in this country used just under five hours' worth of entertainment screen media per day, and teens used an average of just under seven and a half hours' worth—not including time spent using screens for school or homework. Already, in 2019, more than twice as many young people watched videos every day than did in 2015, and the average time spent watching had roughly doubled.[109] The Pew Research Center reported that 53% of children younger than 11 view YouTube daily, with 35% viewing multiple times per day.[110]

Much of the screen time even young kids spend today occurs without their parents. Parental co-use goes down dramatically as the child's age goes up: The proportion of parents who say they use media "most of the time" with their 5- to 8-year-old child ranges from 11% to 19%, depending on the media activity (compared to 37% to 62% for parents of children under 2).[111]

Importantly, children in lower-income households pre-pandemic were spending nearly two hours more with screens than children from higher-income households, and the gap by race and ethnicity had also grown substantially.[112] In addition, lower-income households are more likely to have mobile connectivity and limited bandwidth – these factors make it harder for children to use technology in ways that allow them to create and produce.[113]

The pandemic further increased the time kids spent with devices, when children turned to screens to meet essentially all of their needs (social, educational, even physical). Screen time post-pandemic is up, in some studies 50%.[114] While for older children and teens, distance learning is a big driver, screen time is up for younger kids too. For children under 5, a Morning Consult poll found that whereas pre pandemic, 70% of parents reported 3 hours or less of screen time, post-pandemic, almost 60% of parents reported 4 hours or more of screen time.[115] Television viewing – including smart TVs

---

[109] Rideout, V., and Robb, M. B. (2019). The Common Sense census: Media use by tweens and teens, 2019. San Francisco, CA: *Common Sense Media*. Rideout, V., & Robb, M. B. (2020).; The Common Sense census: Media use by kids age zero to eight, 2020. San Francisco, CA: *Common Sense Media*.

[110] Parenting Children in the Age of Screens, *Pew Research Center*, (July 2020).

[111] Rideout, V., & Robb, M. B. (2020). The Common Sense census: Media use by kids age zero to eight, 2020. San Francisco, CA: *Common Sense Media*.

[112] Ibid.

[113] Alexis Martin et al. Teacher Perspectives on COVID-19's Impact on K-12 Computer Science Instruction, *Kapor Center*, (September 30, 2020).

[114] Sara Fische & Margaret Harding McGill, Kids' screen time up 50% during pandemic, *AXIOS*, (2021).

[115] Sarah Shevenock, YouTube, Netflix and Gaming: A Look at What Kids Are Doing With Their Increased Screen Time, *Morning Consult*, (August 21, 2020).

and streaming – for 2-15 year olds was literally a full day a week in October 2020.[116] YouTube and gaming consoles have seen big spikes in usage.[117] Roblox, a popular online game platform and game creation system, averaged 82% more daily users in the first 9 months of 2020 than it had the year prior.[118] Two-thirds of teens report texting and connecting with friends and family on social media more than before the pandemic.[119] Social media use on mobile devices is up 49%.[120] An online monitoring company used by parents and schools found a 144% increase in online messages sent and received by children.[121] And some predict that the longer the pandemic goes on, the more likely these media habits will stick.[122]

It is important to note that "screen time" is not monolithic, and the pandemic has shown us the variety of ways that technology can be used for good and for bad. Common Sense has joined with other experts in trying to reframe parents' focus to be on quality, not quantity.[123] Nonetheless, in too many instances, the content targeted at and consumed by children is not of high quality. And parents are worried. Pew Research found in October 2020 that 63% of parents with school aged children were more concerned about screen time now than in the past.[124] A national poll found that of the top 10 child health concerns among all parents in 2020, the first three involved the internet: overuse of social media, bullying/cyberbullying, and internet safety.[125]

---

116 Ryan Tuchow, Kid device usage changing as a result of the pandemic, *Kidscreen*, (February 19, 2021).

117 Sara Fische & Margaret Harding McGill, Kids' screen time up 50% during pandemic, *AXIOS*, (2021).

118 Kellen Browning and Lauren Hirsch, Roblox, edging toward I.P.O., reveals surging revenue and losses, *New York Times*, (November 19, 2020).

119 How Teens Are Coping and Connecting in the Time of the Coronavirus, *Common Sense Media* and *Survey Monkey*, (2020).

120 Ryan Tuchow, Kid device usage changing as a result of the pandemic, *Kidscreen*, (February 19, 2021).

121 Heather Kelly, Growing up on screens: How a year lived online has changed our children, *Washington Post*, (March 5, 2021).

122 Ryan Tuchow, Kid device usage changing as a result of the pandemic, *Kidscreen*, (February 19, 2021).

123 Mike Robb, Screen Time in the Age of the Coronavirus, *Common Sense Media*, (April 7, 2020).

124 "Most Parents of K-12 Students Learning Online Worry About Them Falling Behind," *Pew Research Center*, (October 2020).

125 C.S. Mott Children's Hospital National Poll on Children's Health at Michigan Medicine.

Kids' Brains Are Still Developing

Parental – and societal – concerns about screen time, social media, and online safety are more acute for kids because their brains are still developing. Young people are prone to sharing and impulsive behavior, less able to understand the complex data ecosystems that make up the internet, and more susceptible to advertising and other online persuasion.[126]

Both young children and teens are prone to overshare. The UK Children's Commissioner found that, pre-pandemic, children posted an average of 26 times a day to social media, averaging 70,000 posts by age 18.[127] This has implications for their privacy.

Children do not understand the consequences of their sharing.[128] They anticipate that information shared remains at a device level, or within an app or game. They believe that deleting an app or information within an app will delete it from the internet, and do not expect or understand that an app may gather information about them from outside-app sources.[129] They may even view monitoring by others as a positive, especially if they are very young.[130] (While older children may understand some negatives to sharing too much information, in studies this centers around strangers and physical risks, and not commercial surveillance[131]).

---

[126] Children, Adolescents, and Advertising, *Committee on Communications Pediatrics*, (Dec 2006).

[127] Who Knows What About Me?, *Children's Commissioner*, (Nov. 8, 2018). According to the UK Children's Commissioner, on average, 1,300 photos of a kid will be posted before they turn thirteen years old.

[128] Children may not understand what is going on, whereas teens may have a slightly better sense but be more likely to partake in risky behavior.; *see* Adriana Galvan et al., *Earlier* Development of the Accumbens Relative to Orbitofrontal Cortex Might Underlie Risk-Taking Behavior in Adolescents 26 *Journal of Neuroscience* 25 (2006) (teens' brain development can bias them towards risky behaviors).

[129] Anonymous Author(s). 2021. "They See You're a Girl if You Pick a Pink Robot with a Skirt": How Children Conceptualize Data Processing and Digital Privacy Risks. In CHI '21: *ACM CHI Conference on Human Factors in Computing Systems*, May 8–13, 2021, Yokohama, Japan. ACM, New York, NY, USA.

[130] Gelman, Martinez, Davidson, Noles (2018), *Child Development Journal*; Sonia Livingstone, Mariya Soilova, Rishita Nadagiri, Children's data and privacy online: Growing up in a digital age, An evidence review, (December 2018).; p. 18. Children 4-7 view GPS tracking favorably, not as a privacy concern, and even 8-11 year olds can view monitoring as positive to ensure their safety.

[131] Anonymous Author(s). 2021. "They See You're a Girl if You Pick a Pink Robot with a Skirt": How Children Conceptualize Data Processing and Digital Privacy Risks. In CHI '21: *ACM CHI Conference on Human Factors in Computing Systems*, May 8–13, 2021, Yokohama, Japan. ACM, New York, NY, USA.

Even older and literate children struggle to understand privacy policies, which can be long and full of legalese.[132]

Teens, too, are more likely to share without thinking, focusing on the immediate present and not long-term consequences as their brains prioritize rewards and minimize risks.[133] Fifty-eight percent of twelve to fifteen-year-olds think it is easy to delete their information online.[134] What's more, given susceptibility to peer pressure, teens will even stay and share in online communities that are no longer enjoyable to them, as that is where their friends are.[135] Social media is designed in a way that is particularly appealing to teenagers and emerging adults, when individuals are oriented toward others, belonging, groups, and acceptance.[136]

Even when teens have consented to share their information, they may not understand how far the information will go and the lifelong consequences of that sharing. Only a third of teens think social networking sites do a good job of explaining what they do with users' information.[137] When it comes to reading privacy policies, Common Sense research has found only a small minority of people read the terms of service on social networking sites. Only 17 percent of teens say they read the terms of service "almost all the time," compared to 36 percent of parents.[138]

This is entirely rational given that many privacy policies are written for higher grade levels and can be full of legalese.

---

[132] Children's data and privacy online: Growing up in a digital age, An evidence review, Sonia Livingstone, Mariya Soilova, Rishita Nadagiri, p. 15. (December 2018).

[133] Adriana Galvan et al., Earlier Development of the Accumbens Relative to Orbitofrontal Cortex Might Underlie Risk-Taking Behavior in Adolescents 26 *Journal of Neuroscience* 25 (2006); Adriana Galván and Kristine M. McGlennen, Enhanced Striatal Sensitivity to Aversive Reinforcement in Adolescents versus Adults, 25 (2) *J. of Cognitive Neuroscience* 284–296 (2013).

[134] OFCOM, Children and Parents: Media Use and Attitudes Report, (Nov. 2016).

[135] Center for Digital Democracy and the Campaign for a Commercial Free Childhood Comments before the Federal Trade Commission, Competition and Consumer Protection in the 21st Century, Hearing #12: The FTC's Approach to Consumer Privacy (2019), at 12, citing Taylor Lorenz, Teens Are Being Bullied 'Constantly' on Instagram, *The Atlantic* (Oct. 10, 2018), "teens stay on Instagram even with cyberbullying because "quitting wasn't an option"

[136] Zuboff, Shoshana, *The Age of Surveillance Capitalism: The Fight for a Human Future at the New Frontier of Power*, p. 449, (January 15, 2019).

[137] *Common Sense Media*, Privacy Matters: Protecting Digital Privacy for Parents and Kids, (2018).

[138] Ibid.

Parents too feel fairly helpless when it comes to protecting kids' privacy. In many instances, parents would like to make changes to protect privacy and are afraid of privacy consequences and data misuse, but do not know where to begin.[139] And most parents say that social networking sites and apps don't do a good job explaining what they do with users' data.[140] Even before the pandemic, 71% of parents were worried that use of devices at such a young age may do kids more harm than good.[141]

Children and teens' developing brains also have trouble both identifying and understanding advertising, and new technologies and advertising techniques, like native ads and influencer marketing, exacerbates these difficulties.[142] Research suggests children are not aware of advertisements until they reach 4–5 years of age.[143] And even older children still have trouble identifying advertisements: 75% of kids between 8-11 years old cannot distinguish ads.[144] Historically many of these studies have been done with television ads, but other studies have found children are even worse at identifying advertisements on the internet. The lack of separation between sponsored and non-sponsored content online can make it harder for a child to discern an advertisement from entertainment.[145] Online, we see older children very often confuse Google search ads with organic search results, and indeed less than half of young teens in one study understood that the top search results in a Google search had paid to appear, even when the results were labeled with an orange box reading "ad."[146] Companies also hide commercial exhortations in advergames, which are videos and online games that integrate advertising

[139] What's That You Say? Smart Speakers and Voice Assistants Toplines, *Common Sense Media* (May 2019).; Anonymous Author(s). 2021. "They See You're a Girl if You Pick a Pink Robot with a Skirt": How Children Conceptualize Data Processing and Digital Privacy Risks. In CHI '21: *ACM CHI Conference on Human Factors in Computing Systems*, May 8–13, 2021, Yokohama, Japan. ACM, New York, NY, USA.

[140] *Common Sense Media*, Privacy Matters: Protecting Digital Privacy for Parents and Kids (2018).

[141] Parenting Children in the Age of Screens, *Pew Research Center*, (July 2020).

[142] Common Sense Comments to the Federal Trade Commission on Guides Concerning the Use of Endorsements and Testimonials in Advertising, (June 22, 2020).

[143] Ibid.

[144] Ofcom, Children and parents: media use and attitudes report, November 2016.

[145] American Psychological Association, Advertising and Children, February 20, 2004 http://www.apa.org/pubs/info/reports/advertising-children; Hudders, Liselot & Cauberghe, Verolien & Panic, Katarina. (2015). How Advertising Literacy Training Affects Children's Responses to Television Commercials versus Advergames. *International Journal of Advertising*. 10.1080/02650487.2015.1090045.

[146] Common Sense Comments to the Federal Trade Commission on Guides Concerning the Use of Endorsements and Testimonials in Advertising, (June 22, 2020).

into a game to promote products. Children play these without realizing they are engaging with an ad.[147]

Identifying an ad is only half the battle. Even when children can differentiate between ads and other content, they still struggle to understand the commercial purpose of the advertisement. Children under 8 years old lack the cognitive ability to understand the persuasive or "selling" intent of advertisements, and this knowledge of persuasion is still underdeveloped until at least age 12. Some researchers found that children ages 6–7 predominantly view advertisements as informational breaks for the watchers or the makers of a tv program.[148] If ads are harder to identify online, that cannot help children in understanding their commercial intent.

The Status Quo Is Failing Young People

Technology was already failing families before covid. Shutdowns and stay-at-home policies have magnified and multiplied these problems. Technology has intruded into every aspect of our kids' lives and every corner of our homes. And the companies providing technologies and related services have grown unchecked and unaccountable – too many are manipulating children online, misusing their personal information, and exposing kids to harm.

Children Are Growing up Surveilled

Kids today face surveillance unlike any other generation – their every movement online and off can be tracked by dozens if not hundreds of companies. We talk of a digital footprint, but at this point it is more accurately a full-body scan. And we have little reason to think that all of this data collected is being maintained and used in a way that respects children's privacy. As discussed above, children and teens may not think twice before sharing information, and do not understand what happens to their information once shared. They can also be early adopters of invasive and insecure

---

[147] Soontae An, Hyun Seung Jin & Eun Hae Park (2014) Children's Advertising Literacy for Advergames: Perception of the Game as Advertising, *Journal of Advertising*, 43:1, 63-72, DOI: 10.1080/00913367.2013.795123.

[148] Samantha Graff, Dale Kunkel & Seth E. Mermin, Government Can Regulate Food Advertising to Children Because Cognitive Research Shows that it is Inherently Misleading, *Health Affairs* 2, 392-398 2012 . Valkenburg, P. M., & Cantor, J. (2001). The development of a child into a consumer. *Journal of Applied Developmental Psychology*, 22(1), 61–72. https://doi.org/10.1016/S0193-3973(00)00066-6 Most children's understanding of the "selling intent" of television food ads did not emerge until around 7–8 years, reaching 90% by 11–12 years. Owen B.J.Carter et al. Children's understanding of the selling versus persuasive intent of junk food advertising: Implications for regulation, *Social Science & Medicine*, Volume 72, Issue 6, p. 962-968, (March 2011).

technology.[149] One analysis found that more than half of thousands of free children's apps may serve kids ads in violation of federal law.[150] Privacy is an equity issue, and children with low socioeconomic status were more likely to play games collecting and sharing information for advertisements. Among young children's apps, a study found two-thirds collected and shared persistent identifiers for advertising purposes, also not permitted without parental consent under federal law.[151] Yet another study found that popular apps for teenagers included more third-party trackers than apps for adults, and were more likely to seek access to personal information stored on phones.[152] More than half of connected devices do not provide proper information on how they collect, use and disclose users' personal information.[153] In the last five years, millions of kids and parents have had sensitive information – including family chats – exposed by connected toys.[154] Data brokers have sold profiles of children at least as young as two (and identity theft can occur before a child's first birthday).[155] And companies are almost always seeking more – it is not uncommon for companies to use clever design to get as much information as possible out of a user, and then use that knowledge to go back for more.

This poses real concerns for kids. As the head of the UK ICO has noted, "if we have a generation who grow up seeing digital services misuse their personal data, what does that do to their trust in innovation in the future?"[156] Children do not want their data shared: research in the UK and Ireland has found kids are "outraged" when they learn what businesses do with information they collect, and that kids find targeted ads to be "unfair" and "annoying" as "companies ha[ve] no business using their personal data for

149 Johnson, Ariel Fox (2019) "13 Going on 30: An Exploration of Expanding COPPA's Privacy Protections to Everyone," *Seton Hall Legislative Journal*: Vol. 44 : Iss. 3, Article 1.

150 Reyes et al. "Won't Somebody Think of the Children?" Examining COPPA Compliance at Scale. *Proceedings on Privacy Enhancing Technologies*, (2018).

151 Zhao F, Egelman S, Weeks HM, Kaciroti N, Miller AL, Radesky JS. Data collection practices of mobile applications played by preschool-aged children. *JAMA Pediatrics*, accepted for publication.

152 Risky Business: A New Study Assessing Teen Privacy in Mobile Apps, *BBB National Programs*, (October 2020).

153 GPEN Privacy Sweep on Internet of Things, (2016).

154 Jensen, Data Breach Involving CloudPets "Smart" Toys Raises Internet-of-Things Security Concerns, Data Privacy + Security Insider (2017).; and Caroline Knorr, Real-World Reasons Parents Should Care About Kids and Online Privacy, *Common Sense Media*, (2018).

155 Ibid.

156 Elizabeth Denham, From facial recognition technology to children online: regulating data protection in 2021, *Office of the ICO*, (March 3, 2021).

profit."[157] And feelings are similar here: 68% of teens are concerned about how social media sites target them with advertisements.[158] The risks to young people of having all of their information and data collected are manifold, as detailed extensively in Common Sense's report Privacy Risks & Harms.[159] Inadvertent disclosure or misuse of a child's personal information can lead to emotional, behavioral, and safety problems, including: cyberbullying, radicalization, substance abuse, limited educational opportunities, self-harm, contact from strangers, identity theft and increased parent-child conflict. Ultimately, children will self-censor themselves for fear of surveillance.

Tech Manipulates Kids to Be "Always on" and Drives Them to More Outrageous Content

Manipulative design takes further advantage of kids – subverting their choices and autonomy and causing them not only to give up more information than otherwise but also to spend more time clicking and scrolling and taking them down rabbit holes. Indeed, almost half of teens report feeling "addicted" to their phones.[160] Social media platforms offer immediate and variable rewards, just like casino games, and these can lead to compulsion.[161] Infinite scrolls do not offer any visual cues or reminders to young people to stop. "Awards" for repeat use or actions, like Snapchat's "Snapstreaks" for daily communication with friends, encourage unnecessary and excessive engagement. Autoplay videos keep kids glued to the screen even after a show is over.

Video and content recommendations do more than keep kids hooked. They also lead children to increasingly sensationalist, inappropriate, and illegal content (and lead adults to similar, including content involving

---

[157] Sonia Livingstone, Mariya Soilova, Rishita Nadagiri, Children's data and privacy online: Growing up in a digital age, An evidence review, (Dec. 2018).; Know Your Rights and Have Your Say! Stream Two of the DPC's Public Consultation on the Processing of Children's Personal Data and the Rights of Children as Data Subjects under the GDPR, Data Protection Commission, (January 28, 2019).; "Some stuff you just want to keep private!" – Preliminary report on Stream II of the DPC's consultation on the processing of children's personal data and the rights of children as data subjects under the GDPR, (July 29, 2019).

[158] *Common Sense Media*, Privacy Matters: Protecting Digital Privacy for Parents and Kids, (2018).

[159] Kelly, G., Graham, J., Bronfman, J., & Garton, S. (2019). Privacy risks and harms. San Francisco, CA: *Common Sense Media*.

[160] Rideout, V., and Robb, M. B. (2018). Social media, social life: Teens reveal their experiences. San Francisco, CA: *Common Sense Media*.

[161] Zuboff, Shoshana, *The Age of Surveillance Capitalism: The Fight for a Human Future at the New Frontier of Power*, p. 448, (January 15, 2019).

children).[162] Social media can glorify harmful crazes (like swallowing laundry detergent) and violence (children posing with weapons and being virtually cheered on can and has turned into tragedy). A parent reported to us that when the pandemic began and she had no childcare, she turned to YouTube, and was horrified when her nine year old's autoplay of Dora videos turned into a graphic clip of Dora being raped. Kids have moved to digital spaces to connect with friends during the pandemic, and such spaces can be difficult for parents to monitor and easy for kids to navigate into mature content. With little adult oversight either by parents or the companies themselves, these platforms can quickly allow for bad behavior and sharing of explicit content. Almost half (46%) of parents say their child younger than 11 has accessed inappropriate videos on YouTube, and 65% say they are concerned about the types of videos recommended to their child (Auxier et al., 2020).[163] On the user generated gaming platform Roblox, reporters found numerous virtual spaces where underage users created animated pornographic images and naked avatars could engage in simulated sexual acts. A recent report by Fast Company outlined the rise of spaces created for digital sex parties, known as "condo games," to be created and then shared on platforms such as Roblox and Discord. These "condo games" have been strongly criticized by experts on child predators for operating as prime spaces for predators to groom children for sexual abuse.[164]

Online games and social media are also rife with harassment and hate speech. One recent survey found that 65 percent of players experience some form of severe harassment, including physical threats, stalking, and sustained harassment; 38 percent of women and 35 percent of LGBTQ+players reported harassment on the basis of their gender and sexual orientation.[165] A study found 8 in 10 tweens and teens reported witnessing or experiencing bullying in 2020, and 9 in 10 witnessed violent subject matter.[166] A forthcoming report from Common Sense looks at how teens have turned to social media during the pandemic, and in many ways social media has been a lifeline for teens and

---

162 Max Fisher & Amanda Taub, On YouTube's Digital Playground, an Open Gate for Pedophiles, *New York Times*, (June 3, 2019).

163 Radesky, J. S., Schaller, A., Yeo, S. L., Weeks, H. M., & Robb, M.B. (2020). Young kids and YouTube: How ads, toys, and games dominate viewing, 2020. San Francisco, CA: *Common Sense Media*.

164 Burt Helm, Sex, lies, and video games: Inside Roblox's war on porn, *Fast Company*, (August 19, 2020).

165 Free to Play? Hate, Harassment, and Positive Social Experiences in Online Games, *Anti-Defamation League*, (2020).

166 Haley Zapa, Bark's Annual Report: 2020 Research on Teens and Tweens, (January 15, 2021).

young adults in managing their mental health. And yet it remains mired in hate speech and harmful content – for example, the percent of teens who see racist content has nearly doubled in the past two years.[167] This is especially concerning as hate speech exacerbates negative mental health outcomes - and it's already being targeted at vulnerable groups by race, gender, and sexual orientation.

The Commercialization of Childhood Online Is More Insidious Than in Traditional Media

Kids are also subject to a high level of commercialism online. The internet offers frictionless opportunities for endless consumption, be it of ads, content, in-app items, or physical goods. And traditional safeguards – like a parent shopping in a physical store with a child – are lacking.

Ads are pervasive. Recent Common Sense research looking at children's content on YouTube found advertising occurred in 95% of early childhood videos. Over one-third of videos in the early childhood category contained three or more ads, while 59% contained one to two ads. Ad design in these videos was often problematic, such as banner ads that blocked educational content, sidebar ads that could be confused for recommended videos, or ads for video games that showed doctored versions of popular characters, such as Peppa Pig.[168] Past research on advertising in children's apps has shown a high prevalence of manipulative or disruptive ad designs as well as adult-oriented ad content that is easily clickable by child users.[169] And apps encourage ad viewing, including by offering in-app rewards in exchange.[170]

In-app spending is also a big problem. Teen apps are highly monetized – a recent study highlights that teen apps are over three times more likely to support in-app purchases than general audience apps.[171] And even young and pre-literate children are directly encouraged to spend money within apps and games. Beloved cartoon characters berate preschool players for not spending

---

[167] Rideout, V., Fox, S., Peebles, A., & Robb, M. B. (2021). Coping with COVID-19: How young people use digital media to manage their mental health. San Francisco, CA: *Common Sense Media* and *Hopelab*.

[168] Radesky, J. S., Schaller, A., Yeo, S. L., Weeks, H. M., & Robb, M.B. (2020). Young kids and YouTube: How ads, toys, and games dominate viewing, 2020. San Francisco, CA: *Common Sense Media*.

[169] Ibid.

[170] Meyer M, Adkins V, Yuan N, Weeks HM, Chang YJ, Radesky J. Advertising in young children's apps: A content analysis. *Journal of Developmental & Behavioral Pediatrics*. 2019 Jan 1;40(1):32-9.

[171] Risky Business: A New Study Assessing Teen Privacy in Mobile Apps, *BBB National Programs*, (October 2020).

money.[172] Educational games allow children to advance faster than their friends if they purchase subscriptions.[173] Often, the fact that a purchase involves actual money is not made clear to kids, who believe their activities have no "real world" consequences and do not realize they are spending their parents' money. And kids have spent hundreds and thousands of dollars, collectively totalling millions. Indeed, Google, Apple, and Amazon have all settled with the Federal Trade Commission over unfairly permitting minors to make in-app purchases when it was not clear a purchase was being made and when parents were not given a choice whether to allow the purchases.[174] Facebook documents show the company allowing children as young as five unwittingly spending their parents' money, and intentionally making it difficult for children and parents to get refunds.[175]

Children and teens have also taken to commercializing their peers, both inadvertently and very intentionally. On the unintentional side, children are often prompted to share their mobile game progress on social media and rate apps on app stores,[176] which is effective at commercializing friends. Similarly, teens may inadvertently become product ambassadors – as in Facebook's "sponsored stories" program – and encouraged to submit photos and share products and content with friends, all of which is monitored and monetized.[177] Despite having to pay a $20 million settlement in a lawsuit about these[178],

---

[172] Marisa Meyer, Victoria Adkins, Nalingna Yuan, Heidi M Weeks, Yung-Ju Chang, Jenny Radesky, Advertising in Young Children's Apps: A Content Analysis, (January 2019).

[173] Alyson Klein, Popular Interactive Math Game Prodigy Is Target of Complaint to Federal Trade Commission, *Education Week*, (February 23, 2021).

[174] See ruling in *FTC v. Amazon*, 2016 Federal Court Finds Amazon Liable for Billing Parents for Children's Unauthorized In-App Charges., and *FTC v. Apple*, FTC Approves Final Order in Case About Apple Inc. Charging for Kids' In-App Purchases Without Parental Consent, and *FTC v. Google,* FTC Approves Final Order in Case About Google Billing for Kids' In-App Charges Without Parental Consent.

[175] Request for the Federal Trade Commission to Investigate Facebook In-App Purchases for Violating the Federal Trade Commission Act and the Children's Online Privacy Protection Act.

[176] Meyer M, Adkins V, Yuan N, et al. Advertising in Young Children's Apps: A Content Analysis. *Journal of Developmental and Behavioral Pediatrics: JDBP*. 2019 Jan;40(1):32-39. DOI: 10.1097/dbp.0000000000000622.

[177] Josh Constine, Facebook Sponsored Story Ads To Appear In The Web News Feed In 2012, *TechCrunch*, (December 20, 2011).; Brittany Darwell, Understanding the difference between Facebook Sponsored Stories, Page Post Ads, Promoted Posts and Marketplace Ads, *Ad Week*, (January 11, 2013).; Generation Like, *PBS Frontline*, (Feb. 18, 2014), *see also* Workgroup on Children's Online Privacy Protection, Report to the Maryland General Assembly on Children's Online Privacy, 17 (Dec. 30, 2013).

[178] Brain Feldman, Facebook Reaches Settlement in Sponsored Stories Lawsuit, *The Atlantic*, (August 27, 2013).

Facebook still allows for sponsored stories.[179] Additionally, "peers" intentionally push products via unboxing videos and influencer campaigns. Common Sense research has found that a third of children under age eight report sometimes or regularly watching unboxing videos – essentially program-length advertisements – on YouTube.[180] The nine-year old multi-million dollar star of many popular unboxing videos has faced consumer complaints over failures to disclose paid product placement.[181] He recently opened an online world within Roblox where children can make in-game purchases.[182] Host-selling is rampant online, and characters can hawk products in ways that would be prohibited on tv because of children's special relationships with the hosts. Teenagers look to influencers as peers with whom they have their own relationships.[183]

Online promotions cause real world harm. Sales in e-cigarettes amongst middle school and high school students increased drastically when U.S. tobacco companies began exploiting their online ads to children.[184] Children who saw the online ads were significantly more likely to use the products. And rules meant to limit what purchases young people can make are less effective than in physical retailers. Social media companies provide markets for teenagers to find illegal goods, like drugs.[185] Ineffective purchasing gates, such as simply stating in a Terms of Use that a user must be 18, have, for example, allowed children to purchase weapons from Amazon.[186]

---

[179] Facebook states in its terms of service that users give it permission to use their name or photo "next to or in connection with ads, offers, and other sponsored content that we display across our Products, without any compensation to [the user]."

[180] Common Sense Census: Media Use by Kids Age Zero to Eight, *Common Sense Media*, (October 19, 2017).

[181] Tiffany Hsu, Popular YouTube Toy Review Channel Accused of Blurring Lines for Ads, *New York Times*, (September 4, 2019).

[182] Sahil Patel, 9-Year-Old YouTube Star Ryan Kaji Opens Virtual World on Roblox, *Wall Street Journal*, (December 4, 2020).

[183] Common Sense Comments to the Federal Trade Commission on Guides Concerning the Use of Endorsements and Testimonials in Advertising, (June 22, 2020).

[184] Lisa Rapaport, Teens Most Drawn to E Cigarettes by Online Ads, *Reuters Health Report*, (April 2016).

[185] Rachel Paula Abrahamson, Mom warns about drug dealers on Snapchat after son, 16, dies from overdose, *Today Show*, (February 8, 2021).

[186] The Parent's Accountability and Child Protection Act, A California 14 year old purchased a BB gun, throwing knives, and a hunting knife on Amazon without his parent's knowledge, (September 2018).

Children and Teens Face a Toxic Online Environment

The internet and especially social media have changed the way kids view themselves and others. While social media can be a body positive place for teenagers[187], for some it can be detrimental, especially if they are prone to comparing themselves to images.[188] Almost half of girls say social media makes them feel they have to look or act a certain way.[189] According to Common Sense Media's body-image research, teens who are active online worry a lot about how they're perceived.[190] Tweens and young teens have reported pressure to create a "personal brand" and to "be perfect and compare myself to others all the time."[191] And teenagers measure self-worth and happiness in how many likes and comments their posts receive.[192] Many studies have shown a correlation between social media use and mental health issues, though causation still requires further research.

The pandemic has exacerbated concerns about mental health. As detailed in Common Sense's forthcoming report, depression continues to go up, especially among LGBTQ+ and teens and young adults who have had COVID-19 infections in their homes.[193] This is particularly concerning because research has shown social media has an outsize impact – both negatively and positively – on the severely depressed and those at risk for substance abuse. Among the severely depressed, our forthcoming work shows a high number of respondents report that social media made them feel more anxious, stressed, and depressed. Numbers for this vulnerable group are trending in the wrong direction.

---

187 Cohen, R., Fardouly, J., Newton-John, T., & Slater, A. (2019). #BoPo on Instagram: An experimental investigation of the effects of viewing body positive content on young women's mood and body image. *New Media & Society*, 21(7), 1546–1564. https://doi.org/10.1177/146144481982653.

188 Kleemans M, Daalmans S, Carbaat I, Anschütz D. Picture perfect: the direct effect of manipulated Instagram photos on body image in adolescent girls. *Media Psychology*. 2018;21(1):93–110.

189 *Reclaiming the Internet for Girls*, Plan International UK, (2017).

190 Common Sense Media, Children, Teens, Media, and Body Image, (January 20, 2015).

191 Zuboff, Shoshana, *The Age of Surveillance Capitalism: The Fight for a Human Future at the New Frontier of Power*, p. 448, (January 15, 2019).

192 Jessica Contrera, 13, right now: This is what it's like to grow up in the age of likes, lols and longing, *Washington Post*, (May 25, 2016).

193 Rideout, V., Fox, S., Peebles, A., & Robb, M. B. (2021). Coping with COVID-19: How young people use digital media to manage their mental health.San Francisco, CA: *Common Sense Media* and *Hopelab*.

Building a Safe, Empowering, and Equitable Digital Future for Kids

Technology should be a force for equity and opportunity, for connection and creativity. As our CEO and Founder James P. Steyer has said, "we are at a pivotal moment in history, as technology collides with our democracy, our fundamental approach to education, and our mental, physical, and emotional health. Technology's original promise to foster connection has been lost, but it is not too late for us to right the ship." It is high time to right the ship. To do so, Congress must take a holistic view of the interconnected harms young people experience online and support a variety of related solutions that overall can improve the online landscape for kids both today and tomorrow. And technology leaders should do what they can immediately to improve their products.

Congress has long recognized children's special vulnerabilities – including in media and technology specifically – and provided additional protections for kids and families.[194] The Children's Television Act requires a certain amount of educational programming during hours children are likely to be watching, limits commercial time, and requires clear delineations between ads and other content. Congress has also provided for special protections for young children on the internet, with the Children's Online Privacy Protection Act, which sought to re-insert parents as gatekeepers of their children's lives and protect against unwanted contact from strangers and marketers – in an era when children were dialing up the internet on bulky desktops shared with the whole family. Now, the internet is always on, and always within reach in a pocket, atop a bedside stand, or on a kitchen counter. "Simply existing" can subject a child or teen to surveillance and data collection,[195] simply pressing a few buttons or saying a few words can broadcast a child into countless homes, connect a child with someone on the other side of the world, enable a child to watch everything from live streams of other kids playing video games or, much more distressingly, of rapes or murders. There is incredible opportunity, for good and for bad.

---

[194] Other areas are in prohibiting driving, the purchase of dangerous items, special contract protections, minimum-age requirements for work.

[195] Discussing the context of boilerplate language and the internet, Lauren Scholz notes that "Simply existing in the room with ordinary devices may subject individuals to having their movements and data governed by contract." Fiduciary Boilerplate, *The Journal of Corporation Law*, 2020. Vol 46. P. 157.

Protect Families' and Kids' Privacy

First, Congress must act to better protect young people's privacy. This includes passing a comprehensive national privacy law, which will limit the impact of inadvertent gaps in child-specific laws, ensuring at least some coverage for children and teens on any site or service. That said, given children and teens' unique vulnerabilities, they need special protections – no behavioral ad targeting, data minimization by design and default – and, consistent with international precedent and more recent state laws like California's Consumer Privacy Act, those special protections should definitely include teens. Current federal law, COPPA, stops providing protections when a child turns 13, and has other limitations even with respect to children.

Happily, there are already good models. The PRIVCY Act[196] would address many of COPPA's shortcomings: preventing sites from turning a blind eye to young people using their services, offering special protections to and empowering teens to make decisions for themselves, emphasizing the importance of age-appropriate controls and language, and providing bright line rules prohibiting certain particularly problematic practices like behavioral marketing to young children. It would also enable stronger enforcement, allowing parents to sue on behalf of their kids and enhancing the Federal Trade Commission's powers. Enhancing regulators' ability to enforce privacy violations in general is critical, and the Commission should have more resources.

Protecting privacy will go a long way in improving children's overall experiences – companies will be less able to microtarget kids with inappropriate content and advertisements, for example, or use what they have learned to further manipulate children to stay online longer or spend more money. But more is also needed – children's exposure to unhealthy content via social media and algorithmically-curated feeds should be limited, and companies should not be incentivized to push inappropriate ads and disturbing and even illegal content onto kids.

Holds Platforms Accountable in a Digital Age

Congress should pass a Children's Television Act for the internet age. Again, a model exists: the Kids Internet Design and Safety Act or KIDS Act.[197] It would limit kids' exposure to marketing and commercialization by creating rules that limit how commercial content can be recommended to kids. It also

---

[196] H. 5703, PRIVCY ACT, (January 29, 2020).

[197] H. 8372, Kids Internet Design and Safety (KIDS) Act, (September 24 2020).

requires platforms to provide families with better guidance on kid healthy content, label and identify healthy content, and supports no-cost and ad-free access to this material. The KIDS Act acknowledges the reality that how platforms and technologies are designed can be just as impactful as what data they collect and use.

We additionally need to control algorithmic amplification and UX/UI design that undermines users' choices and amplifies negative content. The bipartisan Deceptive Experiences To Online Users Reduction Act (DETOUR Act) in the Senate targets practices by large online platforms to use deceptive and manipulative design practices known as "dark patterns."[198] For large platforms like Facebook and YouTube, the DETOUR Act would curb design interfaces that create compulsive usage among children under the age of 13 years old. It also encourages the creation of professional standards bodies to provide guidance on design practices that undermine user autonomy, places limits on online behavioral and psychological experiments,[199] and promotes the development of independent review boards.[200] In addition, we must hold platforms accountable for their promises to address misinformation, harassment, and harmful content, including via educated, meaningful enforcement and exploring instances where platform intermediaries should be liable for the content they actively host and what changes are needed to current rules like Section 230.

We strongly recommend that Congress advance legislation that holds technology companies accountable. We also believe there is much that industry could do right now to improve children's experiences – -and indeed many of our advocacy efforts include convincing companies that it is in everyone's interests for them to improve. Companies can act immediately to limit information collection from children and teens, design healthier products, and promote quality content for kids. Later this month, the full Committee will hear from social media CEOs on misinformation and disinformation. That is an excellent opportunity to ask them to do the right thing by kids, regardless of limitations in current laws, and on behalf of American families we hope you will take full advantage of that opportunity.

---

[198] S.1084, Deceptive Experiences to Online Users Reduction (DETOUR) Act, (April 9, 2019).

[199] Evan Selinger and Woodrow Hartzog, Facebook's emotional contagion study and the ethical problem of co-opted identity in mediated environments where users lack control, *Research Review at Facebook*, (May 13, 2015).

[200] Ryan Calo, Consumer Subject Review Boards, (2013).

Conclusion

Thank you again for your commitment to understanding the issues children face online during the pandemic. Currently, technology is failing young people. While it is important to recognize the enormous benefits that technology and media have offered to all of us during this time especially – truly a lifeline – kids deserve better. Children and teens deserve to be able to chat with their friends without the conversation and location being recorded, to enjoy a game without being shamed for not purchasing an in-app item, and to watch their favorite cartoons without fear of violence. They also deserve a digital environment not tailor-made to appeal to many of their insecurities. The digital world provides limitless opportunities, and Congress should do all that it can to enable young people to fully take advantage of what technology has to offer while recognizing their still evolving capacities.

* * *

Ms. SCHAKOWSKY. Thank you. And the gentlelady yields back.

We have concluded witness' opening statements at this time. So we are going to move to Member questions. Each Member will have 5 minutes to ask questions of our witnesses, and I will start by recognizing myself for 5 minutes.

So the line between people's online and offline lives has rapidly disappeared. This is particularly true for kids, and as one of our witnesses said, even infants. I have seen babies just holding devices in the airport and other places.

The ability to track children for behavioral advertising, coupled with persuasion design tactics, has been a real problem and a threat to our kids.

And I wanted to ask Dr. Ameenuddin. Can you speak to how children and even teens struggle to identify and resist these manipulative techniques in today's complex online ecosystem?

Dr. AMEENUDDIN. Certainly. Thank you, Chair Schakowsky.

I think your question really gets to the heart of the problem. The fact is that children at different developmental ages have different levels of ability to understand and to resist persuasive programming.

For young children, I do not think that exists, period. They just do not have the sophistication and are uniquely vulnerable to persuasive design.

Even when you look at older kids, teenagers, who may even have some training in digital literacy, media literacy, have a lot of difficulty resisting these very, very persuasive, well-targeted ads.

Frankly, it is hard for adults to resist too, and so that is why the American Academy of Pediatrics feels that it is so important to create structural layers that hold tech responsible.

And we think this is a wonderful opportunity for Congress to help pass laws that protect kids from that kind of predatory targeting and data collection.

Ms. SCHAKOWSKY. Thank you so much.

Let me ask Ms. Fox Johnson. Given that these marketing and design techniques are so sophisticated, thoroughly tested and intentionally directed at children and teens, do you believe that the Federal Trade Commission, FTC, should regulate such practice, predatory behavior, under the unfair and deceptive practices authority?

Ms. FOX JOHNSON. I certainly believe that the Federal Trade Commission could regulate these things as unfair and deceptive, particularly to children under 13 who may not even know they are interacting with an advertisement in lots of scenarios.

I think that a less litigious and perhaps quicker path forward would be Congress making it clear that these practices are not allowed.

Ms. SCHAKOWSKY. And let me ask you this about the platforms' accountability. Dr. Ameenuddin, do you think that we need to have platforms accountable for exposing children to harmful and inappropriate content?

Dr. AMEENUDDIN. I always think that accountability is important, especially when you are creating products that are not necessarily developmentally appropriate but are still exposing children to sometimes highly inappropriate content.

We absolutely believe at the American Academy of Pediatrics that tech companies need to take responsibility for that because we all believe that we have a same general goal of wanting to protect children.

Ms. SCHAKOWSKY. Thank you.

And I wondered if you wanted to comment on that, Ms. Fox Johnson, the accountability of the platforms.

Ms. FOX JOHNSON. Yes. These platforms are incredibly powerful and have an incredible amount of resources at their disposal, unlike many parents. They are not just making content available to kids that is inappropriate, but in many cases actively pushing it on them and taking them into outrageous or concerning scenarios. So they can do a better job at what they push and also a better job at identifying healthy, positive, education content.

Ms. SCHAKOWSKY. Thank you.

And, Dr. Ameenuddin—oh, I did it again—Ameenuddin, I want to ask you. How might this repeated, regular exposure to inappropriate content, often viewed together with appropriate content, harm or affect our children?

And if you could tell us long term, as well, how it could affect our children.

Dr. AMEENUDDIN. So that is a very important question. Thank you so much for addressing that.

Repeated exposure to harmful content, whether it is violent content or, frankly, you know, racist content that kids are encountering online, really can be harmful.

We know from past research that bio space harassment and being exposed to these negative images can really undermine the child's self-esteem. It can cause significant mental distress for them.

And being exposed to that repeatedly, unfortunately, only multiplies that effect, which is all the more reason to be careful and hold tech companies accountable for what they are putting out there.

Ms. SCHAKOWSKY. Thank you so much.

I realize I have gone over my time, and I yield back.

And now I would welcome Congressman Bilirakis to ask his questions for 5 minutes.

Mr. BILIRAKIS. Thank you, Madam Chair. I appreciate very much.

Dr. Ameenuddin, thank you not just for your testimony but your important work on kids' mental health. That is so very important. They are our future.

I believe your contributions here today really serve multiple areas we are working on. So, again, I really appreciate all of the witnesses.

I am concerned about how children being, again, depressed, anxious, and even suicidal this generation has become. You know, you see it on a regular basis when you are in our district.

Can you speak to the isolation that kids have felt since the pandemic began?

And can you provide perspective on what are the most common issues you are seeing that might be driving the sadness of these kids?

And then as a follow-up, would you agree that one of the best ways that we deal with these issues is to curb access to these negative impacts?

Dr. AMEENUDDIN. Thank you, Ranking Member Bilirakis.

Such a critical question. There is no doubt that pediatricians have anecdotally been reporting increased visits for depression and anxiety. I find that those are two of the most common mental health issues that I have personally been seeing during the pandemic.

I do want to make it clear we have been seeing increasing levels of this even before the pandemic hit, but certainly exacerbated by a combination of factors. The pandemic has been very stressful for everyone.

I have had children whose parents have lost jobs. I have had patients who have lost family members to the COVID–19 disease. And so really I think it is multifactorial. Isolation certainly plays into it.

And that is where in some ways we also have to look at the positive benefits of technology where that has allowed them to stay connected to grandparents, to elderly neighbors, to friends, but obviously, you know, we want to maximum the positive benefits without leaving them vulnerable to the negative benefits.

And I apologize. You had a follow-up question.

Mr. BILIRAKIS. Yes. Addressing it, would you agree that one of the best ways that we deal with these issues is to curb access to these negative impacts?

Dr. AMEENUDDIN. So I would agree that the best way to help curb negative impacts is to look at the structural system and to try to minimize those harms through accountability for tech platforms and also legislation to help regulate what children are able to access and what data is collected on them.

Thank you.

Mr. BILIRAKIS. Thank you.

Again, Doctor, for you again, there have been many data and scientifically backed pediatricians, including those at the American Academy of Pediatricians, who argue that schools are safe enough to open. Do you agree with your colleagues that we need to begin opening schools back up for students and teachers?

Dr. AMEENUDDIN. So I appreciate that question. I know that that is a related issue, even if it is not the specific issue of this particular hearing.

I think that the American Academy of Pediatrics has put together a very thoughtful and evidence-based recommendation for school reopening.

We also know that not all schools are equally resourced, and in order to make sure that schools are safe to return, we need to be able to ensure universal masking, hand washing, social distancing. Ideally it would be great to have teachers vaccinated as well. That is an additional layer of protection.

It is never just one thing when we talk about public health or health benefits, but we certainly all can agree that we want to move towards the goal of making it safe for all kids to return to school and to make sure that schools are appropriately funded so that they ensure those safety measures for everybody.

Mr. BILIRAKIS. Thank you, Doctor.

Dr. DeAngelis, would you like to comment on any of the data from Public Health Masters supporting the reopening of schools?

We would appreciate that. Thank you.

Dr. DEANGELIS. Yes. In fact, there was a systematic review of the evidence published just today. So if you want to add it to the record, you can find it at The 74 Million. A reporter named Linda Jacobson actually summarized the study and said, and I quote, "Mounting evidence shows it is safe for reopening schools and that the risk of in-person learning contributing to the spread of COVID– 19 is low," according to a new review of research released Thursday.

That covered 130 different studies. So it is a huge amount of evidence, and then also researchers at the CDC published in a top journal, JAMA, saying that, quote, "The preponderance of available evidence from the fall school semester has been reassuring insofar as the type of rapid spread that was frequently observed in congregate living facilities or high-density work sites has not been reported in education settings in schools."

And quote, "There has been little evidence that schools have contributed meaningfully to increased community transmission."

You can also look at places like New York City, where the school positivity rate is less than a tenth of what the positivity rate in the overall community is. You can look at quotes from people like Anthony Fauci as well saying to close the bars and open the schools and that schools are generally not major contributors of community transmission.

I know I am over time, but there's tons of evidence suggesting that schools can reopen safely, particularly if you have the procedures in place.

And then my latest study in Social Science Research Network suggests there is no relationship between funding and schools re-opening.

Ms. SCHAKOWSKY. We are going to have to call on the next speaker.

I am looking for Frank Pallone. Yes, the chair of the full committee is recognized for questions for 5 minutes.

Mr. PALLONE. Thank you, Madam Chair.

I wanted to start out with Dr. Ameenuddin. My concern is that, you know, you have many of our constituents who work two jobs and have to take care of their family and, you know, just putting food on the table is a challenge.

And there was a recent Common Sense Media survey that showed that children from lower-income households spend nearly two additional hours on screens than those from higher-income households. You know, so while parents can supervise—or, at least, that is the goal—it is really impractical or not possible for many if they are working two jobs and have all of these other things.

So, Dr. Ameenuddin, are children able to self-monitor their own digital consumption?

And do they know when to disconnect? I know parental controls are viewed as an alternative when direct supervision is not possible, but 71 percent of parents say they are not satisfied that the tools they have to use to keep kids safe.

That is my question, to what extent the kids can self-monitor, know when to disconnect or what to do, if you would.

Dr. AMEENUDDIN. Thank you, Chair Pallone.

So, again, I think that is a critical question, whether or not children can self-monitor, and when we look at the circumstances that this pandemic has really brought to the fore, these are not new.

For a long time, for decades, the American Academy of Pediatrics has recognized the unique vulnerability of young children, in particular, but even teenagers to be able to really self-monitor and resist manipulative designs.

And, you know, 20, 30 years ago, as I think one of your members mentioned, it was easy to sort of turn off the TV and for parents to monitor, but these days with the ubiquity of digital devices and the ability to take these devices into bedrooms, it really makes it so much harder for kids to self-regulate and self-monitor.

Young children are not capable. I want to make that very clear. It is just not going to happen without some structural supports and parental supervision, which of course has become even more difficult when you have got a parent in one room working one job, a parent in another room working one job.

So really, again, we have to look at this as a structural issue, as the American Academy of Pediatrics has done for years, to recognize that we need more protections for our kids. Even media-savvy teens have difficulty self-regulating, although it is OK to give them a little bit of flexibility to try to do that.

Mr. PALLONE. Well, thank you.

Then let me ask Ms. Fox Johnson. Can you discuss briefly the different parental control options that are currently available, including how easy they are to use, how much they cost, what that means for low-income families, and any privacy concerns?

And then a second question: Given the limitations that you are probably going to say about these devices, how do you explain why baseline default protections from children are important, if you could?

Ms. FOX JOHNSON. Sure. Thank you, Chairman Pallone.

So there are a variety of parental controls, and just researching all of them it takes a lot of time, time that parents do not have. You can have browserable controls. You can have controls at the device level. Some apps and gaming systems offer controls within them.

Like I said, it takes time to research these, and it takes additional time and effort to try to implement them in effective ways.

They also—especially the better ones that do more than just allow you to block sites but allow you to, say, filter content or see what your kids are doing—cost money, $10 a month, $100 a year, more money if you have more kids.

This plus the time involved make it very difficult for lower-income families, in particular, or families with less digital literacy to use these tools effectively.

And then also, as you mentioned, concerns about kids growing up with surveillance and feeling normalized, and it is normal that someone can constantly follow them. Traditionally a kid could go into a bedroom, shut their door, and have a moment of privacy, but that may not be possible if their parent or someone else is constantly monitoring them.

The U.K. has advised that, with parental controls, companies should make that clear to kids so that they know what's going on and have not sort of secret surveillance given out.

Mr. PALLONE. Baseline default protection, is that important?

Ms. FOX JOHNSON. Yes.

Mr. PALLONE. Did you mention that? Go ahead.

Ms. FOX JOHNSON. Baseline protections are super important because we know that defaults are super important. Lots of people do not take the time to change defaults, and companies make it very difficult to change defaults.

If companies had to put kids' best interests at the front from designing their products from the get-go, it would be less critical for parents to go to the trouble and time and money of putting in extra parental controls.

Mr. PALLONE. All right. Thank you so much.

Thank you, Madam Chair. I yield back, Ms. Schakowsky.

Ms. SCHAKOWSKY. Thank you.

And I recognize Mrs. Rodgers, the ranking member on the full committee, for her 5 minutes.

Mrs. RODGERS. Thank you, Madam Chair. Thank you, Mr. Chairman, for this hearing today. I think it is very important.

I appreciate all of the witnesses being here and sharing your insights with us.

You know, during my opening statement, I highlighted the importance for schools to reopen fully for 5 days a week, for students and teachers both to return to the classroom.

Dr. DeAngelis, you raise some startling statistics in your testimony, especially regarding the disproportionate impact on less-advantaged children in our country, like those with disabilities.

Your testimony states that, in 2020, failing grades in Arlington Public Schools increased 91 percent since the previous year for middle school students with disabilities, and 81 percent for high school students with disabilities.

Can you explain what this means for these families and these students and what it would mean for them to have school in person again?

Dr. DEANGELIS. Well, thank you so much for the question.

It can lead to a ton of long-term negative impacts, in addition to the student achievement negative impacts that we are seeing.

And I want to say there is a nationwide analysis done by McKinsey & Company on two different occasions finding that students have already lost months and months of learning, and Eric Hanushek, an economist affiliated with Stanford University, did a report published by the OECD, estimating that this could have a net present value of a negative impact around $17 trillion in the U.S. alone associated with reductions in lifetime earnings and other negative impacts to GDP.

But then there are other problems that are not associated with learning losses, like mental health problems increasing. I know I think Ranking Member Bilirakis had pointed out that suicides had doubled for students in Clark County Public Schools, Nevada, since the same time last year.

So there are a ton of costs associated with keeping the schools closed. One more district in my area, Fairfax County Public Schools, their failure rate increased by 83 percent relative to last year for students failing two or more classes, and that number was even larger, 111 percent, over a doubling in failure for two or more classes for students with special needs.

So, obviously, reopening the schools would lead to more options for individual families to make that choice of whether they want to do in-person or remote learning going forward and to be able to take the best learning environment for their individual children, which would lead to better incomes later in life and could lead to lower likelihood of criminal activity and better lifetime earnings in the long run.

So these are important things that we need to consider. There are a lot of costs in keeping schools closed, and at first a lot of people were only looking at the cost associated with reopening schools. We have got to look at both sides of the equation.

Mrs. RODGERS. Thank you.

And as a follow-up, the Republican leader on this subcommittee, Gus Bilirakis, mentioned that some of the schools are beginning to open.

Washington State, where I come from, is still largely locked down. Some schools, a small percentage, have opened, but I wanted to ask you about the private and parochial schools, because some of them have opened. More of them have opened, and I wanted to ask if you had any data on the trends of transmission rates in private and parochial schools.

Dr. DEANGELIS. Yes. First, I think it is common knowledge at this point that private schools have been substantially more likely to reopen than traditional public schools in the U.S., if you look nationwide or in particular counties across the country, as well.

And there are data on COVID case rates in private schools collected by Brown University. I think Dr. Emily Oster, an economist over at Brown University, has been compiling this for months, finding that, one, the case rates in the schools are substantially lower than the case rates in the community over time.

But then also you can break it down by public versus private schools and how many people are in the schools. So even with the private schools, with a majority and a vast majority of children returning to in-person learning, the COVID case positivity rates in those schools had been substantially lower than in the overall community, sometimes as much as a tenth or a twentieth below the overall community positivity rate, hovering around .5 percent or less pretty consistently over time.

So the private schools have been able to do it, and some public schools have done a good job at being able to reopen in person as well. So it can be done, and you can see that with the comparison that I pointed out earlier between California and Florida.

Florida spends a lot less, yet they are way more likely to be open than California as far as their schools are concerned, and Florida tends to have a lot less powerful teachers' unions as well.

Mrs. RODGERS. You mentioned in your testimony that, after private and parochial schools open, nearby public schools often follow suit. It seems to me that these schools were safe enough to reopen from the beginning. Even the Director of CDC believes schools could reopen.

So why do you think this is happening?

Dr. DEANGELIS. It could be another reason why Florida is more likely to reopen. They have a lot of school choice and competition through even open enrollment with their public schools and then private school choice programs. It is leading the way on those fronts, which could lead to more competition, as that Brown University study found, where places with low-cost private schools, the public schools were more likely to reopen as well.

So I think this has a lot to do with incentives.

Mrs. RODGERS. OK. Thank you, Madam Chair. I yield back.

Ms. SCHAKOWSKY. Thank you.

I am going to go vote. Before I do that, I want to yield now for 5 minutes to Bobby Rush, my colleague from Illinois, for 5 minutes of questioning, and thank Tony Ca´rdenas, the vice chair of this committee, for taking over while I am gone.

So thank you to both of you, and you are recognized, Bobby.

Mr. RUSH. Well, thank you, Madam Chair.

And I want to thank all of the witnesses for this superb hearing. Ms. Fox Johnson, in your testimony you discuss how children in lower-income households and those from racial and ethnic minority groups are spending more time in front of a screen.

My question to you is, given the very positive and inspirational request from the Biden administration in that the vaccinations will be available to all Americans by the end of May, and then it makes us more optimistic about schools being able to open no later than the fall—but in the interim, how do we use online opportunities to help abrogate or help address the missed condition that a lot of our students have fallen so far behind because of the closure of schools?

Is there any way that we can pivot from what the current situation has been to what the current situation could possibly be, given the fact that we will be opening soon?

Ms. FOX JOHNSON. Sure, and thank you, Representative Rush.

I mean, the numbers about more students of color and more typical and more kids from low-income families spending more time on devices comes from before the pandemic, and children in lower-income households are more likely to also use apps that have ad tracking and other sort of COPPA-violating information collection practices.

I think, as everyone seems to be saying here, it will be great when schools reopen. Screen time was a problem before the pandemic. It will be a problem after. I think we need to create a healthy environment for kids online.

I think Congress can help with this. Companies can help with this. They can move away from business models that prioritize engagement and sensationalist content, and they can move away from behavioral ad targeting that preys on kids' particular vulnerabilities.

They can try to promote high-quality and educational content. I mean, Sesame Street is a media product. That is a good product for kids. So the internet companies can change their business models and work to push high-quality content that respects kids and empowers them to grow and learn.

Mr. RUSH. Dr. Ameenuddin, in your testimony you stated that youth of color can cause additional challenges for digital media and face various assessments of beneficial estimates of technology. And this is something that is becoming more evident over the past year and something I have witnessed here in my own district in Chicago.

Can you please talk about the challenges the youth of color face and what, if anything, can Congress do to help alleviate these obstacles?

Dr. AMEENUDDIN. Yes. Thank you so much, Representative Rush, for that question.

Digital inequity and the digital divide have been a concern of ours for a very long time. Those of us who are pediatricians were interested in this issue and really are seeing why it has become such a problem.

Part of the reason why youth of color are so vulnerable to this is that there is targeted advertising towards them for unhealthy products, and you know, as we are still learning during the pandemic and I anticipate a whole slew of research that will come out as a result of this, I can also look historically back at how, in lower-income neighborhoods or neighborhoods with large minority populations, alcohol and tobacco billboards were often much more prevalent there.

Like a child walking to school in the neighborhood would pass several of these billboards, and again, that is historical. But we have also seen that in terms of digital marketing, whether it is for unhealthy foods or for tobacco, alcohol, or even marijuana advertising, all of which the American Academy of Pediatrics opposes being targeted towards children, which I am happy to recommend our previous policy statements on that.

In addition to that, we have to look at the built environment around children and what is safe. It is not safe to play outside if there are not green spaces. Children are by circumstance, you know, going to spend more time indoors on a screen.

Thank you.

Mr. RUSH. Thank you. I yield back.

Mr. CÁRDENAS [presiding]. The gentleman yields back.

The Chair now recognizes Member Bob Latta for 5 minutes.

Mr. LATTA. I thank my friend for recognizing me and also for the chair for holding today's hearing examining how to protect children in the digital age.

That issue has become amplified by the COVID–19 pandemic. In my home State of Ohio, the Department of Education is reporting significant areas of learning lag. Its reporting shows the decrease in third-grade proficiency was clear among students learning in districts that used a fully remote education model as their primary education model in the fall of 2020.

In fully remote districts, third-grade proficient rates decreased by approximately 12 percentage points compared to decreases of approximately 8 percentage points in districts primarily using a 5-day in-person model and 9 percentage points in districts primarily using a hybrid model.

Students are clearly suffering across our country without in-person learning. Where schools are open, children are proving to be very resilient. However, they are much less resilient to the impacts of remote or distance learning.

And, Dr. DeAngelis, thank you for your testimony and the wealth of data explaining schools are safe to reopen. As you also know, many children are struggling with distance learning for a variety of reasons, including lack of social engagement, difficulty concentrating, and Zoom fatigue.

My colleagues in the majority recently provided over $7 billion to fund remote learning, which makes us more reliant on these small screens.

Now, if we are serious about connecting those without broadband, we should have devoted that money toward improvement of broadband infrastructure and reform our permitting laws to deliver connectivity to these unserved Americans.

Even before COVID, we knew students without connectivity do not have the same chance of success and can be left behind.

Dr. DeAngelis, have you seen distinctions on how broadband can be an important bridge for learning?

Dr. DEANGELIS. Yes, absolutely, and thank you so much for the question.

And one thing I might add is that additional funding for remote learning could disincentivize schools from reopening for in-person instruction if they get more funding with remote services.

But one way to access more broadband within communities is to reallocate the funding from institutions to individual students. There are at least 28 State legislators that have introduced legislation to fund students as opposed to systems in the form mostly of something called an education savings or education scholarship account, which would take a portion of the money that would have gone to the traditional public school that students are residentially assigned to, and if they like the remote learning that is going on in the public school, they can still do that and keep that option on the table.

But they would be able to take some of that funding to go to an in-person private school or a pandemic pod or a micro school or other types of learning scenarios.

And with education savings accounts, it is possible to have State legislatures or even the Federal Government approve the funding to be used to access connectivity and broadband as well. It could be used for any approved, government-approved, education-related expenditure.

I think this could, in theory, fall into that bucket.

Mr. LATTA. Let me ask. Let me follow up. How can schools become responsible stewards of making education more accessible via broadband without that becoming a crutch then?

Dr. DEANGELIS. One way to do it is to incentivize the schools to reallocate the existing resources, particularly because my latest study at Social Science Research Network with MIT's Dr. McCredie finds that resources have not been statistically related to reopening in person even after you control for things like household income, the age and race distributions, and COVID risk in the area.

Meanwhile we did not find significant relationships between COVID risk and reopening schools in person.

We also tended to find that political partisanship was a strong predictor, along with a few other studies have found this as well, of reopening in person.

Mr. LATTA. If I can just follow up again with another question. You know, in my district the majority of our schools are open for a 5-day learning week, and I know that that is not the norm nationally.

In your paper are school reopening decisions related to funding. You examine the impact of per student expenditures on if schools are open for in-person learning or not.

Does the level of funding per student have an impact on the re-opening decisions during the COVID pandemic?

Dr. DEANGELIS. We do not find any evidence, and this is the only existing study on this topic that is done nationwide. We do not find any evidence that is statistically significant between the funding, whether it is measured by revenues per people or expenditures per pupil, even after controlling for a ton of different characteristics in the area. No relationships between funding and being more likely to reopen.

If anything, we find that in some cases the remote districts actually were financially better off than their in-person counterparts, and a Georgetown University study similarly found recently that remote districts were more likely to have surpluses.

In Los Angeles, they had about a half-a-billion-dollar surplus estimated for this school year.

Mr. LATTA. Well, thank you very much.

My time has expired, and I yield back.

Mr. CÁRDENAS. The gentleman yields back.

The gentlewoman from Florida, Kathy Castor, is now recognized for 5 minutes.

Ms. CASTOR. Well, I thank my friend, the vice chair, for recognizing me.

And another big thank you to Chair Schakowsky for calling this very important hearing on protecting kids online.

Ms. Fox Johnson and Dr. Ameenuddin, your testimony really lays out the harmful effect on children caused by predatory data collection and exposure to inappropriate commercial content.

Last Congress I introduced two bills, the Kids' PRIVCY Act and the KIDS Act. The KIDS Act—thank you to my colleague Yvette Clarke and to Congresswoman Wexton from Virginia for joining me in that effort. They both address the harms caused by these kinds of activities online by the big tech platforms.

And our bill proposed to update COPPA and put new safeguards in place to protect kids when they are online.

So just to go over a few of the things that are contained in the bills: expanding protections to young consumers age 13 to 17; requiring opt-in consent for all individuals under 18; banning companies from providing targeted advertising to kids; increasing the FTC penalty authority; repealing provisions that allow industry self-regulation; and changing the knowledge standard from actual to constructive, among a variety of other provisions that really help empower parents and protect kids.

So, Ms. Fox Johnson, do you agree with those updates to COPPA to protect kids online?

And focus in. Are there any that are more important than others, or are they important as a package?

Ms. FOX JOHNSON. I thank you for the question and thank you for your leadership on this issue.

We wholeheartedly agree that these updates are critical to COPPA and think that they are critical as a package. For us, some of the most important ones are extending protections to teenagers, who, as you have heard, have their own set of risks and vulnerabilities.

Ensuring that sites cannot pretend like they do not have kids. TikTok and YouTube pretending like they did not have children on their site for years, even though they had nursery rhyme videos in the case of YouTube or clearly had small tweens and preteens in the case of TikTok.

We also think it is critically important that enforcement gets enhanced. COPPA has been around for over 20 years, and the FTC has brought about 30 cases. So we do not think that enforcement is sufficient right now.

We also think it is critical that certain practices just be flat-out off limits. Behavioral targeting to young kids is unfair, and it should not be allowed no matter what kind of, you know, consent is allegedly given.

Thank you.

Ms. CASTOR. Dr. Ameenuddin, what do you think?

Dr. AMEENUDDIN. Well, thank you, Representative Castor, for being a champion for this issue.

Some of the elements that you mentioned are actually laid out in our most recent digital advertising policy statement, which came out in June of last year from the American Academy of Pediatrics.

I would love to look over some more legislation to see where else we are on the same page.

So thank you so much for that.

Ms. CASTOR. And then, Ms. Fox Johnson, the KIDS Act prohibits companies from using design features like autoplay and push alerts or any feature that unfairly encourages a child to spend more time engaging with the platform.

The bill also prohibits platforms from amplifying harmful content to children.

Are we on the right track here?

Ms. FOX JOHNSON. Once again, a wholehearted yes. Kids get hooked onto autoplay until spending too much time and watching inappropriate content that is pushed on them. They get addicted to the dings and badges that they receive.

I mean, there is a reason that we give stickers to children when we want to train them to learn to use the bathroom. This is how they respond to awards, and this is what tech companies are doing to them now.

Ms. CASTOR. You know, one way I have thought about it and shared it with parents is that if there was a person outside your child's window at home or following them to school, you would call the police. You would not put up with this.

So it should not be any different for our online platforms that just have enormous amounts of influence, and they are profiting off it. So I am really hopeful.

And, again, I want to give a big thank you to Chair Schakowsky for directing the committee's attention to this very important issue.

And then I just add at the end everyone wants kids back in school, and thank goodness President Biden has said all teachers, everyone that works in the school, should be vaccinated, and we passed the American Rescue Plan yesterday to provide the resources for schools and students across the country to operate safely and improve student achievement.

So I think we are all on the same page there too.

Thanks, and I yield back.

Mr. CÁRDENAS. The gentlewoman yields back.

It is my understanding that Chair Schakowsky is back.

OK. The gentlewoman yields back, and the next person who will be recognized for 5 minutes is Member Guthrie.

Mr. GUTHRIE. Thank you, thank you, Mr. Ca´rdenas. I appreciate that very much.

Thanks for having this hearing today. Thanks, Chair Schakowsky and Ranking Member Bilirakis.

You know, since the COVID–19 pandemic began nearly a year ago—or a year ago—kids have been experiencing extended periods of virtual schooling away from their teachers and their friends.

As a result of this increased time, longstanding concerns around digital technology have been brought to the forefront. We continually hear about the need for students to be physically in the classroom learning and the positive, cognitive health benefits it brings to a student.

I just want to point out the schools in my hometown. There are two school systems in my home county. One country school is in Bolling Green. Independent schools have been meeting in person to some degree, not everybody at the same time, since August 24th, the first day of school that was on the books.

Most schools in Kentucky spent the summer preparing to allow kids to come safely. When it came time to start schools, the Governor recommended schools not start, and my two superintendents said, "We prepared. We have been working at it. We have got things in place."

So they went forward, much to a lot of criticism from the Governor and a lot of people. But I can tell you, if anybody wants to see an example of schools meeting and kids in session, right—not every kid every day, I am not saying that—but some form of in-person learning since August 24th, prior to there being a vaccine, without any evidence of any student-to-student spread, then they can come to Bolling Green and see how it can be done because they have been successful with it.

And we still have districts in Kentucky that have not met one day in a public setting, when one just a few miles down the road has met since August 24.

So it is kind of without incident. It is not like, well, we are not going to meet because they have had incidents. They are certainly a great example of schools being open.

But I would start out with some questions for Dr. Ameenuddin. You mentioned in your testimony how digital media can negatively impact a child's health and development. In your practice, how do you help parents or legal guardians find the balance for their children between screen time and physical activity, especially since so many kids are learning online?

Dr. AMEENUDDIN. Thank you, Representative Guthrie, for that question.

I have to admit, you know, it is an ongoing challenge. Every family is a little bit different. I advise them. I try to be a coach for them about finding balance, finding moderation.

You know, I also tell parents to give themselves a break. It is just there is unprecedented stress on everyone right now. Parents are being pulled in multiple different directions, and the last thing that we want to do is create more difficulty, more stress and tension in the home.

So what I have been advising families to do is really not that different from before the pandemic, but maybe with a few caveats, is to really prioritize mental health and physical health.

And you know, way back when, when we just had TVs to worry about, we would recommend no more than 2 hours of entertainment or recreational screen time a day. That is not a hard and fast rule, but it does help to have some rules. It does help to have some guidelines and guardrails up.

But I also tell parents not to be so hard on themselves or their kids, because some days might just be very digital- and screen-time-heavy days, but that is OK. You can work on making the next day a little bit more balanced towards physical activity, towards, you know, in-person interaction with other family members to keep things safe.

So really, I am telling parents to give themselves a break, but to just practice moderation on a wider scale long term.

Mr. GUTHRIE. Well, thanks.

And, Dr. Ameenuddin, have you come across research or data that show reopening schools directly correlates to substantial increases in overall COVID–19 transmissions or hospitalizations from child to child or child to adults spread?

Dr. AMEENUDDIN. So that is an important question. It is not my area of expertise, but I would recommend reading the AAP guidance on school reopening because I think that lays it out very nicely.

Mr. GUTHRIE. OK. So the schools could reopen safely if you follow the guidance, correct?

That is what we did in Bolling Green, and we did it until last August. So I just want to point that out.

Can I also ask questions to Mr. DeAngelis? In your testimony, you state that a Gallup poll found 86 percent of parents said that students being separated from classmates and teachers was a challenge for their children.

From your research, have any studies that indicate that virtual learning is more suited for kids than in-person learning?

And you have about 30 seconds to answer.

Dr. DEANGELIS. In general, the research suggests that in-person learning is better, on average, than virtual learning. So I don't want to say that virtual learning can never work. It can work in certain situations. And it is most likely to work in the best way possible when families voluntarily select into that situation, and they can make those cost-benefit decisions themselves.

But on average we are seeing that there is a lot of harm going on as a result of the forced version of remote learning that we are seeing across the country.

Mr. GUTHRIE. Thank you.

Thank you for that time, Madam Chair. I yield back.

Ms. SCHAKOWSKY [presiding]. I thank the gentleman for yielding back.

And I now want to call on Congresswoman Trajan for her 5 minutes of questioning.

Mrs. TRAHAN. Thank you, Madam Chair.

So children's time spent with screens has increased dramatically during the pandemic. I know this because I have five kids. My two young girls are 6 and 10 years old, and they have essentially grown up with electronic devices, but nothing like we have been this past year.

Can I be clear? It is not because they are home from school as much as it is the go-to during the down time, in the absence of play dates and indoor extracurricular activities.

And we do know that the more time children spend on screens, the more they are pulled away from engagement with me, parents, siblings, and critical activity.

Ms. Fox Johnson, big techs employ mental health experts to use persuasive design techniques aimed to increase engagement. We know this, particularly in apps funded by advertising revenue.

Can you explain the way companies leverage their understanding of our children's cognitive developments to keep children on their platform or in their app or network of apps and why that is so harmful?

Ms. FOX JOHNSON. Sure, and thank you. I would be happy to answer that question.

So, as you said, companies employ all kinds of experts who know how to get to kids and to keep them hooked. They use a variety of different features. One of them is the sort of never-ending scroll feature.

Instagram found that, when they short of put in a natural pause or an end spot, people were spending less time on their product, and so they then decided to move that decision back and put in more content so kids just get a constant stream of new information.

Another feature that is really problematic for kids is seeing how many likes their own photos get or how much engagement from their friends. Teenagers particularly are social creatures. They are looking for validation, and this is a way to have how many people like them and how many people like their friends numerically listed publicly for everyone.

Another way that social media companies keep the kids engaged is through autoplay. They cannot step away because the next video is already starting, and as has been mentioned here, that video is tailor made often to appeal to them.

So there are a variety of ways that social media companies right now are using their design tactics to keep kids hooked.

Mrs. TRAHAN. Thank you.

And I have seen it up close in my own home. I have seen my assistants.

Dr. Ameenuddin, in your testimony, you highlight that increasingly exposure, especially ad-based, is correlated with poor eating habits and loss of sleep, and the American Academy of Pediatrics recommends that parents of children ages 6 and older place consistent limits on the time spent using media, specifically lower-quality media.

I have that right, is that correct?

Dr. AMEENUDDIN. Yes. Yes, absolutely. Of course—sorry. Go ahead.

Mrs. TRAHAN. Just what I am hearing today is that even parents who are trying to do the right thing, trying to keep their children healthy by limiting certain types of digital media, using every tactic they have to deploy, they are coming face to face with products that have been designed to keep our children on their apps longer, an end goal that is counter to the recommendations of our pediatricians.

Ms. Fox Johnson, if products can be engineered to keep users endlessly engaged, I imagine that these same products could be designed to encourage healthy behaviors as well. What policy changes would incentivize, would lead to that shift?

Ms. FOX JOHNSON. Definitely products can be engaged right now to be healthier, but since we do not see companies doing that on their own, we would really like Congress to act and help them along.

In the United Kingdom, the age-appropriate design code requires that companies build the best interest of children into their products from the ground up with their design. You are not supposed to use nudges in ways that harm children. You are not supposed to use their information in targeted ads or in other detrimental ways.

Help kids. Give ways so they can set their own limits. Give them visual cues to stop. Do not use their information to keep them hooked.

These are things companies can do.

Mrs. TRAHAN. Well, I appreciate that. You know, I am not going to have time for my next set of questions, which is not introduce them to Facebook Messenger Kids, which is going to get them hooked and using Facebook at an age earlier than they need to be.

So look. Parenting is hard. Parenting during a pandemic is immensely hard. I can only hope that this last year and this hearing today highlights the need for Congress to address urgently the ad-based business incentives that are pervasive in our economy.

I thank you all for your testimony and your deep knowledge.

And I yield back.

Ms. SCHAKOWSKY. I thank the gentlewoman.

I had no idea when you talk about parenting that you have five children. So I learned something, something new today.

Congressman Bucshon, you have 5 minutes for your questions.

Mr. BUCSHON. Thank you, Madam Chairwoman.

And I am a parent of four children. Three of them are grown, but I still have a high school junior, and so I can tell you that, even with strong parenting, which I think my wife and I have done over the years to help our children deal with the online onslaught of information, that even with that it is a challenge, and I do think Congress needs to address some of these issues as have been outlined today.

You know, but after a year's shutdown and remote learning and the hardships that have arisen from COVID pandemic, we have learned that there are some real costs to being in distance learning all year, physical and mental health costs.

And as I mentioned, I am the father of a high school junior. She is a great student. It is not affecting her much. We do not have to prod her to make her classes, but I can tell you that across my district when I talk to educators, some students, you know, when they do enroll, never get online or only sporadically do and are not really technologically present during the instruction.

In addition, there is access to broadband issues, particularly I can tell you in my area, affecting rural America in the same way that it affects urban America.

If you look at a map of the United States and look at the percentage of students that do not have access to consistent internet, it is shocking, honestly.

So we need to open our schools in person with the best available data, protecting our students and our teachers and employees. But we need to do this, again, based on the science that is out there and the guidance that is there rather than relying on politics.

So, Mr. DeAngelis, in-school learning afforded children access to physical fitness activities that are often not available for millions of students at home. This is something we forget about because my daughter is on a crew team, and they have not been on the water now in almost a year. They are at home on rowing machines, if they have one.

So that could be gym class, extracurricular clubs, activities in sports. What are some of the barriers that you expect in getting these programs and activities back up and running once in-person learning resumes?

And what can Congress do to make sure those efforts go as smoothly as possible?

Dr. DEANGELIS. Yes, this is just another unintended consequence of keeping schools closed. We all kind of anticipated the learning loss, but then we started to see job market impacts, disproportionately impacting women. We have seen mental health issues on the rise, and then now we are seeing also physical problems and increases in obesity probably related to the decrease in sports activity.

So one way to incentivize the schools reopen in person is to not pass stimulus bills that are not contingent upon reopening schools in person and given that all teachers are vaccinated, which I think that water is already under the bridge.

But another way to incentivize the reopening of schools, and there are a couple of bills in Congress floating around right now. I think one was introduced yesterday that would reallocate nearly all Federal education dollars from institutions to individuals, which would provide strong incentives for the public schools to reopen their doors in person, as has been found in the Brown University study finding that competition was generally related to a higher likelihood of reopening the schools in person.

I just want to point out something that you pointed out, which was a great point, that there are a lot of inequities that are a result of this because a lot of the families that are the most advantaged do have choices at the moment. They can afford to pay for private school tuition and fees out of pocket. They can afford to move to a school district that is offering in-person instruction. They can afford to pay for a tutor at home. They can afford to pay for the best remote learning services.

So we are really having a conversation about what kind of access will the least advantaged have when it comes to educational services, because this whole debate has really not affected the most advantaged in society. So it is leading to inequities, and I am glad you pointed that out.

Mr. BUCSHON. Yes. I mean, you know, as we are having a hearing on the dangers of and the online activities our children are exposed to, you know, we are still having a tremendous number of students who had no choice. They have to be online.

And I can tell you, even with my daughter, like I said, who is a good student, we still have to set 10 minutes an hour no social media because, while she is on her computer, she also has her phone.

And so we need to get kinds back into a better environment, and you know, I think that can be done. The American Academy of Pediatrics has put out some guidelines, as has been mentioned.

In my district in southwest Indiana and west central Indiana, schools have mostly been open since last fall with proper guidelines in place. And have there been some COVID cases? A few, but overall consistent with what is happening around the country, and not that many.

So, Madam Chairwoman, I cannot see the time clock. So please remind me if my time is up because I am on my phone.

Ms. SCHAKOWSKY. Your time is up.

Mr. BUCSHON. OK. Then I yield back.

Ms. SCHAKOWSKY. OK.

Mr. BUCSHON. Thank you very much.

Ms. SCHAKOWSKY. Thank you.

Mr. McNerney, you are next. You are recognized now for 5 minutes for your questions.

Mr. MCNERNEY. Well, I thank the chairwoman for holding this hearing.

It is an important issue that tech companies have this hold on our children, and we need to explore that whether there is pandemic or not. I am very concerned about the techniques being used by some tech companies that result in addictive behaviors in children.

Some of this seems like the addictive techniques used in gambling. For example, many video games and apps have children use real money to purchase in-game rewards on so-called loot boxes, and the tech companies often do this in manipulative ways.

So, according to a recent survey in the U.K., one in six children in Britain have stolen money from their parents to play for video game loot boxes. I would not be surprised to see similar statistics like that in the United States.

This is a worrisome sign of what effects these features are having on children.

Dr. Ameenuddin, can you explain how gambling-like games are harmful for children?

Dr. AMEENUDDIN. Sure. Thank you very much, Representative McNerney.

Anything that would encourage kids to stay engaged and, you know, could lead to addictive tendencies is a concern for children's health and mental health.

These in-app purchases are another thing that we as pediatricians believe should be banned, particularly since it is something that is really outside a child's level of ability to resist, and it is very concerning that children in the U.K. were actually stealing their parents' money or using things without permission.

That sort of persuasive design is really dangerous. It is bad for mental health. It is bad for physical health, and we strongly stand against that, but because that really is targeting a very vulnerable section of our society.

Mr. MCNERNEY. Well, do you believe that these loot boxes will set up children for addiction to gambling later in life?

Dr. AMEENUDDIN. So addiction is a very complex issue. It is multifactorial, and it is difficult to say with certainty and with a good evidence base that this would set them up for an addiction.

But it is certainly not good for them. I think we would prefer to call it problematic internet use, and you know, as we look at the DSM–5 manual, the manual of psychiatric issues, they have mentioned, you know, the concern of internet gaming disorder, but have not officially laid a diagnosis to it.

So, just to be clear and precise, I would hesitate to use the actual word "addiction."

Mr. MCNERNEY. Well, thank you.

Moving on, the industry's response to concerns about these loot boxes require disclosure in app stores around video games, that a particular game contains an in-app purchase.

Ms. Fox Johnson, how effective is disclosure in these cases, especially with regard to apps and games intended for children?

Ms. FOX JOHNSON. Thank you for that question, Representative McNerney.

In general, we think disclosures are not that effective. I mean, it is important to put them at the point of purchase, but often these kids cannot read. So they do not know what in-app purchase means, and then within the game, there can often not be disclosures.

The purchases themselves, sometimes it is not clear to kids that they are even using real money because things are referred to as, you know, buy gems or sparkle wands. So we do not think that kids and their parents know that they are spending money.

And I think that is clear from the fact that, you know, millions of dollars of money have had to be refunded to consumers when the Federal Trade Commission brought cases against some of these platforms like Apple and Google and Amazon for sort of bilking kids and their parents out of money.

Mr. MCNERNEY. Well, I am going to talk a little about artificial intelligence at this point. AI and machine learning are used in targeting behavioral advertising and persuasive design tactics that we are seeing today and discussing today.

This practice is everywhere. Compared to adults, children and teens are more trusting of privacy-invasive technology like GPS tracking, and I think that poses a major risk for children divulging sensitive information.

Ms. Fox Johnson, how do platform developers use AI and machine learning in their user interfaces to better target children and monetize their data?

Ms. FOX JOHNSON. As you said, Representative McNerney, they are tracking them everywhere. The kids do not realize that their location is being shared because they think they have not actively put it in. They do not realize that the conversation they had with their smart toy is not staying in their toy, but it is going into a data ecosystem.

And companies use all of this information to figure out precisely what that kid might want to buy or might want to do next and use it to create commercial profiles of kids at very young ages.

Mr. MCNERNEY. Yes. Well, I agree. Thank you.

I am going to run out of time. So I yield back, Madam Chair.

Ms. SCHAKOWSKY. Thank you.

And now, Mr. Pence, it is your turn for 5 minutes.

Mr. PENCE. Thank you, Chair Schakowsky and Ranking Member Bilirakis, for holding this hearing.

And thank you to the witnesses for appearing before us today.

This pandemic has impacted us all. It has been particularly troublesome for our youth, as the witnesses talked about today.

Students learning remotely are missing out on higher-quality instruction from the in-person attention during formative years of their development. I am concerned that those lost opportunities will lead to damaging learning gaps setting back an entire generation.

Instead of having exposure to social connections with their peers at school, students in virtual settings across the country are often isolated, spending more time on the internet and away from their friends.

Comparatively, in my State, Indiana, Hoosiers underwent local community-led efforts last summer to keep our kids in school. Together with parents, administrators, and local health officials, schools in my district developed comprehensive strategies to ensure students and teachers could safely return to the classroom, which they did. And that is exactly what they did.

Every one of the counties in my district have schools that have returned to the classroom with notable success. Having students in person provides structure and stability that is so important for the mental and emotional well-being of children.

Beyond the attention received in the classroom, clubs, sports teams and other student organizations provide an invaluable collected learning environment that cannot be replicated from a Zoom connection, like leadership skills and social skills.

Recently I had the opportunity to meet with bright young students at St. Nicholas Catholic School and Batesville High School, a public school. Both schools are prime examples of how local stakeholders are best positioned to develop school safety strategies that fit the unique educational needs of their community.

From my discussions with these students, their teachers, and administrators, one thing remained clear: Students feel more purpose when they are in school and involved in person.

I share the concerns of my colleagues that the increased online presence of children can be detrimental to their health and safety. Shifting children away from in-person learning and towards a digital life has surely sentenced them to more time for predators to prowl, which is another argument for in-school learning.

Dr. DeAngelis, I am afraid of a scenario of dueling outcomes for students that participate virtually versus students that participate in person. In your testimony you mention substantial achievement gaps between these two groups, specifically leading to increased dropout rates and impacts on their future earnings.

Can you please expand on what this will mean for our future generation of, in particular, community leaders that are losing this sports and social interaction?

Dr. DEANGELIS. Yes. I would first like to point out that, look, this is leading to inequities. So this is hitting the least advantaged in the community the hardest, particularly because the most advantaged have access to in-person alternatives or good versions of remote virtual learning at home or even have more ability to cover the cost associated with home-based education.

But to your point, McKenzie & Company in a nationwide analysis in 2020 on two separate occasions found that they estimated that achievement gaps would increase, and achievement gaps are already a horrible thing in the United States that we need to remedy.

But the gaps by race they estimate to increase by 15 to 20 percent, and they estimate dropout rates to increase by 2 to 9 percentage points, translating to about 232,000 to 1.1 million additional ninth-to-eleventh-graders dropping out of high school, which could translate to about 60 to $80,000 reduction in lifetime earnings, which is a huge problem, obviously.

And there is a lot of evidence, this is just one source from McKenzie & Company finding these exacerbated inequities from keeping the schools closed.

So the best option is to give families options, allow them to choose the in-person or hybrid learning setting of their choice or, even better, allocate the money to the families so that more families can access other in-person alternatives.

Mr. PENCE. Which in Indiana we have school choice.

Thank you. Madam Chair, I yield back.

Ms. SCHAKOWSKY. The gentleman yields back.

And now I call on Mr. Cárdenas for 5 minutes for questions.

Mr. CÁRDENAS. Thank you very much, Madam Chairwoman. I appreciate the honor of being the sit-in chair for just a little bit. It is a bit addicting, but I relinquished it.

OK. Thank you so much. Appreciate your bringing this committee together on this issue, Madam Chairwoman Schakowsky and also Ranking Member Bilirakis.

I appreciate this opportunity for us to hear from many different perspectives about what our families and children are going through, but more importantly, being able to dialogue and discuss maybe what some of the solutions are so we can have a better environment, better world so that our children are less negatively affected by all of this.

I am a father and, more importantly, a proud grandfather, two grandchildren, ages 2 and 4, and, yes, they are on devices already, and we need to protect every child as much as possible.

And, of course, the responsibility of the individual family raising those children is paramount, but at the same time I think it is important that government understands that we do have a responsibility of making sure that the guidelines and the lanes in which these incredibly prolific and lucrative businesses are in our homes and in the eyeballs and the minds and hearts of our families and our children.

And also, I would say that it is unfortunate that we speak of who is negatively affected the most or who in America might not be as prepared as others to protect themselves and protect their children from the potential negative effects and harmful effects of what could be going on, but let me tell you this. I think it is important that everybody understand that these negative effects, they do not see color. They do not see race. They do not see gender. A child is a child is a child.

And I believe that because about 60 percent of all children in America are White, it is disproportionately affecting White children, and I just want to point that out because I think that some people get the misinterpretation that all we care about is Black and Brown children.

We care about all children, and I do not want anybody to think that because we mentioned minority children or poor children in general that we are leaving out the 60 percent of the children in America who are White. We are looking to protect every child, regardless of their background.

Let me just go to my first question because time is fleeting.

Dr. Ameenuddin, in your testimony you mentioned that for infants and toddlers still developing cognitive language, sensory motor, and social-emotional skills, screen time of any kind is typically discouraged. What do you know about the long-term effects early exposure to technology like tablets and smartphones can have on a child's development in this area?

Dr. AMEENUDDIN. Well, thank you for that question, Vice Chair Ca´rdenas.

I will share what we know and what we do not know. Frankly, there are still a lot of unknowns, and research is evolving.

But what we do know from early studies on tablets and devices and apps is that there is very little benefit and there is a strong potential for harm for children under 18 months of age.

For children between the ages of 18 months and 2 years, if it is a high-quality, educational app that involves parental engagement with the app and the child and then the parent teaches back after they have finished using the app, there can potentially be some benefit there.

But we do know, again, from decades of research that early introduction to screen time, even if it is purported to be educational, can actually have the opposite effect.

For example, we had the Baby Einstein videos from several years ago. One of my colleagues in pediatrics actually did a study on that and found that children whose families used the Baby Einstein videos versus those who did not use any kind of screen time were actually having developmental delays in terms of expressive language skills.

So we do know that there can be harms, but that we really recommend, again, mindful, mindful use for older kids because there can certainly be benefits with certain good, educational programming.

Mr. CÁRDENAS. Thank you, Ms. Ameenuddin, for that important information and those facts.

I hope that after today's hearing we will keep these issues in focus, and that is why today, along with my colleague, Representative Trahan, I introduced the Youth Mental Health-Suicide Prevention Act, a bill authorizing the Substance Abuse and Mental Health Services Administration, SAMHSA, to provide funding to school districts for a variety of positive mental health promotion and suicide prevention purposes.

Like I said, we all have the interest of every child at heart, and I think that it is important that Congress play its current—excuse me—its appropriate role and right-sized role in making sure that we create and make sure that the lanes are being followed and the lanes are created so that our children can remain protected.

Thank you. I yield back.

Ms. SCHAKOWSKY. The gentleman yields back.

And now, Congresswoman Lesko, it is yours for 5 minutes for questions.

Mrs. LESKO. Thank you, Madam Chairman, and thank you, colleagues. It is good to see you.

You know, this subject is very important, protecting our children. I have four grandchildren. Two of them are elementary school age, and so protecting them, they are hours on their phones, they are hours on their tablets. This is a very important issue.

I totally agree with the subject, and I have asked my staff during this hearing—actually I left—asked them to write me up decision memos on some of these bills that both the Democrats and Republicans in this subcommittee have said that they have introduced, and so I will do that and get back with you on my decision on those.

I also totally agree with Mr. DeAngelis. I am from Arizona. We have lots of school choice in Arizona. It started in 1994, I think, when we opened up. Not only parents could go to different school districts that were not in their neighborhood with their kids, but also charter schools were legalized in Arizona. And so we have many, many, many charter schools.

I also introduced legislation when I was in the State legislature on empowerment scholarship accounts, which are a way for now special needs children to go to private schools using public funds.

And so, Mr. DeAngelis, I worked with Reason Foundation before on pension reform, bipartisan pension reform, when I was in Arizona, and you guys do great work. I totally agree with the concept of more competition, more choices for parents and students.

I do want to show everybody an article from a Tucson, Arizona newspaper, but it is titled "No Way to Check on Hundreds of Kids Missing from Schools Across Tucson."

And I would like to submit, unanimous consent, to include it in the record, Madam Chairman, but I am going to read some——

Ms. SCHAKOWSKY. All of these will be added at the end of the hearing.

Mrs. LESKO. Thank you. Thank you, Madam Chair.

Some of the things in the article were very disturbing. It says it is unclear what is happening in the lives of over 1,100 young people who never show up for online school or only attend sporadically. The combined total of students unaccounted for in Tucson and seven other major school districts is at least 1,160, with some students missing since last spring.

On average, calls to an abuse hotline run by Arizona's Department of Child Services are down 25 to 30 percent. The agency's director attributes the decrease largely to schools not being held in person. This lack of oversight by teachers and administrators is happening at a time when families and parents are under tremendous stress due to layoffs, social isolation, and sometimes illness.

The largest school district, Tucson Unified School District, is still working to identify how many kids have fallen off the radar. That means the number of unaccounted-for children is likely much higher than the 1,160 number coming out of the other school districts across the county.

Tucson Unified School Districts have had an enrollment decline of 2,600 students since this time last year.

And the reason I bring this up is because what we have talked about, and others, is we need to get kids back in school, and in Arizona my grandkids go to a charter school, and guess what? Their charter school has been open almost the entire time, and they have not had a COVID outbreak.

Also, because some of the district schools would not reopen, parents have been very creative and they are doing these micro schools. So even though they are paying all of the taxes, the property taxes, everything to the schools, they are hiring their own teacher. Like, groups of parents get together and hire their own teacher.

And that is why what Mr. DeAngelis says is so important. You know, I guess I want to give my last 15 seconds to you, Mr. DeAngelis. I took up most of the time, but tell me why that is important.

Dr. DEANGELIS. Yes. I mean, the Wall Street Journal wrote an article about the teachers' union's tiny little enemy, which was tons of micro schools over there in Arizona, and they have been very successful. You can socially distance better with small settings in a micro school.

And the reality is that most advantaged families without school choice already have those opportunities, and they are able to get that one-on-one attention with the kids and also have more social interaction. So we might as well fund the students directly like Arizona does through the education savings account and allow more families to have access to those alternatives.

Mrs. LESKO. Thank you so much.

And I yield back.

Ms. SCHAKOWSKY. All right. And now I am happy to call on Congresswoman Clarke. Welcome back, and it is your turn for 5 minutes.

Ms. CLARKE. Thank you so much, Madam Chair, and I thank our Ranking Member Bilirakis for convening today's hearing.

I thank our witnesses for your expert testimony here today.

As we all know, the COVID–19 pandemic has exacerbated many issues that are plaguing our Nation. We have seen a dramatic increase in the adoption of digital devices due to individuals and families working and learning from home.

However, along with the uptick in digital device usage, there has been an increase in screen time across our Nation during the transition to life online. This transition has had a tremendous impact on one of our Nation's most vulnerable and impressionable populations: children.

With this increase, I am concerned about the exposure of advertisements that children are now bombarded with. These ads are concerningly harmful to a demographic that is unable to comprehend their persuasive impact.

Ms. Fox Johnson, in your testimony, you mention a Pew Research Center report that stated 53 percent of children younger than 11 view YouTube daily, with 35 percent viewing multiple times per day.

Additionally, you go on to support that we have discussed time and time again. Children from low-income communities and communities of color are more likely to utilize mobile devices and have limited connectivity, which limits the productivity of this uptick in screen time. This is all very concerning.

However, as I stated, screen time is up for young kids, and they are being targeted with ads from companies, influencers, kid influencers on social media now more than ever before the pandemic even struck.

So my question is to Ms. Fox Johnson, and I think our chairwoman may have posed something similar to you earlier. In your testimony you mention that children are uniquely vulnerable to digital harms for a variety of reasons, including increased screen time and the fact that their brains are still in development.

What strategies can we use to protect our children from digital manipulation and ad targeting? And how do we hold big tech companies and advertisers accountable?

Ms. FOX JOHNSON. Sure, and thank you, Representative Clarke, for your question and for your leadership in this area.

There are lots of things that companies and advertisers could do to be more accountable to children. First, we need to make any disclosures of ads more meaningful. A surprising number of teenagers cannot even tell that an ad is an ad when it has an orange box that says “Ad” around it.

We also should ban advertising techniques that take advantage of kids’ feelings of special relationships with hosts and with cartoon characters and not allow for product endorsement.

We should ban advertisements and endorsement ads for unhealthy food and drink, which primarily targets or disproportionately targets communities of color.

We should stop companies from allowing kids to get more content or more rewards from viewing more advertisements.

And we should stop companies from turning teenagers and kids into unwitting product promoters themselves by conscripting them into paid posts that feature their liking of a product to their friends.

These are things that Congress can do, and they are also things that the Federal Trade Commission should be able to work on by updating its endorsement guidelines.

And in the meantime, again, we think companies can take some steps themselves and do not need to wait.

Ms. CLARKE. Thank you very much, Ms. Fox Jackson.

Dr. Ameenuddin, kids are not just learning in front of screens. They are spending their leisure time there too. Utilizing platforms like YouTube and TikTok with deceptive or hidden ads may be harder for children to detect.

Due to the rise of social media influencers and kid influencers, should this influencer marketing be allowed to target kids? And what unintended consequences might this have on their development?

Dr. AMEENUDDIN. Well, thank you so much for the question, Representative Clarke.

And I wanted to say that I agree with everything that Ms. Fox Johnson said. I think those are excellent suggestions.

In addition to that, specifically with regard to the question about kid influencers and unboxing videos, that really is a form of deceptive advertising. As Ms. Fox Johnson mentioned, kids feel like they are just watching a friend, yet it is really a targeted marketing technique.

So the AAP supports banning that kind of advertising towards children, paid advertising, and I apologize. It looks like we ran out of time. Sorry.

Ms. CLARKE. Well, very well. If you would just submit your response to our committee, that would be great. We want to be aggressive in this space.

And I thank all of our witnesses for testifying today. Madam Chair, I yield back.

Ms. SCHAKOWSKY. Thank you.

And now, Mr. Armstrong, it is yours for 5 minutes.

Mr. ARMSTRONG. Thank you, Madam Chair.

And I have a 13-year-old daughter. I have an 11-year-old son. I was a high school baseball coach a long time ago, still the best job I ever had.

And so I appreciate the conversation particularly about the—and my kids went to private school. They went for in-person—but I really do appreciate the fact that we are talking about—I mean, just in every single school across the country, there is a kid who that is the grade equalizer in his or her life, and without it we are leaving them behind.

And sometimes it is poverty issues, sometimes it is family life issues, sometimes it is all kinds of different things. But one of the greatest things about COVID and maybe one of the only good things is that it happened now and we are capable of doing these things. The technology has allowed us to do these things.

But there is no doubt in my mind that we have to get them back into sports, into clubs, into school as quickly as possible, or these gaps are going to continue to grow.

But I want to talk a little bit about something that is going to continue to plague us as Members of Congress outside of schools reopening, and that is how we deal with digital information and particularly with more screen time going online.

COPPA covers the collection, use, and disclosure of children's personal information, but FTC regulations pursuant to COPPA define personal information to include, in part, geolocation information sufficient to identify street name and name of city or town.

This definition means that coarse geolocation data on a child, which may be a ZIP code, county, region, et cetera, can be collected without direct notice, verifiable parent [audio malfunction].

I am not convinced we should be collecting any of this data on kids without parental consent, and I understand that ZIP codes are widely used geographic boundaries, but some ZIP codes in densely populated areas narrow it down to a very specific location.

And there might be a few legitimate reasons to collect this information on minors, but I just fear that potential harm may outweigh those reasons, and we cannot view nonconsensual coarse geolocation data collection as stand-alone data points that only show child-specific [audio malfunction] because a lot is covered in COPPA's definition of personal information.

There are so many other data points when viewed in combination with coarse geolocation data—can further specify a child's location, their habits, and identity.

This question is probably for Ms. Fox. Why are we collecting this from minors?

Ms. FOX JOHNSON. Thank you, Representative Armstrong. I mean, that is an excellent question.

Why are companies collecting this information if not to use it to target or profile a kid? There is no reason that they need to know one ZIP code over the other to, say, determine language or country or things like that.

One of the things that we really like in the Kids PRIVCY Act from Representative Castor is that it would update what forms of information are covered in COPPA and ensure that in statute and not just in the FTC rule. They are taking a full look at the modern ways that companies track minor kids and monetize kids these days.

Mr. ARMSTRONG. And then this is another question, because I think we have to start having this conversation as well. Does this conversation change, particularly as you are involving minors, if we look at data through a property lens instead of a privacy lens?

Ms. FOX JOHNSON. There are lots of discussions in the broader privacy landscape right now about if my privacy is my property or, in Europe, if my privacy is more of a fundamental right.

However you look at it, I think for kids it is not something that we think that they should be giving up or be forced to give up. It is not really a choice. It is sort of a false way of looking at consent.

And children should have the right to do what they wish and to learn and to grow without being surveilled and monitored at every step of the way.

Mr. ARMSTRONG. And then just lastly, there is a reason we have juvenile courts. There is a reason we treat juveniles in the court system significantly different than we do adults. There is a reason we seal records when they are 18.

But we are continuing down this path of holding people accountable when their brains are still developing. We have professional athletes getting in trouble for tweets they have done when they were 13.

Ms. SCHAKOWSKY. Mr. Armstrong, Mr. Armstrong, we are going to have to ask for a response in writing to this. You are well over time.

Mr. ARMSTRONG. Well, I am on.

Ms. SCHAKOWSKY. I am sorry. I am looking now at 25, 24. I am sorry. Go ahead. I am sorry.

Mr. ARMSTRONG. In GDPR there are technical challenges with Right to Be Forgotten. California has got a law, and we really have to start having conversations about allowing minors and allowing parents and allowing guardians to be able to block information that children are putting online.

I mean, they have to function. My daughter is 13. I wish she did not have a phone, but if she did not have a phone, she would not be able to communicate [audio malfunction].

So now I am over time, and I yield back.

Ms. SCHAKOWSKY. No, no, no. Give her a couple of seconds to respond. A good time.

Go ahead.

Ms. FOX JOHNSON. Sure. Thank you.

I would say that we fully agree what you do at 10 should not come back and haunt you when you are 40. So we support the rights for kids to be able to erase their information and take control of what they have inadvertently or intentionally shared at a young age.

Mr. ARMSTRONG. And I would just end with this: I think there are probably Members of Congress on both sides of the aisle that may not be here if we all had social media when we were 13 years old.

Ms. SCHAKOWSKY. OK. And now Debbie Dingell. I know you have been waiting patiently, and thanks for sitting with us the whole time, and it is yours for 5 minutes.

Mrs. DINGELL. Thank you, Chairwoman Schakowsky.

And thank you to all of the witnesses for being here today.

I am not the only Member sitting here patiently, because this subject is so important.

Many modern digital media platforms are designed to keep youth users engaged and incentivize the reengagement, leading to compulsive habits or what some refer to as addiction to their devices. A lot of adults too, I might add.

But we have seen an increasing number of reports correlating time on digital media, social media, and electronics to mental health issues in children and adolescents, among a variety of other serious impacts, including obesity, anxiety, and what really deeply disturbs me, electronic bullying.

In an increasingly digital age, we need to be vigilant in reevaluating how online content is consumed by children and ensure that they receive meaningful protection to their privacy and their mental and physical well-being.

So I want to ask some questions focused on these protections.

Influencers' marketing is now a billion-dollar industry and the fastest growing method for acquiring customers online. Many of today's top influencers are children themselves, so-called kid influencers, with massive followings on social media.

Ms. Fox Johnson, has the FTC brought any enforcement actions against influencers or their sponsors that have a significant child audience?

Ms. FOX JOHNSON. Thank you, Representative Dingell. That is a great question.

The FTC has not, and in fact their current endorsement guidelines do not even talk about kids or teens or special issues that might pertain to them.

Mrs. DINGELL. Some influencers, including those targeting children, are just as well-known or even more well-known than the brands that they promote. Yet the FTC had tended to focus its enforcement actions against the brands and not the individual influencers, limiting action against individual influencers to just warning letters.

Ms. Fox Johnson, have the FTC actions been effective? What more should FTC be doing?

Ms. FOX JOHNSON. I would say the FTC actions have not been effective. There have been multiple complaints filed against the kids influencers. Sometimes the folks are making, you know, $20 million a year hawking products to children in ways that appear to not look like advertisements and what appear to be just sort of sharing a game with a friend.

And so I think the FTC, as I mentioned, should update their endorsement guidelines. They should look at banning this endorsement for young kids certainly and ideally for teens, and for all endorsements in general because sometimes teens are watching particularly things that adults might be watching.

They need to make sure that disclosures are effective, because right now the hashtag ad that comes at the end of some long piece of information is not sufficient.

Mrs. DINGELL. I agree.

Social media platforms facilitate and make a lot of money from influencer marketing. Ms. Fox Johnson, what responsibility do social media companies have to protect kids from manipulative marketing? And what can the FTC do to hold them accountable?

Ms. FOX JOHNSON. Social media companies can take more responsibility, particularly when they are dealing with individual influencers or other people. They can do a better job of being more transparent in ways that are proven to be understood by kids and teens about what is an ad and what is native content.

The FTC—who has not done as much as we wish they could have done in all of these areas, in social media, in privacy—they need more resources so they can do more enforcements and they can update and codify the regulations and guidelines.

Mrs. DINGELL. Dr. Ameenuddin, I want to ask you at least one question before my time is up.

Is there concern that the media consumption habits developed by children and adolescents during the pandemic will continue post-pandemic? And should we be concerned by the potential impacts in terms of their health and privacy?

Dr. AMEENUDDIN. Well, thank you, Representative Dingell.

I think it is a huge concern, and I suspect that this will continue to be an issue long after the pandemic. As we have mentioned earlier, increased social media use, increased screen time was an issue well before the pandemic ever started. It obviously increased.

But making little changes will not mean that everything goes back to normal. I think it will continue to be an issue.

We have somewhat mixed data. I am grateful to you for bringing up the concerns about mental health and the connection to social media. We have conflicting information. For some kids, you know, it has led to sadness or I guess it is correlated with sadness, possibly depression, but for other kids, it has actually been a lifeline. You know, for marginalized kids sometimes finding community online can be a huge source of support.

Mrs. DINGELL. Thank you.

Thank you, Madam Chair. I have to yield back, but I will say our children are 100 percent of our future, and it is our responsibility to ensure their safety and security online.

Ms. SCHAKOWSKY. Thank you.

And now I call on Mr. Dunn for 5 minutes for his questioning.

Mr. DUNN. Thank you very much, Chairwoman Schakowsky.

I am glad the committee has convened this important hearing. The long-term impacts on our children are one of the greatest travesties of the COVID–19 pandemic and lockdowns.

As some of our witnesses have noted, the amount of time that kids spend in front of a screen has been a health concern for quite some time. The problem has been vastly exacerbated by the pandemic.

And the science is clear, the evidence is abundant: The schools across the country have the ability to reopen safely today.

I also appreciate Dr. DeAngelis rightly pointing out that the schools in America are largely closed purely due to politics.

I am grateful to Florida Governor Ron DeSantis, who led the way in reopening, and due to that fact all schools in my district, Florida's 2nd District, are safely opened for in-person learning at this time.

Parents across the country know the best thing for their kids is to be in school. This even includes the heads of powerful teachers' unions who drop their own children off at a private school at the same time they are fighting to keep public school kids out of school behind a computer screen at home.

I have been an advocate for school choice for a long time. I think the best thing we can do for school-age children is to empower the parents to seek out the best educational opportunities available. So let me start with a question for Dr. DeAngelis.

Families are especially vulnerable to the economic and educational impacts of COVID–19 and the lockdowns. Many parents have been forced to work longer hours, provide essential services, and work from remote locations. This obviously impacts their ability to provide adult supervision for their own children.

So briefly, would you say school choice allows households of all socioeconomic groups the best chance for parents to place their students in an educational setting that fits the needs of their individual family?

Dr. DEANGELIS. Absolutely, and as I have noted before, the most advantaged families already have school choice. They can already afford to live in the neighborhoods that are residentially assigned to the best public schools in America.

They are more likely to be able to afford to pay out of pocket for private school in-person learning. They are more likely to be able to afford the cost of home-based learning and micro schools and pandemic pods.

Funding students directly through programs like the ones in Florida allow more families to access alternatives so that at least the more equity and more freedom at the same time, and I think that is a lot of the reason why Florida has done such a good job when it comes to reopening public schools.

Mr. DUNN. You are very articulate on that. You shared a statistic, I believe, that is worth repeating. Florida, a State that spends about $10,700 per student per year, has been able to essentially fully reopen its schools, while California, which spends about 38 percent more per student, has kept their doors closed.

With your research on this issue, what role should the Federal Government play to incentivize the State governments to minimize screen time and return to the classroom?

Dr. DEANGELIS. Well, it is not a good idea to pass stimulus bills that do not make the money contingent upon actually reopening the schools, because then the schools can just get more money and then fail to reopen the schools, especially in context of my new study with Christos Makridis from MIT finding no relationship whatsoever in any of our models or analytic techniques between resources and reopening the schools in person.

And as you pointed out, just looking at places like Florida and California, California spends 38 percent more per pupil per year, according to the U.S. Census Bureau, and yet Florida is mostly——

Mr. DUNN. I am going to cut you off, Dr. DeAngelis, because I want to get to a couple more questions, but you have been very articulate, and I appreciate your presence here today.

Dr. Ameenuddin, thank you for your testimony. You work as a pediatrician. As a doctor myself, I know the challenges you face. I appreciate the work you do for our children.

COVID–19 and the lockdowns have drastically changed the lives of all Americans, especially our students who find themselves sitting in front of a computer more and playing outside less, along with a complete absence of formal physical education.

I noticed that Kelly Armstrong had been a high school coach at one time. He knows this.

In your testimony, you recommend specifying times where families turn off the screens and play. Can you speak to the long-term impacts of less outside play and physical education that students have experienced over the last year?

Dr. AMEENUDDIN. Sure. Thank you, Representative Dunn.

Well, I have an opportunity to refer you to another AAP policy on the importance of play and the importance of making sure that children have a safe environment to play in outside.

You specifically asked about the long-term impacts of essentially sedentary activity and lack of physical activity. You know, we have known for years, as we have seen screen time increase, device use increase, that nonactive time is not a good thing for kids.

I have been working with——

Mr. DUNN. I am going to ask you to put that in the written responses, because my time is elapsed.

Dr. AMEENUDDIN. OK.

Mr. DUNN. I am also going to ask you to conjecture in response to that question. You know, we know that a lot of screen time is bad for kids. Is it also bad for Members of Congress?

So I would like to, you know, consider that option, because I think it is. [Laughter.]

I yield back, Madam Chair.

Ms. SCHAKOWSKY. OK. Congresswoman Rice, it is your 5 minutes for questions right now.

Miss RICE. Thank you, Chairwoman Schakowsky.

Ms. Johnson, I would like to ask you a question.

In 2019, the New York State Attorney General and the FTC secured a settlement from Google and YouTube for $170 million for violating the COPPA. The settlement required Google and YouTube to pay $136 million to the FTC and $34 million to New York for violating COPPA.

The $136 million penalty is still, I believe, the largest amount the FTC has ever obtained in a COPPA case since Congress enacted the law in 1998.

Despite that enormous amount of money, two Commissioners voted against it, citing that the penalty did not go far enough, and one of the reasons was because of the cost of doing business. A hundred and seventy million dollars is nothing compared to the billions of dollars that these companies make from ad revenue.

So, in your opinion, Ms. Johnson, have these penalties been an effective deterrent for companies who violate the laws that are meant to protect children's privacy?

And if not, what steps can the FTC take to deter violations?

I hope we really are going to be able to consider Congresswoman Castor's bill because I think it moves to fix just one aspect, but just in your opinion, you know, is it effective? And if not, how can we make it effective?

Ms. FOX JOHNSON. Thank you, Representative Rice.

We agree with the dissenting Commissioners that, in my opinion, it is not effective. Google is still able to profit off of its activity, and for them $170 million was so small that they did not even have to report that to investors.

They also got the sort of first mover advantage of taking a bunch of children's personal information, collecting that in violation of law, and being able to design better targeting and more addictive and attractive products for kids, and that is not something that they are going to give up, you know, even if they delete, which sometimes companies do not always delete, as they are supposed to, the data later on.

I think that we have seen with this settlement and with other settlements in the privacy space—you know, we objected to the Facebook settlement—these are not meaningful deterrents for companies.

And so things that the FTC could do, luckily with COPPA it has several penalty authorities, but those fines could be increased. It could get civil penalty authority from Congress in other privacy situations. It could get rulemaking authority.

Right now, in general privacy cases it does not even have the ability to fine for the first time of a violation.

In addition, we think the FTC needs more resources itself so it can bring cases. Attorneys General get more civil penalty authority and the ability to obtain penalties under COPPA.

And then also, if you let parents sue on behalf of their kids, that is another way to increase enforcement and to improve the landscape.

Miss RICE. So I am glad you brought up the States' Attorneys General. You know, New York has a very big office with enormous resources, but that is not true of every State in the country. And we want, I believe, State Attorneys General to play their crucial role in working with the FTC on these types of cases.

So what tools do State Attorneys General need to continue to bring these cases like New York was able to do?

Ms. FOX JOHNSON. Yes, thank you.

And New York is one of the sort of more technologically savvy Attorney General's Office, and that is something that the Attorney General's Office and the FTC, again, need more of too. They need more technologists to understand what is going on sort of beneath the very opaque veneer of these tech companies, and we hear from Attorney General's Offices all the time because we work in a variety of different States that they do not have resources.

You might get a great new privacy law, but they will only be able to bring, you know, one case a year maybe because they are up against tech companies and they are understaffed and underresourced.

Miss RICE. Well, that is always a big issue not just in this field but in others when you are dealing with cybersecurity issues or the issues that we are talking about today, that these private companies are able to attract all of the talent because of the enormous salaries that they can pay the government agencies like State AGs just simply cannot.

Dr. Ameenuddin, just very quickly: Expanding this protection to children between the ages of 13 and 17, what is the impact going to be?

I mean, I have a 15-year-old niece, and I worry about, you know, the impact that these, you know, living their lives on social media, especially with all of this information coming up, and the impact, how this is going to help 13-to-17-year-old vulnerable kids.

Dr. AMEENUDDIN. Yes, thank you, Representative Rice.

I think the effect will be huge. I mean, so many teens are online. As you mentioned, they are living their lives online, even before the pandemic, but including children under 18 under these protections I think will have a huge impact on mental health, on multiple other issues too. So thank you for asking that.

Miss RICE. Thank you all for being here.

And I yield back, Madam Chairwoman.

Ms. SCHAKOWSKY. The gentlewoman yields back.

And now I call on Representative Soto for 5 minutes of questions.

Mr. SOTO. Thank you so much, Madam Chair.

This hearing is about our children being increasingly brain-washed by sophisticated targeting popup ads, autoplays, and algorithms, among other techniques, and the result is they are spending more and more time online.

Add in video game addiction, and we see a generation of kids becoming couch potatoes, racking up hours of screen time and barely going outside.

This puts our Nation's children, our Nation's future at risk. Parents are outreached and increasingly asking for Congress to act.

Considering the critical subject, I was a little surprised to see an attempt to shoehorn fake GOP talking points about school re-openings into this very important hearing. So it is important to at least go over the facts briefly.

Forty-one States, both Democrats and Republicans, do not have school opening or closing orders in place. They leave it to school districts.

Five States have orders to reopen. Four States have orders to be partially open.

So saying it is a Democratic or Republican trend is an absolute and total lie. The vast majority of States leave this to local school districts to make a decision, as they should because urban districts have different challenges than suburban and rural districts, all in my district.

Affluent families have more resources for their children to learn from home. Many American families have to go to work and need their children to attend in-person schools.

Add in health complexities of students and other difficulties, and local school districts and families need this flexibility.

In Central Florida, I supported schools reopening, like many Democrats in our State. So what are you really talking about? My wife taught in the public schools at the peak of the pandemic in July and August of last year in Central Florida in the classroom with a mask on, socially distanced, with kids having plastic barriers.

She is a member of the teachers' union. She cares about her students and taught them in school without a vaccine, risking her life for the students.

So I find it shocking that no one here today has even mentioned the hundreds of teachers who have died of COVID–19. The students who have died. In Florida, we have already had 45,000-plus cases of students, nearly 5,000 teacher cases of COVID–19, 3,000 COVID staff cases, and 7,000 other COVID-related public and private K-through-12 school cases.

Bashing teachers' unions is so predictable for some of you. Actually fixing the problem takes work. When we passed the bipartisan Coronavirus Stimulus Relief Act in December, some of our colleagues across the aisle joined us. Thank you.

Fifty-three of you, including some on this committee, voted against school coronavirus relief funds. Then just yesterday all of you voted against the American Rescue Act.

So what are you talking about? You are complaining about opening schools, then voting against funding for them to do so safely. That is absolutely absurd, and the American people know it.

Turning back to the subject at hand, many parties have opted for distance learning, and this has exacerbated these online addictions. So I want to go to the KIDS Act briefly that Kathy Castor had put together, and I want to talk to Ms. Johnson first.

What are, you think, the most important parts of the KIDS Act that we need to pass right away, like auto banning and banning push alerts and banning badges?

Ms. FOX JOHNSON. Thank you, Representative Soto.

I think that we need to pass all aspects of the KIDS Act, but the manipulative design that keeps kids hooked and the protections that would prevent against the commercialization of our children and marketing are really important.

I also think it is important to note I would be remiss in not mentioning that schools use a lot of technology, too, and we need to update our student privacy laws and other privacy laws because wherever kids are learning, whether they are in the classroom or not, a lot of these schools have bought computers and new technology, and they are going to keep using it no matter where kids are, and we need to keep kids protected and safe.

Mr. SOTO. Thanks so much, Ms. Johnson.

Dr. Ameenuddin, what do you think are the most critical parts of the KIDS Act that we need to pass right away?

Dr. AMEENUDDIN. Well, thank you for that question, Representative Soto.

Again, I am going to go back to our AAP recommendations, which are nicely outlined in our digital ad policy.

I think number-one thing is to expand COPPA to ban targeted advertising to children under 18 and also to make sure that they have the highest privacy levels possible and to really stop online tracking and data collection of kids. Those are the two most important things.

Mr. SOTO. Thanks so much.

This is a really important subject. I am glad we are handling it today, Madam Chair. We know with kids being at home, distance learning, some of them by parents' own choice, that we have to step up our ways to protect our kids online.

And I yield back.

Ms. SCHAKOWSKY. Thank you. I really want to thank you for your testimony and your remarks, Mr. Soto.

And now Angie Craig, Congresswoman Craig, it is your 5 minutes. Take it away.

Ms. CRAIG. Thank you so much, Madam Chairwoman, and thank you for holding this incredibly important hearing today.

Dr. Ameenuddin, I also want to thank you for representing the Mayo Clinic so well in the great State of Minnesota and for helping to keep our kids and our families safe and healthy. I am just thrilled that you are on our panel and I get to ask you a few questions.

So I would like to start with kids online during COVID and just share that, as the mother of four boys, I know it can be a challenge to consistently and diligently enforce limits on screen time for our kids and particularly during a public health crisis when so many of our children, our students have been learning remotely or partially hybrid.

This, in fact, was the case for our youngest son, who is a senior in high school this year, and I guess our own experience in our family is that it becomes harder as kids get older and they become more independent, which is why I think that trying to instill good habits and stricter limits on younger kids is so important.

But parents trying to do the best thing and start these habits early really do face an uneven playing field as they try to compete in a digital ecosystem that, as you know, is replete with features intended to influence user behavior while maximizing product use and engagement.

So, Doctor, in terms of the policy recommendations to Congress that you have made in your testimony today, would you consider any of them being particularly critical as you sort of segment it to younger children, those age 2 to 10, for example?

Dr. AMEENUDDIN. Well, hello, Representative Craig. I am thrilled to be reaching you from Southeast Minnesota. Thank you for that question.

Number one, I just want to say, you know, I hear you. The concerns you expressed about children and parents having a hard time is absolutely what I have been hearing from pretty much all of my patients here today.

And so in looking at, you know, how to protect kids, you know, around ages 2 to 10, what are the most important things? Again, I think that we should make sure that there are not any loopholes in COPPA. Even though technically they are not supposed to target advertising or gather information on children under 13, there are just huge loopholes.

So I think the more we can do to tighten up those loopholes, to ensure that there is appropriate enforcement, if there is any sort of breaking of those rules, would be absolutely critical.

Ms. CRAIG. Well, thank you so much.

You also mentioned in your testimony the need for more research on the effects of advertising and digital media in children, and I certainly could not agree more with that recommendation as well. I have a followup question, and I want to direct this to Ms. Fox Johnson. I appreciate that you have provided us with a number of policy recommendations as well from your perspective at Common Sense.

Are there any of these recommendations, again, that you feel would be particularly helpful for parents with younger children who could be thinking about limiting their screen time and what they are exposed to online?

Ms. FOX JOHNSON. Thank you, Representative Craig. That is a great question.

I think the KIDS Act would be particularly beneficial for young children, and another thing that would be particularly beneficial for young children would be the CAMERA Act, the Children and Media Research Advancement Act. In passing that, it would give funding so we could better study the long-term longitudinal effects of all kinds of technology on kids, including really young kids.

As you have heard today, there is discussion about how social media affects teens, which way, and that would be really incredible to have studies funded, you know, not by the industry.

Ms. CRAIG. Well, I appreciate so much the two of you being here.

And with that, Madam Chair, I will yield back a minute of everyone's life.

Ms. SCHAKOWSKY. Next, let me call on Mrs. Fletcher. Are you still here?

Mrs. FLETCHER. Yes. Thank you so much, Ms. Schakowsky.

Ms. SCHAKOWSKY. Thank you for waiting. Five minutes for questioning.

Mrs. FLETCHER. Thank you.

I am here, and I really appreciate you organizing today's hearing. I have appreciated the testimony of our witnesses. Both the written testimony that has been submitted and hearing from you all today has been really very helpful in working through these issues that communities across the country, including mine, are facing throughout this pandemic, and more broadly these concerns about keeping kids online safely, increasing use of digital media, and how we move forward is really important.

So I have a few questions, and I want to follow up on some of the things some of my colleagues have asked. Ms. Fox Johnson, I want to start with you.

In your testimony, you shared that 75 percent of children between the ages of 8 and 11 cannot distinguish ads from other content, and I think this is really important to kind of throw down on this.

You also mentioned that students or children who see only apps are significantly more likely to use those products, and you touched on this briefly in response to Representative Dingell's questions.

One of the things you mention is that kind of the hashtag-ad-sponsored media post just is not sufficient.

So can you talk a little bit more about what research has been done to indicated change in consumer habits, especially in children, about when an ad is properly identified or when it is not, and maybe even more broadly kind of research efforts that you would recommend to be able to determine what we can do that will be sufficient?

Ms. FOX JOHNSON. Thank you, Representative Fletcher.

So research shows that really young kids, 4, 5, you know, they do not even know that an ad is an ad, and as kids get older, they do not know that an ad's purpose is to sell them something.

A lot of these studies were done with traditional media. So now it is even more confusing with native content on the internet. You might think you are reading a Teen Vogue article and then not realize that Facebook has, in fact, sponsored it. You might be playing a game and not realize that Coca-Cola has paid for the game. You may be watching a boxing video and not realize that that is product placement.

So the research shows that kids do not understand this stuff, and the internet has made it much more confusing, and also these ads can be more problematic for kids because they are personally targeted to them, designed specifically to appeal to that individual based on what they have done in the past.

We need more research. As I mentioned, we need things like the CAMERA Act. We need research that is funded by NIH and by independent entities so that it is not all the companies knowing what is most effective based on their own research.

Mrs. FLETCHER. Thank you.

And kind of on a related note, I agree. I think a lot of this legislation is really important for us to be looking at and moving, and especially when it comes to the research and making sure that we're looking at research at NIH.

But, you know, one of the challenges we face in Congress is that it does take a while to respond, and so, yes, technology continues to adapt and change. You know, how do we make sure that the tools that are in place stay up to date?

How do we make sure that COPPA, for example, is inclusive of new developments and can respond to the quickness of technology that moves a whole lot faster than Congress and that is for the [audio malfunction]?

You mentioned better resources for the FTC earlier. What do you think we can and should do?

Ms. FOX JOHNSON. If you give the FTC more funding, they will be able to hire more technologists. They will be able to hire more attorneys and other experts. We and others have proposed having a division specifically focused on kids or specifically focused on privacy and technology at the FTC.

Another really important tool for the FTC that we have seen with COPPA is the rulemaking authority. You know, COPPA was passed over 20 years ago, but happily it was at least updated in 2013 by the FTC. So any future laws should give them the ability to be a little more nimble even though they are, you know, not as nimble as tech companies.

Mrs. FLETCHER. Thank you very much.

And I just have a few more seconds, but I would like to direct my last question to Dr. Ameenuddin.

What do you wish had been in place, both in terms of digital infrastructure and safeguards, prior to the pandemic in order to help families manage this difficult time?

Dr. AMEENUDDIN. So thank you, Representative Fletcher. Essentially what I wish for is what we have outlined and recommended from the American Academy of Pediatrics for years, which would be stronger protections, no targeting for kids under 18, and really kind of closing those loopholes that unfortunately tech companies can exploit.

So, yes, ideally, everything that has been on our wish list for years, but thank you.

Mrs. FLETCHER. Well, thank you for that, and it coincides with the end of my 5 minutes.

So, Madam Chairwoman, thank you so much. I yield back.

Ms. SCHAKOWSKY. Thank you. The gentlelady yields back.

So welcome people who are not on the subcommittee to come and ask questions, and in this case, we have two people, and I am going to call first on Congressman Walberg.

Five minutes of questioning for you.

Mr. WALBERG. I thank the gentlelady, and I appreciate the opportunity to join this subcommittee today on a very, very important hearing that I think that we hear a lot of bipartisanship about as well. So I appreciate that.

Families in my district tell me day after day that their children are frustrated. They are lonely and sad. Kids who once were good students and athletes are now struggling with depression and anxiety.

One parent who wrote me recently described the feeling as simply being trapped, totally trapped, and I have been advocating to safely open schools since last summer. I think it is time, frankly, to do it. It is unacceptable for leaders in charge to be dragging their feet for political purposes at the expense of our children. Again, my opinion.

I would though like to give Dr. DeAngelis a moment to respond to some of my colleague's statements regarding his testimony. Dr. DeAngelis is an expert witness on how our kids are being impacted by constantly being online. He has important evidence from medical and academia professionals about this having the impact it is having on them. He deserves to be heard.

So, Dr. DeAngelis, would you like to speak briefly, and please briefly, about the political dynamics regarding school reopening decisions?

Dr. DEANGELIS. Yes, absolutely. We cannot just sit here and cover our ears acting like the teachers' unions have had nothing to do with fighting against the reopening of schools for in-person instruction every step of the way in so many places.

In every single study that has been done on the topic—and there have been about a handful, and I have done one or two of them— have found that the strongest indicators of reopening in person, all else equal after throwing in a ton of controls into the models, is political partisanship and strength of the teachers' unions in the local area.

There has been a Brown University paper on this. There is a full upcoming publication in Social Science Quarterly that has looked at this. Brookings University Scholar has also. Jon Valant has also found, using the national data, that COVID risk did not predict the reopening of schools, but that the political partisanship in the air [audio malfunction].

Mr. WALBERG. Did we lose him? Am I still on?

Ms. SCHAKOWSKY. Yes, Mr. Walberg, you are still on.

Mr. WALBERG. But we lost Corey.

But I think he made some strong points there, and I am not going to suggest that there was any untoward action to cut him off at all.

Ms. SCHAKOWSKY. Thank you for that.

Mr. WALBERG. That is the challenge we face with this, you know. So I get it. I get it.

Madam Chair, as I mentioned at the beginning of this hearing, I am proud to introduce, reintroduce, the Protect Kids Act with my good friend and colleague Congressman Rush. The bill represents, I believe, a reasonable, commonsense, and bipartisan agreement that better reflects the realities of today's online world and strengthens children's digital safety.

Currently the Children's Online Privacy Protection Act, or COPPA, imposes requirements on website operators that specifically deal with information, personal information, of children 13 years of age and younger.

I would like to turn to Ms. Fox Johnson, and thank you for being here. I understand that my time is limited. So, if you could answer me just yes or no—and I hate that request, but I have to ask you this time.

Do you agree that the COPPA law has by and large succeeded in Congress' intent to protect children's digital footprint and remains to a great degree relevant today? Yes or no.

Ms. FOX JOHNSON. No.

Mr. WALBERG. Thank you.

I understand you have also authored a piece called "Thirteen Going on 30." One of your conclusions is to extend COPPA beyond 13 years of age, to include adults as well.

Is it fair to say that you would support a strong national standard without a private right of action, as COPPA has succeeded in doing?

Again, be brief if you can.

Ms. FOX JOHNSON. I can't speak to whether the private right of action without knowing what is in the bill, but one of COPPA's shortcomings is that it does not cover anyone over 13 and sites can pretend like it does not apply to them, and so if it applied to everyone, they could no longer pretend that.

Mr. WALBERG. Well, thank you.

Madam Chair, I would just like to point out that, while there are much-needed reforms, COPPA has been a fairly effective law for 23 years without any private right of action.

It needs to be amended. It needs to be updated. I agree. But I certainly would ask my Democratic colleagues to work in a bipartisan manner as Congressman Rush and I have done to modernize this law. Reforming the law with a provision aimed at helping trial lawyers certainly does not help kids.

And with that, I appreciate being involved and I yield back.

Ms. SCHAKOWSKY. The gentleman yields back.

And now I call on last but certainly not least, Congresswoman Blunt Rochester.

Ms. BLUNT ROCHESTER. Thank you so much, Madam Chairwoman. Thank you for this important hearing, to Ms. Castor for your leadership on updating COPPA, and to the witnesses for attending this hearing, and also for your patience waiting for me to go last.

When I chose to lead the House version of Senator Warren's DETOUR Act, it was because I was worried that everyone, especially children, would increasingly be exploited by manipulative digital practices known as "dark patterns."

Sadly, the testimony today confirms these concerns and these fears, and as a few of our witnesses testified, these trends are worse for lower-wealth households, as children in them may spend significantly more time with screens than those of households with greater wealth.

Worse still, this gap grows when considering race and ethnicity.

And, as many have noted, we all should have serious concerns for ethical and public health reasons. We may soon have a tech-pessimistic generation that only sees the exploitive potential for the innovative technologies of the future.

And so my question, and I will start with you, Ms. Fox Johnson, and it really follows up on the previous question that we just heard, some of the line of questioning.

I believe Congress needs to act and address "dark patterns," such as design choices that are intended to manipulate individuals into using products or services without their consent or for a little personal gain, especially when applied to children. And we often see tech designs subverting parental choice, but you mentioned a troubling though natural parent-child relationship. As children grow older, their parents naturally supervise their behaviors less.

So my first question is: For older kids and teens, do you believe that the subversion of their choice is a unique problem, and why?

Ms. FOX JOHNSON. Thank you for that question, Representative Rochester.

So we think that children and teens need to be recognized for their evolving capacities. So you should not treat a teenager exactly the same way that you would treat a young child.

Teens still need special protections and safeguards, and we can think of them like training wheels or like your temporary driver's permit, right? They still need help, but they should be empowered and learning how to make more choices for themselves.

The U.K. age-appropriate design code is an excellent example of this. It breaks kids into five different age groups and talks about meeting kids and teens where they are and doing things appropriate to their mental capacity.

Ms. BLUNT ROCHESTER. Excellent. And do we need more research to better understand how dark patterns affect teens?

Ms. FOX JOHNSON. One hundred percent. We need more research to understand how dark patterns affect teens, affect kids, affect adults, and that is one thing, especially with kids and teens, that the CAMERA Act would support.

Ms. BLUNT ROCHESTER. Do we know anything about how tech companies today are designing their products in relation to teens, such as making specific design choices or products that are targeted to this age group?

Ms. FOX JOHNSON. Yes. I mean, teens are like the canary in the coal mine, and they are also a very attractive commercial target for these tech companies, and they are designing their products to hook kids early and to keep them for life.

Ms. BLUNT ROCHESTER. I think my last question kind of goes to the issue of transparency with many of these tech companies. As you and my colleagues have identified, often personal information of minors is mined by these apps for commercial purposes, but it seems to go deeper than this in ways that we do not know.

A few years ago Facebook gained infamy for conducting psychological experiments and behavioral studies on its users without their consent.

Do these experiments and studies pull in children? And do we know if these studies have stopped, or has the lack of transparency continued to be a significant problem?

Ms. FOX JOHNSON. These studies have definitely involved teenagers, and they have probably involved, for all we know, everyone on Facebook and social media company sites.

One of the biggest problems with these studies is we are just finding out about them because there will be a leaked new report or a rogue employee. There is so much data that these companies have.

You know, a researcher would have to get consent and go through processes. These companies can largely do whatever they want with all of the massive stores of data they have and conduct behavioral research on all of us without our knowledge.

Ms. BLUNT ROCHESTER. Thank you so much for answering that question.

I will just say that I think one of my colleagues mentioned that there are opportunities for bipartisanship here. This is a vital area. I am so glad that Ms. Castor is, again, taking up the mantle on this.

Thank you so much, Madam Chairwoman, for your leadership as we look at these issues that affect everyone, but particularly affect our children.

Thank you, and I yield back the balance of my time.

Ms. SCHAKOWSKY. I thank you.

And now I would like to give a hearty thank you to our witnesses for their participation in today's hearing.

Before we conclude, I request unanimous consent to enter the following documents into the record, and there is quite a list:

A written statement from the National Center for Missing and Exploited Children; a letter from Prevent Blindness; an article from Vox; an article from the Chicago Sun-Times; an article from the Globe and Mail, Inc.; an article from NPR; an article from All About Ann Arbor; an article from the World Health Organization; an article from the New York Times; an op-ed in the Chicago Tribune; an op-ed in the Los Angeles Times; an article from the Wall Street Journal; an article from USA Today; an article from the Arizona Daily Star.

If there are no objections—and I hear none—so ordered. [The information appears at the conclusion of the hearing.[201]]

Ms. SCHAKOWSKY. I remind Members that, pursuant to committee rules, they have 10 days to submit additional questions for the record to be answered by the witnesses who have appeared. I ask each witness to respond promptly to any questions—and I know there were some because people were running out of time— that you may receive.

And at this time, with a lot of gratitude for the participation by the Members and by the witnesses, the subcommittee is adjourned.

[Whereupon, at 1:25 p.m., the subcommittee was adjourned.] [Material submitted for inclusion in the record follows:]

Prepared Statement of The National Center for Missing and Exploited Children

Background on NCMEC and Its Programs to Combat Online Child Sexual Exploitation

The National Center for Missing & Exploited Children (NCMEC) is a private, non-profit organization created as a grassroots response to an unthinkable tragedy. In 1981, 6-year-old Adam Walsh was with his mother in a Florida shopping mall when he vanished without a trace. The search for Adam revealed many inadequacies that plagued missing children investigations at the time. There was no coordinated response to search for Adam, no AMBER

---

[201] *The Arizona Daily Star* article has been retained in committee files and is available at https://docs.house.gov/meetings/IF/IF17/20210311/111298/HHRG-117-IF17-20210311-SD006.pdf.

Alert system to quickly deliver critical information to the public, and no place for families to go for guidance or emotional support.

Revé and John endured 10 excruciating days searching for Adam before he was found murdered 100 miles away. The Walshes channeled their grief and came together with other child advocates to create NCMEC in 1984. Over the past 37 years, NCMEC has grown to become the leading nonprofit organization and the nation's congressionally designated clearinghouse on missing and exploited children issues. Today NCMEC has more than 370 employees who work to prevent child abduction, recover missing children, and combat child sexual victimization through five main programs of work relating to: (1) missing children; (2) exploited children; (3) community outreach; (4) training and education; and (5) family resources.

NCMEC's CyberTipline

As the Internet became more accessible to the general public in the 1990s, NCMEC started to see a growing threat to children being sexually exploited, enticed, and groomed into abusive situations by online predators. In 1998, in response to this trend NCMEC created the CyberTipline to serve as the online mechanism for members of the public and electronic service providers to report incidents of child sexual exploitation, including: child sex trafficking; online enticement of children for sexual acts; child sexual molestation; child pornography[202]; child sex tourism; unsolicited obscene materials sent to children; misleading domain names; and misleading words or digital images. NCMEC's two primary goals in running the CyberTipline are: (1) to prioritize reports indicating imminent danger to a child; and (2) to determine where the reported incident is occurring so a report can be made available to the appropriate law enforcement agency for its independent review. Today the CyberTipline is a key tool in helping ESPs; members of the public; international, federal, state, and local law enforcement; and prosecutors to combat online child sexual exploitation.

To date, NCMEC has received over 87 million CyberTipline reports, and the volume of content reported to the CyberTipline continues to increase. In 2019, NCMEC received over 16.9 million reports. In 2020, NCMEC received more than 21.7 million reports containing 65.4 million images, videos and

[202] The term "child pornography" is used in NCMEC's CyberTipline reports because this is the term designated by U.S. federal, and most state, laws. Outside of this legal context, NCMEC refers to these images and videos as "child sexual abuse material" to most accurately reflect what is depicted – the rape, sexual abuse, and sexual exploitation of children.

related contents, with the COVID pandemic being a significant factor in last year's increase in cases.

Impacts of COVID-19 on Online Child Sexual Exploitation

Beginning in March 2020, when COVID-19 stay-at-home orders were first put into place nationwide and in many countries around the world, NCMEC witnessed explosive increases in the number of reports submitted to the CyberTipline. For the first three months of the pandemic (March, April, and May 2020), the number of reports submitted to NCMEC's CyberTipline increased by 106%, 308%, and 126%, respectively, compared to the number of reports submitted to the CyberTipline for the same months in 2019. Overall, reports to NCMEC's CyberTipline increased by 28% from 2019 to 2020.

CyberTipline Reports in 2019 Compared to 2020

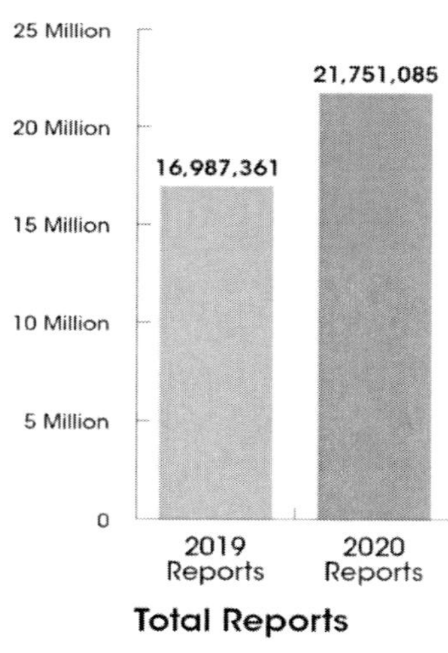

Based on NCMEC's analysis to date, there are several factors specific to the COVID pandemic that fueled this increase in CyberTipline reports in 2020:

- Children and adults have been spending more time at home and online due to school closures, cancellation of social activities, and general social distancing measures.

- Children have been online without adequate levels of prevention and safety education and, in many instances, with less supervision and monitoring than in pre-COVID times.
- Offenders on the dark web have openly discussed taking advantage of social distancing measures to entice and lure children into producing sexually explicit material.
- A general increase in online activity has heightened circulation of "viral videos" where members of the public share child sexual abuse images out of outrage and to try to help identify and rescue a child victim.

While the majority of reports submitted to the CyberTipline involve the distribution of child sexual abuse material, NCMEC has witnessed alarming increases in offenders using social media and chat platforms to engage in the online enticement of children for sexual activity. Online enticement occurs on any online platform and app that an offender can use to lure a child to share sexually explicit images, meet in person for sexual purposes, engage the child in sexual conversation or role-playing, compel the child to engage in sexually explicit conduct alone or with another child via live-streaming, or, in some instances, sell or trade the child's sexual images to others.

The number of enticement-related reports submitted to NCMEC's CyberTipline increased by 97.5% from 2019 to 2020, as shown below. For the first three months of the pandemic (March, April, and May 2020), the number of online enticement reports submitted to NCMEC's CyberTipline increased by 62%, 108%, and 163%, respectively, compared to the numbers submitted to the CyberTipline for the same months in 2019. While the report totals are small with respect to the total CyberTipline report volumes, these increases highlight the immediate impact of COVID-19 on this particular crime:

CyberTipline Reports Relating to Online Child Sexual Enticement in 2019 Compared to 2020

There are multiple reasons why reports of online enticement increased so dramatically in 2020, but one of the most evident is that safety precautions adopted due to the COVID-19 pandemic moved both children's and adults' lives online more than ever before. Many children switched to virtual learning and have spent more time on social media or online gaming in lieu of seeing friends or meeting new people in person. This left children and teenagers more susceptible to the dangers of the internet.

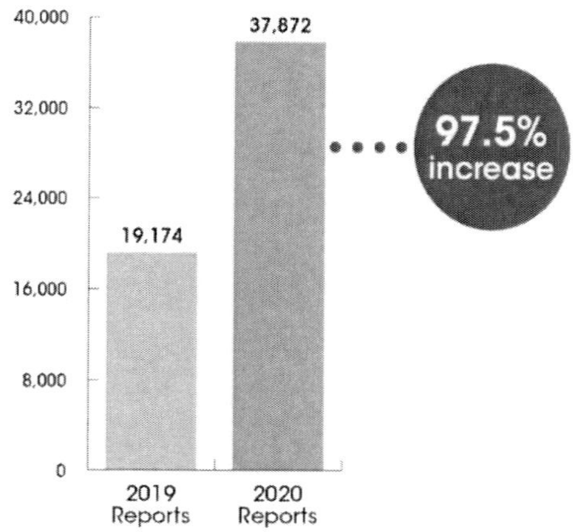

Online Enticement Reports

While the correlation between the increase in reports of child sexual exploitation and the COVID-19 pandemic remains fluid and continues to evolve, one especially alarming development has been a marked increase in offenders actively discussing on the dark web how to entice children who are spending more time online without adult supervision. Examples of these discussions are provided below:

> "Speaking of corona...I hope you guys are developing some online lesson plans for all the cute boys stuck at home. They are in dire need of structured learning activities."

> "... but with all those young girls stuck at home there must be a lot of camming going on now... hopefully some nice self-productions wll show up ;\)"

> "hello fellow pedos, think of all those young boys stuck at home in their bedroom with nothing to do but explore their bodies.."

> "I've been wondering, with hundreds of millions of boys stuck at home, does that mean that capping/finding boys has become much easier?"

> "BTW I don't know if you notice, but due to coronavirus and closed schools, it's like during the summer break. Very easy for find kids in social media."

NCMEC's Efforts to Prevent and Disrupt the Impact of COVID-19 on Online Child Sexual Exploitation

Prevention education and awareness is especially essential in unpredictable times, such as the COVID pandemic, when there are increased threats to child safety online. In response to the growing number of reports relating to online child sexual exploitation, NCMEC has been diligently promoting and expanding its child safety prevention education for children, their families, and child-serving professionals. NCMEC provides free-of-charge, age-appropriate safety and prevention resources focusing on the topics of online and real-world safety, including abduction and child sexual exploitation prevention.

Since the emergence of the COVID-19 pandemic, NCMEC has produced a series of blogs and related educational materials addressing our child safety response and resources to the COVID-19 situation. We also have used our social media platforms to engage with the public and our national safety partners on child safety issues and to provide enhanced educational resources for parents/guardians, many of whom are managing their children's online education and activities in more intensive ways during the COVID-19 stay-at-home timeframe. NCMEC's education messaging has focused on general safety awareness as well as education on how to handle suspected child sexual abuse material online.

Conclusion

Offenders have seized on the opportunity created by COVID pandemic to exploit and entice children for sexual activity. These offenders have moved inside the safety of our own homes via the Internet to seek children to victimize. This alarming trend has underscored the urgency for NCMEC to promote our educational programs on online child safety both for children and their parents. NCMEC continues to closely monitor and assess the impacts of the COVID-19 pandemic on online child sexual exploitation, while providing expanded services to address the needs of vulnerable children, their families and child-serving professionals. Through this time of national crisis caused by the COVID-19 pandemic, and beyond, NCMEC will continue to carry on its mission to prevent and disrupt online child sexual exploitation.

* * *

Letter from Jeff Todd, President and CEO, Prevent Blindness, to Ms. Schakowsky and Mr. Bilirakis

March 10, 2021

The Honorable Jan Schakowsky
Chair
United States House of Representatives
Committee on Energy and Commerce
Subcommittee on Consumer Protection and Commerce
Washington, DC 20515

The Honorable Gus Bilirakis
Ranking Member
United States House of Representatives
Committee on Energy and Commerce
Subcommittee on Consumer Protection and Commerce
Washington, DC 20515

Dear Chair Schakowsky and Ranking Member Bilirakis:

Prevent Blindness is the nation's leading nonprofit, voluntary organization committed to preventing blindness and preserving sight for Americans of all ages, backgrounds, and circumstances. We appreciate that the Committee has called a hearing for March 11, 2021 ("Kids Online During COVID: Child Safety in an Increasingly Digital Age") to examine the impact that increased screen time has on children's health and safety, and we would like to take the opportunity to elevate another harmful aspect of increased and prolonged screen time and digital device use in children: the impact of digital device usage and screen time on children's vision and eye health.

Vision has a critical role in children's physical, cognitive, social, and emotional development. Unlike other senses, which are fully functioning at birth, a child's vision develops throughout early childhood years and is therefore significantly vulnerable to their visual environment. Most visual disorders that lead to permanent blindness are preventable; yet, up to one in 17 young children and 1 in 5 children enrolled in Head Start has an undiagnosed vision disorder. According to the Centers for Disease Control and Prevention (CDC)[203], 63.5% of children between ages 3 and 5 years had not

[203] https://www.cdc.gov/nchs/data/databriefs/db353-h.pdf.

yet seen an eye care provider. This same study also found that 1.6% of children in the United States (roughly 1.1 million children) suffered from blindness or had visual impairment, even with the use of glasses. Vision disorders are the 4th most common disability in children in the U.S.[204] The cost of children's vision disorders amounts to $10 billion per year, with families shouldering 45% of these costs.[205]

The ongoing nature of the COVID-19 pandemic has required Americans to prolong the transition from in-person work and education to online platforms as workplaces and schools continue to determine the feasibility of returning to in-person settings while also mitigating community spread of the virus. Digital device usage has not only increased in frequency during the pandemic, but devices are also being used for longer periods of time throughout the day and every day as we continue to rely on them to work, attend school, connect with others, engage in recreational interests, seek entertainment, and consume information. This extensive reliance on digital devices and prolonged time spent in front of screens has led to a substantial increase in digital device use in children ages 6 to 12 years.[206] Alarmingly, children younger than six years are also increasingly becoming reliant on devices and spending greater time in front of screens.

Digital device usage in children continues to raise a myriad of concerns about the effects of screen time on children's developing and susceptible eyes and the extra visual effort required to read small print overcome screen glare. Notably, children who engage in activities using digital devices and screens lack self-awareness about how long they have been staring at screens or the understanding of how to accommodate their surroundings for more comfortable or disciplined viewing.[207] Extensive screen time can lead to symptoms such as eye strain, dry eye, blurred vision, headaches, or fatigue. Even more worrisome, children who spend many hours doing close visual work, such as learning via electronic devices without frequent breaks or time spent outdoors, also have a higher risk of developing myopia or worsening

---

204 https://preventblindness.org/wp-content/uploads/2020/07/Snapshot-Report-2020condense d F.pdf.

205 Wittenborn JS, Zhang X, Feagan CW, et al. The economic burden of vision loss and eye disorders among the United States population younger than 40 years. *Ophthalmology*. 2013;120(9):1728-1735. doi:10.1016/j.ophtha.2013.01.068.

206 https://www.axios.com/kids-screen-time-coronavirus-562073f6-0638-47f2-8ea3-4f8781d 6b 31b.html.

207 https://www.ncbi.nlm.nih.gov/pmc/articles/PMC2776336/#:~:text=issue%20in%20children. -,Children%20can%20experience%20many%20of%20the%20same%20symptoms% 20related%20to,and%20other%20symptoms%20of%20eyestrain.

existing myopia. If left uncorrected, myopia causes far-away objects such as a classroom board to appear blurry which can cause not only discomfort, but also reduced school performance and behavioral problems related to a child's inability to focus. Myopia is an increasing public health concern as myopia can also lead to life-long sight-threatening complications such as glaucoma, myopic maculopathy, retinal detachment, and cataract in addition to problems seeing clearly in adult life that may limit access to certain jobs.[208] Left unaddressed, all of these conditions could lead to difficulties in learning and compound disparities in health care, decrease academic success, exacerbate the impact of social determinants of health, and reduce quality of life.

Vision problems in children are likely worsening due to the pandemic, which is exacerbated by many families being unable or feeling unsafe to access the necessary care to detect and treat vision disorders in children. This point is underscored by recent data from the Centers for Medicare and Medicaid Services[209], showing that COVID-19 has led to a drastic decline in essential child health services such as screenings for developmental delays in physical, cognitive, or sensory (including vision) health, childhood vaccinations and immunizations, and routine primary and preventive care. In addition, national surveillance of children's vision and eye health is a significant public health challenge as there is currently no system in place to track children's vision screenings, follow-up eye exams, treatment, or outcomes of care; thus, making it difficult to measure progress, close gaps in access, address disparities to achieve equity in vision and eye care, and facilitate coordinated care across systems.

Many of the consequences of the COVID-19 pandemic on children will be long-term in nature and may not be understood or even recognized for years. However, the drastic rise in digital device usage and screen time underscores an important and timely opportunity for Congress to fully address children's vision and eye health by promoting federal-level programmatic efforts pertaining to the development, coordination, and promotion of evidence-based best practices (such as by age, and based on *Bright Futures* guidance from the American Academy of Pediatrics) and to provide states with technical assistance to promote children's vision and eye health as an essential component of childhood development and growth and successful learning.

---

[208] https://www.aaojournal.org/action/showPdf?pii=S0161-6420%2820%2931043-5.

[209] https://www.cms.gov/newsroom/fact-sheets/fact-sheet-service-use-among-medicaid-chip-beneficiaries-age-18-and-under-during-covid-19.

We appreciate the Committee's consideration of this important and timely matter. Please do not hesitate to contact Sara Brown, Director of Government Affairs, at (312) 363-6031 or sbrown@preventblindness.org if you or your staff would like to discuss these issues.

Sincerely, Jeff Todd

President and CEO, Prevent Blindness

Cc: The Honorable Frank Pallone, Chairman Energy and Commerce Committee

The Honorable Cathy McMorris Rodgers, Ranking Member, Energy and Commerce Committee

The Honorable Anna Eshoo, Chair, Subcommittee on Health

The Honorable Brett Guthrie, Ranking Member, Subcommittee on Health

"I'm an Epidemiologist and a Father. Here's Why I'm Losing Patience with Our Teachers' Unions," by Benjamin P. Linas For *VOX*

Feb 15, 2021, 10:00am EST

The evidence is clear: We can open schools safely now.

Source: Paul Bersebach/MediaNews Group/Orange County Register via Getty Images.

A student does at-home learning in Orange, California, in December 2020. After months of at-home learning, school districts are grappling with bringing students back to campus for in-person teaching.

Millions of students across America have now been stuck in remote learning for nearly a year. This situation, which has hurt learning and widened gaping disparities, is in large part because many teachers fear returning to the classroom in person. But in this past year, we have also learned how we can keep schools open safely.

Educators' anxiety is based on reasonable concerns. Covid-19 is a serious illness. And schools are an indoor group setting with the potential to spread infection. But schools, it turns out, with a few basic safety measures, including masks and reasonable distancing, are not a high-risk venue for Covid-19 transmission. In fact, they appear to have far lower rates of the virus than their surrounding communities. Still, some education union leaders are beginning to lay the foundation for schools remaining shuttered into the 2021-22 school year.

For the better part of the past year, I've been living inside the tempest that is Covid-19 and schools. I am a father of three girls, ages 11, 13, and 17, all of whom go to public school. I am also an infectious diseases physician and epidemiologist. I understand teachers' fear — it is real and I have felt it myself as a front-line doctor. But I also know that America needs to have its schools open for in-person learning and there are safe, affordable ways to do this — right now.

And if educators and their unions don't embrace the established science, they risk continuing to widen gaps in educational attainment — and losing the support of their many long-time allies, like me.

The Agonizing Choice between Science and Teachers Didn't Have to Exist

Since March 2020, I have been a front-line pandemic health care provider, adviser to my hospital, and consultant to my religious congregation and a local community college — all with the aim of preventing the spread of Covid-19. Toward that goal, I have also been a volunteer member of the public health and safety advisory panel to the Public Schools of Brookline, Massachusetts, where my family lives.

Unfortunately, our panel's expertise — and that of national and international health groups — has been frequently dismissed by the local educators' union in favor of their own judgments about best health practices and the safety of in-person learning. In the process, they have misinterpreted scientific guidance and transformed it into a series of litmus tests that keep our district in hybrid learning. These litmus tests are not based on science, they are grounded in anxiety, and they are a major component of the return-to-school quagmire in which we are stuck.

One sticking point, for example, has been the union's early and continued insistence that desks remain at least 6 feet apart at all times. This requirement mathematically determines whether there is enough space for learners in the building. Distancing is absolutely critical to Covid-19 mitigation, but there is no magical threshold that makes 6 feet the "safe" distance and 5 feet "dangerous."

In settings like school, where everyone is wearing a face covering, there really is no measurable difference in risk between being 3 feet and 6 feet apart. That is why there is no official guidance from any relevant public health body that mandates 6-foot distancing at all times. Even the new Centers for Disease Control and Prevention (CDC) school strategy, released February 12, doesn't address the key problems in the existing guidance to move us forward.

The union also named a lack of asymptomatic testing for teachers as a major barrier to returning to in-person learning. To get kids back to school, we implemented such a routine testing plan, at great cost and logistical effort. We discovered that since testing began in January 2021, the positivity rate among teachers and staff has been approximately 0.15 percent — while cases were surging in the Boston metro area — and our contact tracing efforts have not identified any cases of in-building transmission.

Even so, the union continues to resist a return to full in-person learning. What's more, the goalpost seems to have shifted again, now to universal vaccination of teachers.

All of this is frustrating, especially to me as an epidemiologist. Generally, union leaders tie their position to public health guidance from bodies like the CDC. But so far, the implementation of these recommendations by our district's union — and by many others across the country — has been opportunistic, and their stance does not align with current guidance from the World Health Organization, CDC, Massachusetts Department of Public Health, or the Massachusetts Department of Education.

This tension has been agonizing. Because not only do I support organized labor, having previously stood with my town's educator union in negotiations with the district, but also because union representatives are among our family's most beloved teachers.

I want our teachers to be safe — and feel safe — at work. I also empathize strongly with the fear and anxiety that they feel. That fear is real. I felt it too when I entered the hospital for work last spring. That fear traumatized me and still makes me tearful when I recall those early, terrifying days of the pandemic.

But as we approach the one-year anniversary of remote education in America, I find that I am losing sympathy for the educators' position and their myopic vision this far along into the pandemic. We can open schools safely, and we have the evidence in hand to prove it.

Source: Angela Weiss/AFP.

A schoolyard is closed outside a public school in the Brooklyn, New York, on November 19, 2020.

We Have the Science to Safely Reopen — And Know the Stakes

When Covid-19 began to spread in the US last year, teachers were right to be worried about schools. We knew almost nothing about the virus's spread. Operating schools under business-as-usual conditions very well could have led to more infections among teachers, students, and people in the community.

But since then, we have accumulated a massive amount of data about how to keep schools open safely.

First, last spring, we observed the experiences of other countries like Scotland, Singapore, and France, where schools reopened and masks and social distancing seemed to prevent large-scale transmission.

In the US, epidemiologists compared the timing of school closures to changes in Covid-19 incidence. Some studies found that school closures might have reduced the spread of illness, but the findings are complicated because we were also making other major public health changes at the same time. And overall they failed to find a strong link.

Data and patterns also began to emerge about children's Covid-19 test results and their exposures. Playdates with friends emerged as the common exposure among the infected; time in school did not.

Still, as reassuring as the data was, it was all indirect. The gold standard to learn if schools can open safely is fairly simple: Open schools, measure Covid-19 incidence, and see what happens. Many US school districts have now done this, and we have the data.

First, researchers in North Carolina published results from 11 school districts and more than 100,000 students and staff. Schools in those districts employed mandatory masking and 6-foot distancing where feasible, but no major capital improvement to HVAC systems or buildings. In the first quarter of this school year, they found the rate of transmission of Covid-19 in schools was dramatically lower (roughly 1/25) than the level of transmission in the community. Among all of the Covid-19 infections observed in schools, the state health department's tracers found 96 percent were acquired in the community, and there were no documented cases of the virus passing from child to adult in schools — zero.

Second, a similar study followed 17 schools in Wisconsin. Like North Carolina, those schools required masks indoors, 3-foot distancing with an effort to distance farther whenever feasible, and no major capital improvements. Between August 31 and November 29, with more than 4,500 students and 650 staff, they found seven cases of coronavirus transmission to children and also found no cases of coronavirus transmission to educators in the buildings. Further, these schools eliminated transmission at the same time that the surrounding community saw a rapid rise in Covid-19 cases.

A third important preprint study analyzes data from two schools in Atlanta. This study is small, but it is important because the schools were conducting routine asymptomatic screening of students, teachers, and staff. In Atlanta, 72 percent of the limited number of transmission events in one school were known to be the result of noncompliance with masking. And again here, there were no cases transmitted from students to teachers.

Sadly, at the same time that we are learning definitively that we can open schools safely and essentially prevent Covid-19 transmission, data is emerging about the real damage being done to children by prolonged remote learning, including a rise in the use of pediatric emergency rooms for psychiatric illnesses, increasing anxiety and depression symptoms, losses in learning progress, and large racial disparities in the availability of in-person instruction and educational achievement.

Furthermore, most private and parochial schools across America have been successfully open for the school year — many having seen an increase in enrollment for this reason — while most public school districts have been either partially or fully remote. We cannot allow these repugnant inequities to fester any longer.

We Don't Need to Wait for Universal Vaccination — or More Time — to Reopen Schools

I appreciate that returning to in-person learning carries some risk for educators. There is no immediately foreseeable scenario in which there will be truly no risk of Covid-19 infection in school settings.

However, insisting on a zero-risk scenario for school reopening is a commitment to long-term remote learning, which most people agree is not acceptable. We owe it to educators to do everything we can to mitigate risk.

Vaccines can help lower this risk even further but do not save the day just yet. It will take time to vaccinate all teachers (who are only currently eligible for shots in just over half of states) and, still longer, students. And even when people are vaccinated, we do not yet know for certain that the vaccine prevents transmission of the virus (which has been a sticking point for educators and their unions because it means that, theoretically, they could pick up the infection without getting sick and transmit it to others, like unvaccinated family members).

Still, all states need to immediately put teachers at the head of the vaccine line. If we are asking teachers to assume any risk and return to classrooms for the sake of education and our society, then our society should treat them as the essential individuals they are.

At the same time, teachers also need to recognize that full vaccination is not a prerequisite for safe schools, as some educator unions have called for. We did not have a vaccine in North Carolina or Wisconsin when they safely opened schools in August 2020.

We must also not let other demands, such as universal asymptomatic testing or large-scale capital improvements to buildings, stymie the return to in-person learning. Yes, we should be working to implement more screening in schools and improving air exchange, but we can do that in parallel with reopening. We know now from good data that we can effectively stop Covid-19 at the school doors and get American education back on track without these things. Essentially, all we need to safely reopen schools are mask mandates, reasonable distancing of at least 3 feet, minor and affordable upgrades to existing HVAC systems, and teachers.

Many educators and their representatives have proposed we wait out this school year in whatever form it is taking and assess the prospects for reopening public schools over the summer. But for millions of Americans, "the next few months" are a crisis of lost income, unstable housing, and mental health disorders that cannot wait until next year.

It is also true that many people of color whose communities have been hardest hit by Covid-19 are worried about the safety of returning to school, and a lot of urban Black and Latinx families have elected to remain in remote learning even when an option for in-person school exists. To bring families back to school, we need to earn trust. The best way to do that is to open our school buildings and establish an empirical track record of safety while families still have the option of remote learning.

If we hope for our schools to be open full time in fall 2021 and for all families to feel more comfortable in the building, our best chance for success will be if we begin the ramp-up now.

A realistic plan for reopening schools is to immediately begin bringing the youngest learners back to full-time in-person learning with strict guidance for masking indoors, 3-foot minimal distancing with effort to maximize distance as much as possible. Districts can certainly conduct air-exchange surveys in classrooms as an extra precautionary measure and use simple and affordable mitigation strategies for suboptimal conditions, such as upgrading HVAC filters, opening windows, and deploying portable HEPA filters in problem spaces.

Over the course of the rest of February and March, successive waves of older learners can return to school with the same guidelines, in a stepped process that allows teachers and administrators to adapt to growing numbers of students in their buildings.

With this approach, we could have every public school child back to safe in-person learning by April — without optimal screening, before wide-spread vaccination, and without community transmission benchmarks that reflexively trigger school closures.

So, here we are, nearly one year into our national project in remote learning. It is clear that we did what was needed when Covid-19 struck. But it is also quite clear that our solution — remote learning — is failing our children and our families.

I love my kids' teachers and believe in my core that they want what is best for my girls, but I am losing patience. The time has arrived to open our schools for in-person learning — now. We should be working to quickly implement universal asymptomatic testing of teachers as well as universal vaccination, but we cannot wait for those things to be in place before we begin moving. And the science shows that we don't need to. At stake is the 2021-22 school year and, arguably, the future of American public education itself.

Millions turn to Vox to understand what's happening in the news. Our mission has never been more vital than it is in this moment: to empower through understanding. Financial contributions from our readers are a critical part of supporting our resource-intensive work and help us keep our journalism free for all. Help us keep our work free for all by making a financial contribution from as little as $3.

"As Medical Doctors, We Believe Reopening Chicago's Schools Is Essential and Safe," by Michael Angarone, et al. For *Chicago Sun Times*

Dec 29, 2020, 5:34pm CST

We cannot understate the serious psychological harm that prolonged virtual school has had on many children.

An open letter from 17 Chicago physicians

Source: Pat Nabong/Sun-Times.

Chicago Public Schools CEO Dr. Janice Jackson puts on her mask during a press conference earlier this fall.

The COVID-19 pandemic is among the worst public health crises of our lifetimes. Over the past 10 months, healthcare and public health professionals have worked tirelessly to overcome the unprecedented challenges COVID-19 has presented.

The magnitude of cases and deaths related to COVID-19 has been devastating, and we are still far from the finish line in ending this pandemic.

Another serious consequence of this pandemic is the effect it has had on school-age children.

The educational, psychological and financial hardships of remote learning have had serious consequences for our children and their families, and those children with educational or behavioral challenges have been even more seriously affected. We cannot understate the serious psychological harm that prolonged virtual school has had on many children. We are seeing an epidemic of serious psychological illness that has reached a crisis point.

Furthermore, lack of daytime structure and lack of access to school amenities such as hot lunches, especially for younger students from disadvantaged communities, has had significant health consequences.

In March 2020, Chicago and Illinois recognized the immediate threat that the community spread of COVID-19 posed. At that time, we were a facing a new virus with very little understanding of how it spread, how to prevent it and what risks the virus posed to children. This was compounded by limited access to personal protective equipment, diagnostic tests and medications to treat and prevent COVID-19.

A weekly overview of opinions, analysis and commentary on issues aQecting Chicago, Illinois and our nation by outside contributors, Sun-Times readers and the CST Editorial Board.

For that reason, most schools went virtual. However, we have learned a lot over the last 10 months about children safely returning to the classroom. For example, we have discovered that in-school spread of COVID-19 is rare when proper precautions are taken. Furthermore, we know now that children, and especially young children of elementary school age, are much less likely to transmit infection to adults than the other way around.

The American Academy of Pediatrics and many of the world's most prestigious children's hospitals published guidelines over the summer in an attempt to keep schools open. Such rules have enabled many public, parochial and private schools in neighborhoods across Chicago and its suburbs to remain open for in-person learning over the last three months. In our collective experience, there have been few, if any, schools that have fully enforced public health mitigation guidelines that had to close because of secondary transmission. Simply put, layered mitigation strategies at schools have been proven effective.

The mitigation strategies are by now familiar to all. Masks are worn by all individuals at school.

Students and teachers are spaced three-to six-feet apart. Hand hygiene is consistently performed and environmental controls such as adequate ventilation are assured. Children are kept together as much as possible in small classes (pods), so that if there is an exposure, it is limited to a single class and not the entire grade or school. Transition of children between classrooms and crowding of hallways is limited. Lunch time is staggered, and lunches are often eaten in classrooms quickly and quietly. Recess has been modified. Parents are instructed not to send children with any COVID-19 compatible symptoms to school and are required to fill out a daily screener. Contact tracing and quarantining of exposed children and family members is strictly enforced, and proper behavior outside of school is reinforced. Access to testing for those who require it (such as symptomatic students or family members), either at school or locally, is also crucial.

The reality is that these strategies have been successfully implemented at many schools across Chicagoland. Understanding that our children's education is of vital importance, with the support of administration, teachers, students and parents, these schools have safely been open for in-person learning all school year.

The past few weeks have brought a ray of hope. With vaccines being distributed to healthcare workers and high-risk adults, and soon to follow to the general public, we now have a tool that has high potential to lead us back to the lives we knew before COVID-19. As vaccines become more widely available over the coming weeks to months, vaccination campaigns will also help maintain a safe school environment.

It is widely agreed upon by the medical community that in-person classroom learning is both optimal and safe using the layered mitigation strategies described above. The healthcare professionals authoring this op-ed strongly advocate for schools to return to some form of in-person learning as soon as possible. We would be happy to help schools implement this vital and time sensitive recommendation for the benefit of our children.

Michael Angarone, DO, Division of Infectious Disease, Northwestern Medicine

Allison H. Bartlett MD, Section of Pediatric infectious Diseases, University of Chicago Comer Children's Hospital

Virginia DePaul MD, pediatrician, North Suburban Pediatrics

Cathy DiVincenzo MD, pediatrician, Kids First Pediatric Partners

Mary Dobbins MD, president, Illinois Chapter of the American Academy of Pediatrics (representing the chapter)

David Dobkin MD, pediatrician, North Arlington Pediatrics

Daniel Evans MD, Internal Medicine, Northwestern Medicine

Shannon Galvin MD, Division of Infectious Disease, Northwestern Medicine

Mary C Hall MD, pediatrician, Kids Health Partners

Daniel Johnson MD, Chief, Section of Pediatric infectious Diseases, University of Chicago Comer Children's Hospital

Ben Katz MD, Pediatric Infectious Disease, Lurie Children's Hospital

Valerie Kimball MD, pediatrician, Chicago Area Pediatrics

Latania K. Logan MD, MSPH, Chief, Pediatric Infectious Diseases, Rush University Children's Hospital

James Mitchell MD, pediatrician, Section of Academic Pediatrics, University of Chicago Comer Children's Hospital

James Olson MD, pediatrician, Kids Health Partners

Bruce Rowell MD, pediatrician, Lawndale Christian Health Center

Dov Shapiro MD, pediatrician, Associated Pediatric Partners

"Canadian Doctors Call for Schools to Return to In-Classroom Learning," by Caroline Alphonso For the *Globe and Mail*

Caroline Alphonso, Education Reporter

Published February 2, 2021

Updated February 3, 2021

A group of more than 100 doctors across Canada are advocating for in-classroom learning through the second wave of the pandemic, just as the Ontario government prepares to release its reopening plans for students in the hardest-hit regions.

In a letter to federal and provincial governments on Tuesday, the physicians wrote that while protecting the public should be a priority, so should recognizing the "unique needs and rights" of children, who are generally not at risk for serious outcomes if they contract COVID-19.

"Current responses to the pandemic continue to include measures that infringe on these rights. More concerning, these interventions, chief among them school closures, stop our children from reaching their full potential and harm their health (physical and mental) and general wellbeing," wrote the doctors from various hospitals and universities, including Toronto's Hospital for Sick Children, McMaster University in Hamilton and Montreal Children's Hospital.

Ontario is the only province that has kept many of its schools closed to in-person learning. Its Education Minister, Stephen Lecce, is expected to announce on Wednesday reopening dates for schools in the hardest-hit areas, including Toronto, Peel and Windsor. Students in 18 out of 35 public-health units in the province have returned to classrooms since the December holiday break, including those in Ottawa and London, who were back on Monday.

There are few more divisive issues in this pandemic than keeping classrooms open. Almost a year in, there is still no conclusive evidence regarding transmission in schools and to what extent children drive the spread of the virus.

The U.S. Centers for Disease Control and Prevention suggested in a recent paper that outbreaks in schools have been "limited," but highlighted that in order to keep them open, community transmission must be under control and mitigation strategies, including masks, must be implemented.

Martha Fulford, an associate professor in the division of infectious diseases at McMaster University and one of the signatories on the letter, said that although almost every province has reopened its schools, the letter was a plea from doctors not to shut them. The letter said that classrooms should remain open to in-person learning "unless there is high quality evidence to show that doing otherwise is more dangerous for the overall physical and mental health of children." It also called for improvements to services that support children who suffer from mental health and academic difficulties.

Data has shown that schools do not amplify transmission of the virus, but rather reflect what's going on in the community, she said. "When we are planning these measures, children deserve to be considered as a unique population with their unique rights."

Dr. Fulford added: "As we move forward, a fundamental right of children is the right to an education, and an in-person education. This shouldn't be compromised."

"The Coronavirus Crisis: U.S. Pediatricians Call for In-Person School This Fall," by Anya Kamenetz For *NPR*

June 29, 2020, 12:33 PM ET

The nation's pediatricians have come out with a strong statement in favor of bringing children back to the classroom this fall wherever and whenever they can do so safely. The American Academy of Pediatrics' guidance "strongly advocates that all policy considerations for the coming school year should start with a goal of having students physically present in school."

Source: Ross D. Franklin/AP.

Kristina Washington, special education staff member at Desert Heights Preparatory Academy, walks past desks and chairs at the closed Glendale, Ariz., school in early June.

The guidance says "schools are fundamental to child and adolescent development and well-being."

The AAP cites "mounting evidence" that transmission of the coronavirus by young children is uncommon, partly because they are less likely to contract it in the first place.

On the other hand, the AAP argues that based on the nation's experience this spring, remote learning is likely to result in severe learning loss and increased social isolation. Social isolation, in turn, can breed serious social, emotional and health issues: "child and adolescent physical or sexual abuse, substance use, depression, and suicidal ideation." Furthermore, these impacts will be visited more severely on Black and brown children, as well as low-income children and those with learning disabilities.

The guidance for returning to in-person schooling includes recommendations about physical distancing, cleaning and disinfection, hand-washing, and using outdoor spaces whenever possible.

The AAP argues that offering elementary school children the opportunity to go to school every day should be given due consideration over spacing guidelines if capacity is an issue: "Schools should weigh the benefits of strict adherence to a 6-feet spacing rule between students with the potential downside if remote learning is the only alternative."

And, it also argues that masks are probably not practical for children younger than middle school unless they can wear a mask without increased face touching.

The guidelines do note that adult school staff are more at risk compared to young children and need to be able to distance from other adults as much as possible — no in-person faculty meetings, no class visits by parents. And they emphasize the need to make accommodations for students who are medically fragile or have special health care needs or disabilities.

However, these guidelines don't necessarily address the health concerns of America's teachers or their willingness to return to in-person teaching. Federal data show nearly a third of teachers are over 50, putting them in a higher risk category when it comes to the disease.

Fairfax County Public Schools in Virginia, for example, recently announced its reopening plans, offering families a choice between two days a week of in-person classes or an all-remote schedule plus extra intervention on a third day for students who need it. The county's three educator unions resisted, arguing in a statement that remote learning should continue. "Our educators are overwhelmingly not comfortable returning to schools," said Tina Williams, president of Fairfax County Federation of Teachers. "They fear for their lives, the lives of their students and the lives of their families."

"Hundreds of Physicians, Psychologists Call for Ann Arbor Public Schools to Reopen," by Meredith Bruckner For *All About Ann Arbor*

Group urges AAPS to reopen by Gov. Whitmer's March 1 goal date

Meredith Bruckner, Community News Producer, All About Ann Arbor.

Published: February 8, 2021, 1:13 pm

Updated: February 9, 2021, 10:12 am

ANN ARBOR – More than 350 local physicians and psychologists have signed an open letter and petition to the Ann Arbor Board of Education and Ann Arbor Public Schools Superintendent Dr. Jeanice Kerr Swift, urging them to reopen schools for students who choose to learn in-person by Gov. Gretchen Whitmer's recommended deadline of March 1.

Citing data and recommendations from the American Academy of Pediatrics, Centers for Disease Control and Prevention, World Health Organization, Dr. Anthony Fauci and more, the group maintains that it is safe to return to schools for those who choose to do so.

"The scientific, health and psychological consensus is clear: It is possible for children and teachers to safely return to school with proper mitigation measures. Giving parents this choice is the best course of action for our children and community," Kimberly Monroe, a pediatric hospitalist and one of the lead organizers of the letter said in a statement.

"My own experience of seeing the devastation caused by school closure among Ann Arbor's children has been eye-opening and heartbreaking. The letter supports a choice for return to in-person learning to reduce these impacts."

The health professionals criticize AAPS for its decision to remain fully virtual since last March. It is the only school district in Washtenaw County – and one of the remaining districts in the state – to have yet to set a firm start date to return to school buildings.

"My colleagues and I feel so strongly that science and the best interests of children should guide the Ann Arbor Public School's decision that we needed to speak out," Joanna Spencer-Segal, an internist with a subspecialty in endocrinology said in a statement.

"It's time for Ann Arbor to make the rational decision to allow students and families a choice of in-person schooling. There are thousands of successful models around the country that AAPS can follow – what is needed now is leadership that is willing to stand up for science and our children."

AAPS Superintendent Swift announced on Jan. 8 that while preparations are in place to offer a hybrid learning model, the reopening of schools depends on low local infection rates, vaccination progress and regular antigen testing.

While the petition supports "aggressive vaccination of all teachers," the group of medical professionals said: "We agree with Governor Whitmer that school reopening should not wait on vaccination progress."

Ahead of the Jan. 27 Ann Arbor Board of Education meeting, Swift wrote a letter to the school community announcing that all schooling will remain virtual due to a high number of cases in Washtenaw County, a slowed effort to vaccinate teachers due to low vaccine supply and the emergence of the new COVID-19 B.1.1.7 variant in Ann Arbor.

"The health and safety of our staff and students, parents and community remain paramount; this commitment will not change," wrote Swift. "There will not be an announcement of an upcoming transition to open in-school hybrid learning at this current time."

The letter from area medical professionals cites data that shows school closures are having a profound impact on the most vulnerable students.

According to the group, this includes negative impacts on learning and "physical or sexual abuse, substance use, anxiety, depression and suicidal ideation." Students with special needs and their families are particularly underserved and are in urgent need of returning to schools, said the group.

"We understand that in the fall, there were many unknowns, and school districts were left to make an educated guess as to the safety of reopening schools," reads the letter. "That is no longer the case. We are disappointed that the district continues to delay reopening, despite considerable data and government guidance indicating that it is safe to reopen.

"The district has also not surveyed AAPS staff and families or gathered data on their willingness to return to face-to-face instruction at this time. AAPS students deserve better."

This is the third letter that Ann Arbor healthcare providers has sent to AAPS and coincides with efforts by parents to reopen the schools due to negative impacts their children are facing during the closures.

"New Checklist Supports Schools to Reopen and Prepare for COVID-19 Resurgences," World Health Organization News Release

11 December 2020

A new WHO *Checklist to support schools re-opening and preparation for COVID-19 resurgences or similar public health crises,* lists 38 essential actions to be considered by different stakeholders as they work together to agree school reopening plans.

According to data collected by UNESCO, classrooms for nearly 1 in 5 schoolchildren globally – or 320 million – are closed as of 1 December, an increase of nearly 90 million from 232 million on 1 November.

In some places, children have been out of school for 9 months or more. Prolonged school closures in response to the COVID-19 pandemic are presenting an unprecedented challenge to children's education, health and well-being worldwide. The longer a student stays out of school, the higher their risk of dropping out.

As school closure numbers continue to soar and many schools break for holidays, a new WHO checklist aims to support the different levels of decision-making (national, local, and the schools themselves) that are needed in order to reopen schools safely.

The checklist also aims to help improve adherence to existing COVID-19-related public health and social measures designed to protect children under the age of 18 years in educational settings.

"Schools can reopen safely," says Dr Ruediger Krech, WHO Director of Health Promotion. "Decisions to reopen schools should be driven by data and the safety measures in place, but also address the concerns of students, parents, caregivers and teachers. These concerns are best addressed if reopening approaches are co-designed with students, parents, caregivers and teachers."

Developed in accordance with the health-promoting schools principles, the checklist aims to enhance compliance and adherence to the public health measures outlined in the recently updated Considerations for school-related public health measures in the context of COVID19. It focuses on protective measures such as, hand hygiene and respiratory etiquette; physical distancing; use of masks in schools; environmental cleaning and ventilation; and respecting procedures for isolation of all people with symptoms.

Of the 38 essential actions, 21 focus on individual school-level measures to ensure the school returns to equitable and high-quality education while safeguarding the health and well-being of all students. Some of these school-level actions include reorganizing school layouts to space desks or changing school schedules to stagger recesses and breaks, depending on the local context.

There is one set of actions to prepare to reopen schools and another to prepare schools for COVID-19 resurgences.

WHO encourages active engagement with concerned stakeholders – including students, parents and caregivers – in all decisions that impact their lives, families, safety and education. Students can be strong allies in strengthening efforts and reinforcing or amplifying public health messages.

The actions specific to preparing for COVID-19 resurgences aim to support schools to design plans, protocols, and trainings in anticipation of potential resurgences that might result in a reclosure, such as increased transmission and/or prevalence of COVID-19-related illness or hospitalizations following a period of cessation or interruption.

The checklist is not intended to suggest either uniform or all-or-nothing approaches. Users are urged to constantly adapt the checklist and specific actions – or combinations of actions – in accordance with the changing local social, epidemiological, economic and cultural contexts.

The checklist was developed by WHO, in collaboration with UNESCO, the World Food Programme, UNICEF and members from the health-promoting schools expert working group.

"In Their Own Words: Why Health Experts Say Elementary Schools Should Open," by Margot Sanger-Katz and Claire Cain Miller for *The New York Times*

March 2, 2021

With proper safety measures, doctors and scientists said in a survey, the benefits outweigh the risks.

Source: Naima Green/The New York Times.

Students at the Child Center of N.Y. in Corona, Queens, last month.

Scientists and doctors who study infectious disease in children largely agreed, in a recent New York Times survey about school openings, that elementary school students should be able to attend in-person school now. With safety measures like masking and opening windows, the benefits outweigh the risks, the majority of the 175 respondents said.

In some ways, they were more supportive of broad reopening than the Centers for Disease Control and Prevention was in recently published guidelines. But the experts pointed to the large share of schools in the United States and worldwide that have opened with minimal in-school spread while using such precautions.

Below are a representative range of their comments on key topics, including the risks to children of being out of school; the risks to teachers of being in school; whether vaccines are necessary before opening schools; how to achieve distance in crowded classrooms; what kind of ventilation is needed; and whether their own children's school districts got it right.

In addition to their daily work on Covid-19, most of the experts had school-aged children themselves, half of whom were attending in-person school.

They also discussed whether the new variants could change even the best-laid school opening plans. "There will be a lot of unknowns with novel variants," said Pia MacDonald, an infectious disease epidemiologist at RTI International, a research group. "We need to plan to expect them and to develop strategies to manage school with these new threats."

What Do You Wish More People Understood in the Debate over School Reopenings?

Most of the respondents work in academic research, and about a quarter work as health care providers. We asked them what their expertise taught them that they felt others needed to understand. Over all, they said that data suggests that with precautions, particularly masks, the risk of in-school transmission is low for both children and adults.

> "We need to rely on science and not emotions to make these decisions. Expert guidance can get our children back to school safely. Keeping them out of school will result in irreparable harm to their education, particularly for minority children and those from lower socioeconomic backgrounds."
> *Archana Chatterjee,* Dean, Chicago Medical School

"It will never be — and never has been — 100 percent risk-free to return to school. We know a lot more than we did last spring about how to prevent transmission, and vaccination is on the rise. There are significant deleterious effects on children who are learning remotely, and that needs to get equal attention."
Allison Bartlett, Associate Professor of Pediatric Infectious Diseases, University of Chicago Medicine

"I wish that school reopening wasn't subject to such politicization and fear, and that decisions could be made based on data and facts. Data would suggest that children, particularly younger children, can safely go to school, and that neither the children nor the teachers are at particularly higher risk."
Anne Blaschke, Associate Professor of Pediatrics and Pediatric Infectious Diseases, University of Utah

"There is some risk in everything we do. Teachers are not at higher risk than other essential workers."
David Rosen, Assistant Professor of Pediatric Infectious Diseases, Washington University in St. Louis

"Closing schools can benefit adults but mainly hurts children. Surely we should *close* casinos and bars and ban international travel before we close schools."
Joan Robinson, Professor and Director, Division of Pediatric Infectious Diseases, University of Alberta

"I am an infectious diseases physician, respiratory virus researcher, pediatric hospitalist and mother of two. I have taken care of children with Covid-19 and seen its devastating complications. I have engaged in this work while taking care of the academic and social-emotional needs of my children. I had to make the difficult choice to abandon the public school system, of which I was a strong proponent. My children needed to be in school. I needed them to be in school. I knew this could be done safely. I wish the same for everyone else."
Suchitra Rao, Associate Professor, Pediatrics, University of Colorado School of Medicine; Pediatrician, Infectious Disease, Children's Hospital, Colorado

"I wish people trusted the science. I wish people trusted the medical professionals and public health experts who have dedicated their careers to taking on these exact issues of school reopening. The science is clear. Kids are suffering. Families are suffering, trying to navigate as workers, parents, teachers, psychologists and social workers, all simultaneously."
Mitul Kapadia, Associate Clinical Professor, University of California, San Francisco; Director, Pediatric Physiatrist, Benioff Children's Hospital

"This is a debate like climate change: The science and data are clear that we can reopen schools safely and successfully. However, media and the unions have fostered uncertainty and fear. We should all find a way to do right by our children with innovation and creativity, but above all, science."
Kim Newell Green, Pediatrician; Associate Clinical Professor, University of California, San Francisco

"The mental health crisis caused by school closing will be a worse pandemic than Covid."
Uzma Hasan, Division Director Pediatric Infectious Diseases, Saint Barnabas Medical Center

"Education is absolutely essential for child health and development. Young children are not a driving force in community spread of Covid; non-masked, non-distanced adults gathering indoors are."
Brian Campfield, Assistant Professor of Pediatrics, University of Pittsburgh School of Medicine

Do You Think Your Local School District Made the Right Decision About Opening?

About 85 percent of the experts who lived in places where schools were open full time said their district had made the right call. Just one-third of those in places where schools were still closed said that had been the right choice.

"I believe our schools could have opened earlier in a limited fashion with appropriate mitigation efforts, rather than continuing to await vaccines for teachers."
James H. Conway, Professor of Pediatrics, Division of Pediatric Infectious Diseases, University of Wisconsin-Madison

"Initially, yes. They decided to do a hybrid model. But now with clear data that transmission is not as high in schools as in the community, I think they should open for full in-person education."
Sheila Nolan, Chief of Pediatric Infectious Diseases, Maria Fareri Children's Hospital/Westchester Medical Center

"As a mother of two, I have personally observed the huge difference in my kids' mental, physical and social well-being since our schools safely reopened with medical professionals, including me, on the reopening committee. We have identified no in-school transmission, despite strict

protocols and extensive testing. In fact, we saw a dramatic increase in cases among students and staff over the holiday break."
Megan Ranney, Director, Brown-Lifespan Center for Digital Health

"My school district delayed any kind of in-person learning way after many other districts in my state had opened. An overabundance of caution probably exacerbated social isolation and the other deleterious effects on children – many students simply never logged on. We could have reopened relatively safely much earlier than we did."
Gregg Gonsalves, Assistant Professor, Epidemiology of Microbial Diseases, Yale School of Public Health

"Absolutely not. School closure in Spring 2020 was the right decision. We now know schools can open safely. We see it in private and parochial schools all over San Francisco. We see it in public schools all over the state, country and world. Fear is guiding decisions even against the guidance and recommendations from the medical and public health community. Absolutely not!"
Mitul Kapadia, Associate Clinical Professor, University of California, San Francisco; Director, Pediatric Physiatrist, Benioff Children's Hospital

"This issue has been politicized, and the unions have inappropriately focused on fear and misinformation. San Francisco public schools could have been successfully reopened in August had the district, unions and others come together to support children."
Kim Newell Green, Pediatrician; Associate Clinical Professor, University of California, San Francisco

"In Philadelphia, public schools have been fully closed since March 2020 while private schools have been open since September 2020, thus exacerbating existing disparities."
Mayssa Abuali, Pediatrics Attending, Einstein Medical Center Philadelphia

"School reopening decisions have been decentralized and deferred to local school boards that generally do not have expertise in public health and safety, leading to prioritization of perceived safety and comfort over what the data actually show to be safe."
Jayme Congdon, Assistant Professor of Pediatrics, University of California, San Francisco

Other Than the Virus, What Is Your Biggest Concern about Children's Well-Being during Closures?

The group expressed great concern that other aspects of child health and well-being had been neglected during the pandemic, with the potential for dire long-term consequences.

> "Food insecurity. Socialization. Depression. Isolation."
> *Andrew Janowski,* Assistant Professor of Pediatrics at Washington University School of Medicine in St. Louis; Pediatric Infectious Disease Specialist
>
> "While parents can testify to this on a household level, there are many studies now confirming that children are suffering academically, emotionally, socially and physically by not being in school. They've essentially lost a year of peer interactions, and the long-term consequences may not be fully realized for years."
> *Kristin Moffitt,* Infectious Diseases Physician at Boston Children's Hospital; Assistant Professor of Pediatrics, Harvard Medical School
>
> "Child abuse."
> *Sruti Nadimpalli,* Pediatrician; Clinical Assisant Professor, Pediatrics, Infectious Diseases, Stanford University
>
> "They suffer socially when they are not in school. They suffer intellectually learning remotely. It puts pressure on working parents. It denies students access to a school lunch that may be their only nutritious meal all day. There are so many downsides to closing schools that have nothing to do with the virus."
> *Saul Hymes,* Assistant Professor of Clinical Pediatrics, Stony Brook University Renaissance School of Medicine
>
> "The impact is far worse for children of color and those living in poverty, increasing already devastating racial and economic disparities in educational outcomes and potential for future careers and income. It is unconscionable to continue to prioritize the opening of in-person dining and bars over children's education."
> *Rebecca Same,* Pediatrician; Assistant Professor, Washington University School of Medicine in St. Louis

"Worsening educational disparities, which I'd like to see creative solutions to address, like year-round school or mandatory summer school."
Leana Wen, Visiting Professor of Health Policy and Management, George Washington University

"Distance-based learning deprives children of meaningful and developmentally appropriate interactions with peers, adults and the broader community."
Pia MacDonald, Infectious Disease Epidemiologist, RTI International

"Childhood education and development. That should be goal No. 1."
John V. Williams, Professor of Pediatrics, University of Pittsburgh School of Medicine; Chief, Infectious Diseases, UPMC Children's Hospital of Pittsburgh

"I am concerned about children's overall mental and physical health. Not just the impact of being away from peers and less physically active, but the stress of parents losing jobs, families without adequate food and loss of monitoring for signs of abuse."
Taylor Heald-Sargent, Assistant Professor of Pediatrics, Infectious Diseases, Northwestern University; Attending Physician, Infectious Diseases, Lurie Children's Hospital

"We are going to have a lost generation — a set of children who will fall behind educationally, with deficits that could affect their entire life course."
Gregg Gonsalves, Assistant Professor, Epidemiology of Microbial Diseases, Yale School of Public Health

"Not only do children need academic instruction, but schools also provide the socialization, peer support and emotional development that is critical to a child's growth. School closure has led to a wave of mental health problems in children, with disparate numbers in those in minority racial and ethnic groups."
Suchitra Rao, Associate Professor, Pediatrics, University of Colorado School of Medicine; Pediatrician, Infectious Disease, Children's Hospital, Colorado

"My biggest concern is the massive fault lines of equity — socio-economically, racially, developmentally, disability-focused — that have widened even more this past year. I worry how we will be able to give these kids an opportunity to catch up."
Mitul Kapadia, Associate Clinical Professor, University of California, San Francisco; Director, Pediatric Physiatrist, Benioff Children's Hospital

"We are witnessing a significant public health crisis in our children, who are experiencing unprecedented mental illness and physical ailments during this time. This would be mitigated, if not completely alleviated, by in-person schooling."
Kim Newell Green, Pediatrician; Associate Clinical Professor, University of California, San Francisco

"Categorically closing schools has caused more harm to children than Covid has."
Sameer J. Patel, Associate Professor of Pediatrics (Infectious Diseases), Northwestern University; Attending Physician, Lurie Children's Hospital of Chicago

"Obesity, depression, anxiety, regression. Kids going hungry."
Uzma Hasan, Division Director Pediatric Infectious Diseases, Saint Barnabas Medical Center

"Social networks for older children are critically important, and school closures and quarantines may have much greater negative effects in these age groups."
Anthony Flores, Associate Professor, University of Texas Health Science Center at Houston/McGovern Medical School

"Less detection of child abuse and likely increased risk due to worsening child behavior and parent or caregiver frustration with the ongoing situation."
Alison Tribble, Assistant Professor of Pediatrics, Pediatric Infectious Diseases, C.S. Mott Children's Hospital, University of Michigan

"Children are incredibly adaptive. However, there is no question that many groups are being adversely affected in their academics, general nutrition, psychological health."
Sarmistha B. Hauger, Pediatric Infectious Diseases, Dell Children's Medical Center, Austin, Texas

"We are seeing alarming rates of anxiety, depression and suicidal behavior. It is also increasing educational disparities and leaving a generation of learners behind."
Allison Eckard, Professor of Pediatrics, Division Chief of Pediatric Infectious Diseases, Medical University of South Carolina

"Social isolation is damaging the children and making life extremely difficult for parents."
Chad Sanborn, Pediatric Infectious Disease Specialist, Palm Beach Children's Hospital

Should Vaccinations of a Certain Group — Such as Teachers, Parents or Students — Be a Precondition to School Openings?

The experts felt strongly that, while vaccines were important, they shouldn't be required of any population for schools to open as long as other precautions were followed to keep both teachers and students safe. (This, along with much of what the panel said, aligns with new federal government recommendations for opening schools.Like the C.D.C., the panel thought more precautions were necessary before older students could return, because they are likelier to spread the virus.) Many recommended prioritizing teachers for vaccines, along with frontline workers.

"Many studies have demonstrated that transmission in congregate settings for children can be eliminated with masking, distancing and hand washing, even in the absence of vaccines."
Sallie Permar, Chair of Pediatrics and Pediatrician-in-Chief, Weill Cornell Medical School/NewYork Presbyterian

"Teachers should be prioritized for vaccination, but it need not be a precondition for opening. There is growing research that shows that non-pharmacological interventions — masks, plexiglass, distancing, ventilation – are more than sufficient to keep school infection rates quite low."
Saul Hymes, Assistant Professor of Clinical Pediatrics, Stony Brook University Renaissance School of Medicine

"Teachers may have a fear that they are at risk in the classroom. This is not backed up by the data. Teaching is one of the safest essential occupations."
David Rosen, Assistant Professor of Pediatric Infectious Diseases, Washington University in St. Louis

"There are many teachers who are hesitant about being back in school for in-person learning. Vaccines should be offered to them, especially if they are in areas of high community transmission and other mitigation measures may not be in place."
Leana Wen, Visiting Professor of Health Policy and Management, George Washington University

> "While I would not make vaccination a required precondition to reopening schools, I think we should place an extremely high priority on providing immunization for teachers and other school personnel."
> *Gregory Storch,* Professor, Pediatrics, Washington University School of Medicine in St. Louis

> "The evidence is clear that schools can and have opened safely without vaccinations. However, teachers who commit to in-person learning should be prioritized for vaccinations when available."
> *Mitul Kapadia,* Associate Clinical Professor, University of California, San Francisco; Director, Pediatric Physiatrist, Benioff Children's Hospital

> "Teachers and school staff should receive a Covid vaccine. Once a Covid vaccine is available for children, it should be required for school entry."
> *Theresa Barton,* Associate Professor of Pediatrics, University of Texas Health Science Center San Antonio

> "They should be required once groups are eligible, but school should not be delayed if they are not yet eligible, if precautions are in place."
> *Daniel Blatt,* Assistant Professor-Pediatric Infectious Diseases, University of Louisville

How Important Is Ensuring Adequate Ventilation in the School, Such as with Open Windows or Air Filters?

Many of the experts agreed that ventilation in school buildings — along with masks and distancing — was important to minimize the spread of the virus. But they specified that good airflow did not require major renovations or expensive air filters; it could be achieved with open windows, box fans and outdoor classes.

> "Of all interventions, rapid air exchange with good filtration can probably accomplish the most in preventing transmission, in some cases even more than masking."
> *Saul Hymes,* Assistant Professor of Clinical Pediatrics, Stony Brook University Renaissance School of Medicine

> "HEPA filters and other air filtration systems are beneficial, but may not be feasible in many public schools. Air exchange and circulation can be

enhanced in more inexpensive ways with open windows, outdoor classrooms or tents."
Suchitra Rao, Associate Professor, Pediatrics, University of Colorado School of Medicine; Pediatrician, Infectious Disease, Children's Hospital, Colorado

"Keeping doors open is important. New HVAC systems are not important."
Jeanne Noble, Director of Covid Response, University of California, San Francisco, Medical Center Emergency Department; Associate Professor of Emergency Medicine, U.C.S.F.

"This is nice if it is possible, but is less important than masking and distancing."
Matthew Kronman, Associate Professor of Pediatric Infectious Diseases, University of Washington

"Probably this is an underappreciated need. Ventilation can make a major difference in spread of this virus."
Paul Spearman, Director, Division of Infectious Diseases, Cincinnati Children's Hospital

How Important Is It to Divide Students into Small, Fixed Cohorts Who Attend School on Alternating Schedules?

Many school districts have been splitting classes in half and bringing each half back part-time, to minimize exposure to the virus. The experts said such strategies could be helpful in situations where it was impossible to maintain distance, and for contact tracing. But many urged other solutions instead.

"This is only important if appropriate distancing cannot be achieved with larger cohorts."
Saul Hymes, Assistant Professor of Clinical Pediatrics, Stony Brook University Renaissance School of Medicine

"There is no data that these fixed cohorts are any better for public health. What are the kids doing when they are not in school? They are being exposed to others in the community who could have Covid. Instead, we should keep all kids in school every day where we can ensure proper mitigations."
David Rosen, Assistant Professor of Pediatric Infectious Diseases, Washington University in St. Louis

"This depends very much on facilities. Small and fixed is key. Part-time may not be."
Kim Newell Green, Pediatrician; Associate Clinical Professor, University of California, San Francisco

"Other creative solutions, like the use of open-air classrooms, should be considered to allow the full cohort of students to return."
Vandana Madhavan, Clinical Director, Pediatric Infectious Disease, Massachusetts General Hospital

"This is important to reduce the number of kids who need to quarantine if there is an exposure, but not as important as masking and distancing."
Isaac Thomsen, Associate Professor, Pediatric Infectious Diseases, Vanderbilt University Medical Center

How Much Distance Should Schools Require between Students, Assuming They Are Masked?

Even though most respondents said it was not crucial that classes be divided in half, most preferred a standard of six feet of distance between children in classrooms — which can be impossible to achieve with full classes. This is an example of how opening schools requires creativity and weighing various risks: Many said the six-foot standard could be relaxed in situations where ventilation was good, and especially among younger children, who are less likely to spread Covid-19.

"Schools should attempt six feet, and if successful in opening school with mitigation policies in place, can move on to try three feet."
Sahera Dirajlal-Fargo, Assistant Professor, Pediatrics, Case Western Reserve University Medical School; Pediatric Infectious Disease Specialist

"There isn't really a lot of evidence for six feet versus three feet, and the masks are much more important than the distance. Three feet would allow much more capacity in schools."
John V. Williams, Professor of Pediatrics, University of Pittsburgh School of Medicine; Chief, Infectious Diseases, UPMC Children's Hospital of Pittsburgh

"This issue requires an individualized approach. For example, in a building with very good ventilation, there may be a higher tolerance for closer spacing."
Gregory Storch, Professor, Pediatrics, Washington University School of Medicine in St. Louis

"With other precautions in place, for younger kids of elementary age, three feet is sufficient, as the evidence has shown. Older kids still should try to maintain six feet."
Mitul Kapadia, Associate Clinical Professor, University of California, San Francisco; Director, Pediatric Physiatrist, Benioff Children's Hospital

"If the area is properly ventilated, perhaps a smaller distance would be acceptable. Ventilation is the key."
Sarmistha B. Hauger, Pediatric Infectious Diseases, Dell Children's Medical Center, Austin, Texas

How Worried Are You That New Variants Could Disrupt Plans for In-Person School This Spring and Fall?

The emergence of Covid-19 variants around the world has raised fears that the current evidence about school safety may no longer apply. Over all, the experts in our survey said the variants could interfere with school opening plans. But few thought they were sure to cause substantial problems, in part because of the current rollout of effective vaccines.

"There is the potential that variants could cause major problems, almost like we're starting the pandemic over again, but it's too soon to really say that. We might not have much time left to get this pandemic over with – we need widespread vaccine uptake right now before it's too late."
Jessica Ericson, Assistant Professor of Pediatrics Division of Infectious Diseases; Pediatric Infectious Disease Specialist, Penn State Children's Hospital

"I think this is more based on fear from the teaching and general communities. With increased vaccinations that also protect us from these variants, schools should still be able to reopen safely."
Mitul Kapadia, Associate Clinical Professor, University of California, San Francisco; Director, Pediatric Physiatrist, Benioff Children's Hospital

"I am worried about our inability to translate these concerns intelligibly to families and teachers' unions; I am worried that pseudoscientific hysteria over mutant viruses will keep schools closed until the end of 2021."
Shom Dasgupta-Tsinikas, Physician Specialist, L.A. County Department of Public Health

"I worry both about actual spread of virus – and the fear of worsening spread. Both could be quite harmful and impact school reopening."
Alison Tribble, Assistant Professor of Pediatrics, Pediatric Infectious Diseases, C.S. Mott Children's Hospital, University of Michigan

"The new variants have the potential to increase the risk of transmissions that occur at school. We need to stay vigilant to this possibility and continue to monitor the case transmission risk in the classroom."
Allison Eckard, Professor of Pediatrics, Division Chief of Pediatric Infectious Diseases, Medical University of South Carolina

"Op-ed: As Parents and Doctors, We Call on CPS to Open Schools with Safety Measures," by Anna Volerman Beaser, et al. For the *Chicago Tribune*

By Anna Volerman Beaser, Chrisoula Andressakis Chuchro and Preethi Raghupatruni

Jan 26, 2021 at 1:29 PM

Source: Brian Cassella/Chicago Tribune.

About 6,500 CPS students in pre-kindergarten and special education were due to arrive to schools for in-.

We are parents of Chicago Public Schools students and doctors, writing on behalf of a group of CPS parents who are health care professionals across this city. With both our medical experience during the pandemic and our experience as parents, we strongly advocate for schools to reopen for in-person learning with multilayered mitigation strategies to minimize spread of COVID-19.

The pandemic has been devastating. In Chicago, there have been more than 230,000 cases and more than 4,500 deaths. Since the beginning, many of us have been on the front lines caring for individuals with COVID-19. We also have helped our patients and their families manage exposures, symptoms and risks.

At the same time, we have witnessed the irreparable harm of this pandemic on children, harm exacerbated by keeping schools closed. More families are facing hardship, including food insecurity, housing instability and unemployment. The pandemic has negatively affected children's mental health with increased rates of depression, anxiety and suicide. There are less clearly measured impacts on children, such as exposure to domestic violence and abuse as well as dropping out of school to care for siblings or go to work. These effects will plague children well beyond the pandemic, yet a return to school has potential to lessen their impact.

We know not all families are ready to go back to in-person learning right away. That is OK. However, this does not mean that schools are unsafe spaces. Rather, it creates an opportunity to meet children and families where they are and to implement and refine safety protocols before large numbers of students return in person.

Some families and school personnel believe it is unsafe to be in school. We understand and grieve the losses our communities have suffered. We acknowledge the anxiety about the return to in-person school. We are writing to help lessen the fear for children and parents, teachers and staff, as well as their families. We want people from all communities across Chicago to know that with mitigation strategies in place schools are safe.

CPS has put together a reopening plan in alignment with Centers for Disease Control and Prevention and Illinois Department of Public Health guidelines. It includes key elements to prevent COVID-19 transmission, including wearing masks, social distancing, health screening and contact tracing. None of these layers are perfect alone but together these elements strengthen our defense in the spread of COVID-19. They reflect best practices, similar to those taken in hospitals/clinics as well as other schools around the country and the world. Here in Chicago, parochial and private schools, as well as day cares, have reopened and stayed open for months without significant outbreaks and without impacting local COVID-19 rates.

Now let's be frank: There have been cases of COVID-19 among individuals in schools, both in Chicago and nationally. CPS is no different. Given ongoing community transmission, it is inevitable that there will be some COVID-19 cases among students and school personnel. Fortunately, the risk of COVID-19 transmission in schools can be effectively reduced with symptom screening, hand hygiene, universal masking and distancing. The goal is to prevent the spread of COVID-19. In fact, local schools have done this effectively as the overall transmission rate within Chicago Catholic schools was lower than the community rates. Local and national data also show that outbreaks within schools are acquired outside of the school building. Importantly, in-school transmission is rare, with minimal student-to-teacher spread, when safety measures are in place.

The Chicago Teachers Union has made various demands for reopening, some of which do not align with scientific evidence. The 3% positivity rate is problematic, and schools, such as those in New York City, have safely reopened in communities with higher positivity rates. Given the rapidly changing landscape, the CDC has shared dynamic metrics for opening. While we wholeheartedly believe all school personnel should be vaccinated, school reopening should not be delayed while vaccination is in process. Vaccines are not the only strategy to prevent COVID-19, and it is unlikely all CPS personnel will consent to vaccination, just as up to 40% of health care workers have opted not to receive the vaccine to date.

In addition, while we support CTU's efforts to reduce housing insecurity and homelessness, its demand to make reopening contingent on certain support services seems unrealistic, particularly when in-person learning can help alleviate some of those challenges.

While the district and union continue to battle over reopening, our children are caught in the crossfire. Teachers, staff and administrators across the district have been incredible during a complex and difficult time. Rather than debating about whether to reopen and taking votes about returning in-person, it's time to shift focus. The primary efforts right now should include:

- Identifying and addressing specific needs at each school for safe reopening, including equipment and staffing, with creative models to ensure equity across the district.

- Sharing scientific information with school personnel and families about preventing COVID-19 spread to help ensure safety as well as lower fear and anxiety.
- Adopting best practices for classrooms and schools, including using appropriate personal protective equipment and enforcing safety measures. Raising awareness about COVID-19 vaccine among school personnel.
- Educating parents, students and school personnel about their shared responsibility in safely reopening schools, as everyone must maintain COVID-19 safety measures (masks, distancing, hand hygiene) outside of school.
- Disseminating clear protocols for quarantine and testing in case students or school personnel have symptoms, are exposed or test positive.

If school reopening is approached collaboratively, with all stakeholders — including parents — at the table, schools can be opened safely. As a city, we must prioritize our youth and invest in their future. During this challenging time, getting children back in the classroom is the No. 1 way to show this commitment. CPS should disseminate evidence-based information to families, share data transparently and ensure schools have necessary equipment and clear protocols. CTU should use its voice to share evidence-based information about COVID-19 and the vaccine with its members.

Given the hardships children have endured due to the pandemic and remote learning, plus the robust data supporting reopening with safety measures in place, we strongly support efforts to have children back in schools. We want to see our city's children — including our own — learning in person with their teachers and socializing with their peers. We stand prepared to help support the reopening of CPS to in-person learning.

"Op-ed: Kids Are Suffering. Follow the Science and Reopen Schools Now," by Alice Kuo For the *Los Angeles Times*

February 6, 2021

For the last 10 months, most public schools in this state have shut their doors and opted for remote education. Kids have been forced to limit their social interactions to a Zoom square on their computer if they are lucky enough to have a stable internet connection. Playgrounds have been locked and spending time with friends and family isn't allowed.

To a child, this feels like an unbearable punishment that's lasting a lifetime. They feel alone, in the dark. Many lack the coping resources and connection to caring adults to help them make it through this difficult time.

I see it every day. The negative impacts of school closures are compounding and taking a toll on the emotional, physical and mental health of our kids.

The Centers for Disease Control and Prevention recently reported that compared with 2019, the proportion of mental health-related emergency department visits for children aged 5-11 and 12-17 increased approximately 24% and 31%, respectively.

In Northern California, UCSF Benioff Children's Hospital Oakland has seen an alarming 75% increase in the number of children brought in for emergency mental health services that required immediate hospitalization.

Studies also show that the shutdowns are linked to increased risk of obesity among children and adolescents, and higher rates of depression and anxiety during and after isolation ends.

Even worse, researchers from the UCLA Fielding School of Public Health and the University of Washington concluded that declining educational attainment due to school closures may be associated with a decrease in life expectancy in U.S. children.

These data are real, and a generation of kids is suffering.

At the same time, extensive research and data from across the globe show schools can be reopened safely for both students and teachers.

According to an American Academy of Pediatrics study, schools can reopen safely without causing larger community spread if proper mitigation measures such as masking, physical distancing and hand washing are in place. Studies from Europe, the United Kingdom, Norway, Spain and other countries echo these findings that schools have not seen superspreader events.

And yet, public schools in California remain largely closed and millions of children are left behind. It's a tragedy.

This isn't a partisan issue. Our state and local leaders are failing to stand up for our children — their most vulnerable constituency — and do what's right. Listen to the science. Read the data. Follow the facts and reopen public schools now.

Earlier this week the Biden administration's new CDC director, Rochelle Walensky, told reporters in a White House briefing that "There is increasing data to suggest that schools can safely reopen, and that safe reopening does not suggest that teachers need to be vaccinated. Vaccinations of teachers is not a prerequisite for safely reopening schools."

And she's not alone. The nation's top infectious disease expert, Anthony Fauci, along with Gov. Gavin Newsom, have said that we can open schools safely.

So, what are we waiting for?

We can't afford one more mental health breakdown, one more suicide or one more unnoticed child abuse case. Or even one more student falling behind.

The data show that the damage done to children is widespread and will be long-lasting. Our kids are suffering and it's time to reopen public schools, which we can do safely.

"School Isn't Closed for Lack of Money," by Corey A. DeAngelis and Christos A. Makridis For the *Wall Street Journal*

March 9, 2021 6:26 pm ET

Teachers union influence, not government funding or the latest science, drives reopening decisions.

The new Covid-19 relief plan, passed by the Senate over the weekend, includes $123 billion for K-12 public schools, supposedly to help them reopen. That's almost the amount the U.S. dedicated, in real terms, to the Marshall

Plan to rebuild Europe after World War II. And it's on top of the mostly unspent $54 billion federal bailout for public schools from December and the $13 billion allocation from last spring.

Source: Robyn Beck/Agence France-Presse/Getty Images.

A student learns remotely in Culver City, Calif., Sept. 10, 2020.

Major teachers unions have claimed repeatedly that public schools need gobs of cash to reopen in person. American Federation of Teachers chief Randi Weingarten protests that "countless places lack the resources to implement the necessary safety provisions." But our new analysis suggests funding isn't the reason teachers unions are keeping schools shut. In fact, our prior work has found that union influence, rather than scientific concerns about the spread of the virus, is the primary driver behind reopening decisions.

Private schools have either been open for most of the past year or have been fighting to reopen. Kentucky private schools took the fight to the U.S. Supreme Court to return to in-person instruction, and private schools in Ohio and Michigan pursued similar legal action. A private school in Sacramento, Calif., even rebranded itself as daycare to get around the government's arbitrary closures.

Many teachers unions, by contrast, have been fighting to stay at home. The difference is one of incentives. Public schools get their funding regardless of whether they open their doors.

A study published by Brown University's Annenberg Institute found that public schools with more Catholic school competition nearby were more likely to reopen in person in 2020. It also found, and three other studies confirm, that public school districts with stronger teachers unions are substantially less likely to reopen in person.

Our new analysis throws another wrench in the teachers union narrative. We examine data from more than 12,000 school districts nationwide, covering more than 90% of school-age children, and find no evidence to suggest that higher revenue or expenditures per student are associated with a higher probability of reopening schools for in-person learning.

Instead, we find that public school funding is either uncorrelated or even negatively correlated with in-person instruction. Some models suggest that schools that went fully remote were better off financially than their in-person counterparts in the same state.

These results hold across various analytic techniques and specifications that control for district size and a rich set of county-level demographics such as political tendencies, Covid-19 risk, household income, educational attainment, and race and age distributions.

Like other studies, ours didn't find a consistent negative relationship between Covid-19 risk in the community and the probability of reopening in person. School reopening was strongly related, however, to county-level voting patterns in the 2016 election.

The contrast between Florida and California is a prime example. This month's data from Burbio indicates that in Florida, which spends about $10,700 a student each year, nearly all public schools offer full-time in-person instruction. In California, which spends about 38% more per student and has much stronger teachers unions, most public-school students still don't have access to in-person learning options.

Another analysis, from researchers at Georgetown University, found that public school districts that decided to teach remotely generally had financial surpluses. The researchers estimated that Los Angeles public schools, which opted to keep their doors shut, had a more than $500 million funding surplus, or about $1,100 a student, for the 2020-21 school year.

The Congressional Budget Office estimates that only about 5% of the $123 billion in school "relief" funding will be spent this fiscal year, while the rest would be paid out through 2028. If the goal is to reopen schools in person now, and the relief money is urgently needed, then why spend up to 95% of the money after the pandemic? And why did Senate Democrats vote unanimously to block an amendment from Missouri Republican Roy Blunt that would have made relief funding conditional on reopening schools in person if all teachers were vaccinated?

Something doesn't add up. From Virginia to California, some school districts have opened public-school buildings for in-person child-care services but not for in-person learning. A California teachers union leader working to delay school reopening took his own daughter to an in-person private preschool. A Chicago union leader urged teachers to refuse to return to the classroom while vacationing in Puerto Rico.

This suggests that the school reopening debate has always been more about politics and power than safety and the flourishing of the next generation. For that, children have paid the consequences and will continue to pay in the decades ahead. Parents haven't had it easy either.

The basic problem isn't new: Incentives are misaligned. Taxpayers fund schools rather than students. The only way to fix the system is to give families real options by funding students directly and letting them choose where to spend the education dollars. This would force schools to respond to the needs of students, not the other way around.

"CDC Misinterpreted Our Research on Opening Schools. It Should Loosen the Rules Now," by Dr. Tara O. Henderson, et al. For *USA Today*

March 9, 2021

Keeping schools closed or even partially closed, based on what we know now, is harming children.

Dr. Tara O. Henderson, Dr. Monica Gandhi, Dr. Tracy Beth Hoeg, Dr. Daniel Johnson

"The only thing we have to fear is fear itself — nameless, unreasoning, unjustified terror which paralyzes needed efforts to convert retreat into advance." — Franklin Delano Roosevelt

The recent school reopening guidance released by the Centers for Disease Control and Prevention is an example of fears influencing and resulting in misinterpretation of science and harmful policy. In the United States, about half of schools are either in person or a hybrid. President Joe Biden ran on a campaign indicating that science and data would guide his policy. As we approach the anniversary of the first COVID-19 shut down, this approach is needed more than ever, especially when it comes to schools.

Like in so many states, California and Illinois schools are being hamstrung by the CDC guidance. The guidance does not take into account the data we have regarding little disease transmission in schools. Nor, although the guidance cites the work performed across Wisconsin districts performed by our group and published in the Morbidity and Mortality Weekly Report, does it take that data and new analyses from that data set into account.

Keeping schools closed or even partially closed, based on what we know now is unwarranted, is harming children, and has become a human rights issue.

The Facts about COVID and School

Here are the facts:

First, children are not at significant risk of poor outcomes from COVID-19. As of Tuesday, 288 children have died from the disease in the United States, compared with more than 500,000 adults. While the death of any child is devastating, this is similar to the number who dies from influenza each year.

And COVID-19 deaths in children and adolescents are magnitudes smaller than deaths from suicide, some now driven by school closure. Coronavirus in children can cause potentially dangerous complications — e.g., multi-inflammatory syndrome in children (MIS-C) — but this is very rare and in nearly all cases treatable.

Second, viral spread is minimal in schools with appropriate safety precautions, even in communities with a high disease prevalence (significantly higher than the CDC red zone that the CDC suggests middle and high schools be all virtual and elementary schools hybrid).

Dr. Hoeg led a study of 4,876 grade K-12 students and 654 staff members in Wisconsin school districts last fall. COVID-19 test positivity rates reached 41.6% in the community during the study. Notably, despite the majority of ventilation systems not being replaced, with 92% of students wearing masks (no mask wearing during recess), and with variable distancing, there were only seven students (five children grades K-six, and two in grades seven-12) and zero staff who contracted the virus in school.

Similar experiences are published from North Carolina, South Carolina, Chicago and other cities and countries.

Third, no science supports mandating 6 feet of distance with children wearing masks. A 6-foot distance between students creates space constraints for schools to open in entirety. There is data supporting at least 3-foot distancing.

In Dr. Hoeg's study, more than 90% of elementary school children were less than 6 feet apart in the classroom and while eating (~80% of grades seven-12 were 6 feet apart in classroom but less in hallways and while eating). Recently, the CDC cited data of clusters of COVID-19 cases in Georgia. In this study, students sat less than 3 feet apart (not just less than 6 feet), there were small group instruction sessions in which teachers sat next to students, and many did not wear masks or wore them inappropriately.

States are getting the message and passing rules allowing for 3-6 feet of spacing in schools using masking, why hasn't the CDC?

Fourth, despite fearmongering regarding variants in America, we have not seen evidence that variants are spreading through in-person schools. France, Spain, Switzerland and Belgium have demonstrated that K-12 schools can remain fully open safely even as the United Kingdom variant becomes dominant. Moreover, masks and over 3-feet distancing will protect against variants like it does against all forms of the virus. Therefore, at this time, variants are not reasons to keep schools closed.

Science Shows We Can Open Schools

Vaccination is on the way for teachers and staff. Vaccination is expected to work against the variants. There are two major arms of the immune system: antibodies and T-cells. Vaccines work in multiple ways, most transiently by inducing antibodies that usually provide more short-term protection or protection from mild illness. The COVID-19 vaccines also generate strong T-cell immunity directed against the virus. These T-cells work against multiple parts of the virus, including those that are conserved across variants. A recent paper shows the ability of COVID-19 specific T-cells to protect against multiple variants.

School closure comes with long-term individual and societal costs. Many children cannot effectively learn, group, engage, socialize, be active, eat healthy food or get support until schools physically reopen. Children with special needs and from disadvantaged backgrounds are, in general, paying the largest price. As most private and parochial school districts are open for in-person instruction, the divide between the haves and have-nots is exponentially growing. We are observing a significant psychological epidemic in children with depression and anxiety due to the isolation associated with school closure, with suicidal behaviors.

Subsequent lost wages for families translates into poverty, eviction and food insecurity. Recent research assessed there are greater risks to life expectancy with schools closed versus staying open.

We must act for children, and we can do this while keeping staff and teachers safe. This can be accomplished with appropriate distancing (3-6 feet for students in schools), masking, hygiene, cohorting and increasing ventilation when possible — all of which can be achieved readily and immediately in classrooms and schools. Teachers and staff will have increased safety when vaccinated, and the Biden administration has prioritized this group.

The best way to overcome fear is to follow the science, and the science shows we can safely open our schools now for full-time (nonhybrid) learning and keep them open.

Responses from Nusheen Ameenuddin, MD, MPH, MPA, FAAP, US Congress Subcommittee on Consumer Protection and Commerce, Hearing on March 11, 2021, "Kids Online during COVID: Child Safety in an Increasingly Digital Age," Respectfully Submitted April 8, 2021

The Honorable Lisa Blunt Rochester (D-DE)

1. The technology platforms our kids use undermine a child or teen's ability to moderate their use of digital media. And the prominence of

digital media is not going away, even when we return to normal learning environments – about 3 in 4 teachers and parents are likely to support continue online learning at home or in the classroom. But your testimony suggests it's imperative that we foster moderation with digital media.

a. Can you discuss why this is so important and what the practical effects are of a digital environment that fosters compulsion and overuse instead of moderation?

Thank you for these thoughtful questions, Rep. Blunt Rochester. You are correct in stating that the prominence of digital media is not going away. It was an issue before the pandemic and was further exacerbated during the pandemic. Pediatricians know that time spent on recreational media is part of the lives of children and teens, but if not applied in moderation, can displace other activities that are critical to mental, physical, social and emotional health and development for children. With children spending an average of over 7 hours a day on entertainment media, it is very important that this mostly sedentary activity does not displace time spent playing outside, being physically active, learning and completing homework, relaxing or sleeping. Moderation is key so that children do not miss out on these important activities that are vital for healthy development.

Unfortunately, the practical effect of a digital environment that fosters compulsion means that this is an uphill battle for children and their parents with the deck stacked against them due to manipulative design of products that encourage unending media use. Even with the best intentions and parental engagement, it is extraordinarily difficult for children and teenagers, particularly younger children who are not sophisticated enough to recognize persuasive advertising, to resist built-in features of technology that keep them interested and online indefinitely. As a result, children lose sleep and they lose out on opportunities to grow and develop skills offline, while also being constantly tempted to spend more money to continue the game.

b. You distinguished the compulsive behaviors associated with unmoderated digital use from a medical disorder such as substance use disorder. Can you describe some recommendations Congress should consider when developing legislation to address compulsive behaviors that accounts for the distinction with medical disorders you made in your testimony?

The most important thing to remember when considering compulsive behaviors associated with unmoderated digital use is that the products youth are using are specifically designed to feed compulsive behaviors through persuasive and manipulative design that keeps them engaged well after they have completed what they originally logged on to do. For example, if the child wants to watch a 30 minute episode, the auto play feature will automatically load the next episode even after the first one is completed. There will also be suggestions that pop up at the end of a show or game that encourage further time spent on the platform. More time spent on the platform generates more income for the tech company through advertisements and in-app purchases. The data that is collected without the knowledge or permission of the child and family is used to create recommendations that are specifically designed to maintain their interest and engagement with the product they are using. With this understanding, we recommend that Congress strengthen regulations for technology companies to prevent them from collecting information on children, ban data-driven behavioral advertising to young people under 18, make privacy settings default at the highest level, and address auto-play and other design features that encourage overuse.

The Honorable Robert Latta (R-OH)

1. Dr. Ameenuddin: How can we transfer the power back to parents, and by extension, students to make media consumption decisions that benefit their mental health and cognitive development?

Thank you, Rep. Latta. Right now, the entire onus of media decisions rests on parents and children who are facing an unequal battle between moderation and technology that is designed to keep people engaged for as long as possible. This situation has been unsustainable with the amount of time children spend using devices to access media. Even prior to the pandemic, this presented a challenge for families trying to moderate media consumption and make healthy media decisions. We believe that due to manipulative design and platforms that require youth to opt out of design features intended to increase media use, more responsibility needs to be shifted towards platform developers in order to give parents and children the help that they need to have more control over the type and amount of media used.

While the AAP offers free tools including the Family Media Use Plan to aid families in this shared goal, it is simply not enough to overcome multiple persuasive and manipulative features built in to media platforms, which is why we are asking Congress to help protect children through legislation that ends these harmful practices and holds tech companies accountable for the products they create.

Responses to Questions for the Record, Ariel Fox Johnson, Senior Counsel, Global Policy Common Sense Media, Regarding "Kids Online during COVID: Child Safety in an Increasingly Digital Age," March 11, 2021, Hearing before the United States House of Representatives, Committee on Energy and Commerce, Subcommittee on Consumer Protection and Commerce, April 12, 2021

The Honorable Lori Trahan (D-MA)

1. Facebook launched Messenger Kids in 2017, a video messaging and chat app for kids that offers parental controls. After the launch, advocacy groups including Common Sense Media asked Facebook to discontinue the product. Can you explain your concerns with this application?

Messenger Kids has gotten more young children onto Facebook's services– and we have not seen evidence that it has moved anyone who lied to get on Facebook off of it. We are concerned about normalizing social media use for younger children, because of the mental health and privacy harms that have surfaced in older more studied populations.

Social media has different mental effects on different teens – but recent research shows that teens who are depressed tend to use social media more, and that social media can have an outsize influence on them (both negatively and positively).[210] Social media can lead to anxiety and stress among teen girls who compare themselves to others.[211] And teens who are active online can

---

[210] Rideout, V., Fox, S., Peebles, A., & Robb, M. B. (2021). Coping with COVID-19: How young people use digital media to manage their mental health.San Francisco, CA: *Common Sense* and *Hopelab*.

[211] Kleemans M, Daalmans S, Carbaat I, Anschütz D. Picture perfect: the direct effect of manipulated Instagram photos on body image in adolescent girls. *Media Psychology*. 2018;21(1):93–110.

worry a lot about how they are perceived.[212] We do not want children, especially young girls, to begin internalizing these worries even earlier. In addition, the younger kids are when they start sharing data with Facebook, the more data that company will have about them in perpetuity. And Facebook does not have the best track record of protecting user data. Facebook has refused to state in its privacy policy for Messenger Kids that it will never use children's information for targeted advertising. Messenger Kids for a time unwittingly allowed children to chat with unknown adults, exposing kids to strangers.[213] And while initially Facebook strictly limited how parents could find other children for their own children to connect with, the company appears to be continually loosening these limits, and now allows for a setting whereby Facebook will suggest kids to other kids (via name and profile photo). This is a very slippery slope.

2. During the first few months of the COVID-19 pandemic, the number of daily active accounts on Messenger Kids grew over 3-fold. Have organizations like Common Sense Media learned more about how Messenger Kids has impacted children's relationship with social media?

Common Sense does not have research specific to Messenger Kids at this time. And frankly, the amount of research academics and nonprofits are able to do pales in comparison to that done internally by social media companies themselves. We believe that more research about tech and kids is critical and that Congress is in a position to support independent research into the longitudinal effects of technology and media on all types of children and teens. The Children and Media Research Advancement Act (CAMRA)[214] provides an excellent vehicle for doing so, and we thank you for your leadership on this issue.

3. When children turn 13, they can create their own social-media account without their parent's permission. Can you describe the

[212] *Common Sense Media*, Children, Teens, Media, and Body Image, (January 20, 2015).

[213] Russell Brandom, "Facebook Design Flaw Let Thousands of Kids Join Chats with Unauthorized Users," *The Verge* (July 22, 2019).

[214] H.R.2161, To amend the Public Health Service Act to authorize a program on children and the media within the National Institute of Health to study the health and developmental effects of technology on infants, children, and adolescents. (Representative Raskin, 117th Congress).

mental health risks associated with joining a social media platform too young?

Early adolescence (age 10 to 14) is an especially sensitive time for children. It is when mental health symptoms often first emerge *and* many adolescents begin to use social media frequently. We are concerned about children's exposure during these important years to inappropriate content, cyberbullying, inappropriate sharing of personal info, commercialism and exposure to ads, and the uncertainty of what companies may do then or in the future with their data.

Offline risks and changes in behaviors often coincide or overlap with online risks, as young adolescents with existing mental health vulnerabilities report more negative online experiences and patterns of social media use that may be potentially more harmful.[215] Adolescents who are especially sensitive to social evaluation, who may have "low" status offline, and/ or a history of victimization or bullying may have unique vulnerabilities as they transition into online spaces – and this is something to consider when determining whether children are "too young" for social media.[216] (Our research has also shown that for some teens and young adults social media can be a place they turn to for support[217]). Research demonstrates some of the particular susceptibility of those on the younger spectrum: For example, tween girls in particular are vulnerable to the social comparison that happens on social media and prolonged use may contribute to anxiety.[218] Also, a recent study of tweens found that exposure to "kidfluencers" is associated with a desire to emulate such individuals.[219]

---

215 Rideout, V., Fox, S., Peebles, A., & Robb, M. B. (2021). Coping with COVID-19: How young people use digital media to manage their mental health. San Francisco, CA: *Common Sense* and *Hopelab*.

216 Rideout, V., Fox, S., Peebles, A., & Robb, M. B. (2021). Coping with COVID-19: How young people use digital media to manage their mental health. San Francisco, CA: *Common Sense* and *Hopelab*.

217 Rideout, V., Fox, S., Peebles, A., & Robb, M. B. (2021). Coping with COVID-19: How young people use digital media to manage their mental health. San Francisco, CA: *Common Sense* and *Hopelab*.

218 Jean M. Twenge, Gabrielle N. Martin, Gender differences in associations between digital media use and psychological well-being: Evidence from three large datasets, *Journal of Adolescence*, Volume 79, 2020, Pages 91-102, ISSN 0140-1971, https://doi.org/10.1016/j.adolescence.2019.12.018.

219 Eric E Rasmussen, Rachel E. Riggs & Willow S. Sauermilch (2021) Kidfluencer exposure, materialism, and U.S. tweens' purchase of sponsored products, *Journal of Children and Media*, DOI: 10.1080/17482798.2021.1910053.

4. Buzzfeed recently leaked an internal Facebook post which states it is "building a version of Instagram that allows people under the age of 13 to safely use Instagram for the first time." While the product details have not been released, what design features and data protections should Members of Congress inquire about?

We are deeply concerned about attempts to reach even younger children with Instagram, and appreciate the inquiry you sent to Mark Zuckerberg on this issue on April 5, 2021.[220] Design features and data protections Members of Congress should inquire about include:

Privacy:

- What defaults are in place when it comes to privacy with respect to other users and the public – what is shared publicly (e.g., posts, locations, followers), who can contact whom, and how?
- What information does Facebook require, what does Facebook do with this information (e.g., is it added to existing profiles, used for commercial profiling and ad targeting), how long will Facebook keep this information and how can users delete and correct it?
- How will Facebook connect the information on Instagram Kids with its other information collected from its products or across the internet?
- How does Facebook explain its privacy and data practices to parents and to children?

Manipulative Design:

- What design features are in place to help children limit time spent on the app?
- What design features encourage consumption and infinite scrolling?
- Are there design features that encourage children to give up more information than is necessary?

Digital Well-Being

- What kinds of popularity metrics are there (e.g., likes, number of followers)?

---

[220] Press Release. Senator Markey, Rep. Castor, Senator Blumenthal, and Rep. Trahan Press Facebook on Plans to Develop Instagram for Children, (April 5, 2021).

- What types of image alteration are available within the app, and how is this disclosed to impressionable children?
- What types of monitoring and moderation occur?
- How do users report abuse or misuse?
- What can parents see and how is this messaged to children?

Commercialization:

- Is advertising allowed and how is it identified from native content?
- Are influencers allowed on the app, and how are those disclosed to users?
- Are in-app purchases allowed?

The Honorable Lisa Blunt Rochester (D-DE)

1. We often see tech designs subverting parental choice. But you mentioned a troubling, though natural, parent-child relationship – as children grow older, their parents naturally supervise their behavior less.
   a. Regulating manipulative practices that affect teens is crucial – are there any teen patterns of use or design choices that are unique to this age group that we should be aware of?

We know that teens tend to prioritize immediate rewards over long-term risks[221], have difficulties self-regulating[222], and that they are particularly attuned to the opinions of others as they are developing their own sense of self.[223] This indicates teens may be especially susceptible to design features or nudges that advise them to "act now" or indicate they will miss out on opportunities if they do not act immediately. Teens may also have more trouble resisting design features that encourage compulsive use, like points for daily communications with friends, auto-play, and other nudges to sign in again to devices. Further, teens are likely to be acutely aware of measures of

[221] Adriana Galvan et al., Earlier Development of the Accumbens Relative to Orbitofrontal Cortex Might Underlie Risk-Taking Behavior in Adolescents 26 *Journal of Neuroscience* 25 (2006).

[222] Casey, B., & Caudle, K. (2013). The Teenage Brain: Self Control. *Current Directions in Psychological Science*, 22(2), 82–87. https://doi.org/10.1177/0963721413480170.

[223] Zuboff, Shoshana, *The Age of Surveillance Capitalism: The Fight for a Human Future at the New Frontier of Power*, p. 449, (January 15, 2019).

popularity, including design features that attempt to quantify popularity (e.g., "likes" or numbers of followers) or indications that online friends are hanging out without them or ignoring them (seeing a friend read your message or logged on but did not respond).

Congress is in a position where it can act to curb many of these harmful practices, as technology companies appear unwilling to act on their own. We are grateful for your leadership in addressing manipulative design that subverts user choice and compels compulsive usage, and applaud efforts like the DETOUR Act[224] and the KIDS Act[225] which would curb companies' abilities to use harmful manipulative design on teenagers.

[224] H.R. 8975, Deceptive Experiences to Online Users Reduction Act or the DETOUR Act (Representative Lisa Blunt Rochester, 116th Congress).

[225] H.R. 8372, Kids Internet Design and Safety Act or the KIDS Act, (Representative Kathy Castor, 116th Congress).

Chapter 2

Children's Online Privacy and Data Protection in Selected European Countries*

The Law Library of Congress

Comparative Summary

Clare Feikert-Ahalt
Senior Foreign Law Specialist

I. Introduction

This chapter surveys how selected countries from the European Union (EU), namely France, Denmark, Germany, Greece, Portugal, Romania, Spain, Sweden, the United Kingdom (UK) and the laws of the European Union (EU) itself, provide privacy rights for children online.

The EU introduced the General Data Protection Regulation (GDPR) in 2016. As a regulation, the GDPR is directly applicable in all Member States, but most Member States have introduced legislation to ensure consistency and compliance with the GDPR in their domestic laws. The GDPR also contains clauses that permit derogation in certain areas to allow Member States to incorporate elements of the GDPR into their national law "as far as necessary for coherence and making it comprehensible." While the UK is no longer a

* This is an edited, reformatted and augmented version of The Law Library of Congress, Global Legal Research Directorate Report for Congress, Publication No. 2021-020137, dated April 2021.

In: Keeping Our Children Safe Online
Editor: Joyce B. Dew
ISBN: 979-8-88697-659-5

Member State of the EU, it incorporated all EU law as it stood on December 31, 2020, into a new body of domestic law known as "retained EU legislation."

The EU's GDPR regulates the processing of personal data and establishes several principles that those processing personal data must comply with: lawfulness, fairness, transparency; limitation of purpose; data minimization; accuracy and keeping data up to date; storage limitation; and integrity and confidentiality. Article 6 provides the circumstances under which data processing is lawful; the most common circumstance is where consent has been provided by the data subject.

France, Denmark Germany, Greece, Portugal, Romania, Spain, Sweden, and the UK have introduced legislation that serves to implement or codify the GDPR in the country's domestic legislation. Germany amended its Federal Data Protection Act to incorporate elements of the GDPR into its national law. Denmark introduced a new Data Protection Act. Spain enacted the Organic Law on the Protection of Personal Data and Guarantee of Digital Rights (LPDP), which aims to protect the privacy and integrity of the individual and comply with the Spanish Constitution. The UK incorporated the GDPR into its national law through the Data Protection Act 2018. Portugal enacted Law No. 58 of 2019, which applies to the processing of personal data carried out within its territory. Greece enacted Law No. 4626/2019 to implement the GDPR. Romania amended over 1,500 of its laws and regulations to ensure its domestic laws complied with the GDPR. Sweden codified the GDPR in Swedish law through the Law on Additional Provisions to the EU Data Protection Regulation. France's Civil Code provides for a right to privacy, and it has also adopted the Loi Informatique et Libertés (Law on Information Technology and Freedoms), which states information technology "should not infringe upon human identity, human rights, privacy, or public or individual freedoms."

Denmark, Greece, Germany, Spain, and Sweden have constitutional provisions that provide additional protections to data collection and processing to protect an individual's right to privacy. Denmark's Constitution protects the right to privacy. Greece's Constitution protects against the unauthorized collection, processing, and use of personal data, and enshrines a persons' right to participate in the information society as well as the right to protect against unauthorized collection, processing and use of personal data. Germany's Constitution provides individuals with the right to decide which personal data they would like to disclose and how such data will be used through the basic rights to confidentiality and integrity of information technology systems and informational self-determination. Spain's Constitution provides that the use of information technology must guarantee the personal and family privacy of citizens. Sweden's Constitution protects against the unlawful compilation of personal data.

II. Data Protection for Children

The EU's GDPR provides that consent from a parent or legal guardian must be provided to enable companies to process personal data for children under 16 years of age, and this age is used in Germany and Romania. The GDPR allows countries to provide lower ages of consent. France and Greece require the consent of a legal guardian for children under 15 years of age; Spain considers minors to be under 14 years of age; and Denmark, Portugal, Sweden and the UK set this age for consent at 13 years of age. The EU's GDPR requires that information provided to children about the processing of their personal data must be presented in clear and simple terms that are easily understood.

In the UK, the data controller has a duty to verify that the individual providing consent for the child has parental responsibility for the child. Portugal requires permission from a legal guardian to be obtained through a secure means of authentication. Germany and Romania require data controllers to make reasonable efforts to verify that the person with parental authority has given consent on behalf of the child; however, both countries do not specify and have not issued any guidance over how the age of children should be ascertained. A recent court decision from Germany has noted that a barrier requiring the input of a passport or ID number or credit card number with a minimal amount withdrawn from the account is insufficient and recommended instead the use of other, more technical measures, such as biometric information.

Other than requiring the consent of a legal guardian to process data for children, France, Greece, and Spain do not distinguish between children and adults for data protection rights, which are contained in the EU's GDPR and include the right to be forgotten, right of access, right to rectification, right to limit treatment, right of portability, and the right to object to the use of personal data for marketing purposes. Spain places a duty on legal guardians to ensure that children use digital devices and online information in a manner that "guarantee[s] the adequate development of the [child's] personality and preserve[s] their dignity and fundamental rights."

The UK is the only country surveyed to have issued a code specifically designed to protect children online. The UK's code, titled Age Appropriate Design: A Code of Practice for Online Services, was introduced in September 2020 and has a 12 month transition period, entering into force in September 2021. The Code aims to put children's interests first and protect them from within the digital world. It is comprised of 15 design standards, firmly placing responsibility on information society services to "take responsibility for ensuring that the way their services use personal data is appropriate to the child's age, takes account of their best interests, and respects their rights." The Code will be overseen by the UK's Information Commissioner, which has the power to take action, including issuing fines, to ensure compliance. The Code is not new law and sets out 15 cumulative, interlinked standards of design, detailing how the principles, rights and obligations provided for in the UK's Data Protection Act apply to children, defined as anyone under 18 years of age. It is anticipated that most internet society services that are likely to be accessed by children will have to be redesigned to comply with the Code.

In Sweden, government agencies have issued combined guidance for children's rights online. The guidance provides that nudging techniques should not be used except to increase protection for personal data, and that age verification measures should be in place to ensure that a child does not misrepresent their age.

Denmark's Data Protection Authority has not issued guidance specifically relating to children and data protection, but has instead included them under guidance detailing how personal data collected from vulnerable groups should be handled. According to this guidance, an impact assessment must be conducted over how data collected from these groups should be processed.

In Spain, the Law on Services of the Society of Information and Electronic Commerce provides that public administrations must promote voluntary codes of conduct that take into account the protection of minors. No such code has yet been published. Portugal has also not introduced any code on the standards of age appropriate design that applies specifically to children.

With respect to enforcement, the EU's GDPR provides countries with the ability to issue fines of up to 4% of a company's worldwide revenue for violations of the provisions of the GDPR. Sweden has capped fines for certain violations at US$600,000 and US$1.2 million. Depending upon the severity of the infraction, infringements of Spain's data protection laws can be enforced through a series of monetary penalties, warnings, and disciplinary sanctions. The national regulator in Romania has the ability to apply both sanctions and corrective measures to both public authorities and private data operators that violate the provisions of the GDPR, including fines for each day that the data controller fails to comply with measures required from the regulator. In Denmark, the regulator considers violations involving the consent of children to be among the most serious infringements and this is taken into account when determining any fines, which in accordance with the EU's GDPR are required to be "effective, proportionate and dissuasive."

In France, mishandling personal data in or through a computerized system is punishable under the French Penal Code. Infringing the rules of the GDPR or the Loi Informatique et Libertés can result in substantial fines and up to five years in prison.

III. Advertisements on Platforms Designed for Children

The EU, Denmark, Germany, Greece, Portugal, Spain, Sweden, Romania, and the UK have laws that prohibit advertisements to minors on certain age-restricted products, such as alcohol, tobacco, e-cigarettes, and gambling. The age range of minors varies according to the type of product, but the restrictions typically apply to those under 16 or 18 years of age. In the UK, a code that applies to online advertisements provides that no age-restricted advertisements should appear in media directed to a protected age category and that measures should be used in directed advertisements to ensure children in the protected age categories do not receive them. Spain's laws include prohibitions on advertising on vending machines and information society services to children. Germany, Greece, Portugal, and the UK prohibit the advertisements for food and beverages with high fat, salt or sugar content to be aimed at children aged under 16 years. Greek law encourages video-sharing service providers to adopt industry codes of conduct or take other measures to prevent minors from excessive consumption of food and beverages that are not appropriate for them.

Denmark has special rules that apply to advertisements directly targeting children, prohibiting the promotion of violence, and requiring them to be designed with "special consideration to the child or youth's natural credulity and lack of experience and critical sense." Germany, Greece, Portugal, and the UK have similar laws, requiring advertisements directed at children to take into account a child's psychological vulnerability.

The EU's Audiovisual Media Services Directive (AVMSD) aims to protect children, and has been extended to cover video sharing platforms and audiovisual content shown on social media sites. Video sharing platforms are under an obligation to take measures, such as age-verification or parental control systems, to protect minors from advertisements that may impair their physical, mental, or moral development. The EU's AVMSD prohibits audiovisual advertisements from directing minors to purchase goods or services; from encouraging minors to persuade their parents to purchase goods or services; from including elements that endanger a minor's physical or moral integrity or health and safety; or from exploiting the special trust that minors have in their parents, guardians or teachers. Greece and Spain prohibit advertisers on video sharing platforms from such advertisements. Germany, Portugal, Romania, and the UK apply these prohibitions to any form of advertising. Romania and the UK further provide advertisements featuring children should not encourage dangerous or irresponsible practices or utilize unsuitable, offensive, or distressing material.

Greece requires video sharing platforms to take appropriate measures to ensure that children are protected from "programs, user-generated videos and audiovisual commercial communications which may impair their physical, mental or moral development" and requires the most harmful content, such as gratuitous violence and pornography, be subject to strict access control measures. Any personal information collected through age-verification processes or parental control measures may not be used for commercial purposes, such as marketing or behavioral advertising.

In Sweden and Denmark, advertising rules are based on good practice and custom. In Sweden, advertisements targeting children are, in practice, prohibited. This applies to advertisements placed online, including those that are part of a game. Sweden, Denmark, and the UK require online advertisements, including those on blogs and social media, to be clearly marked to indicate they are advertisements. In Sweden, these types of advertisements may never target children.

France does not appear to currently have any specific laws or regulations that govern online advertising targeted at children.

In Greece, Sweden, Romania, and the UK, advertisements are self-regulated and compliance is enforced by domestic bodies. In Denmark, the Consumer Ombudsman is responsible for enforcing these laws.

IV. Future Plans to Protect Children Online

The EU is currently in the process of replacing its ePrivacy Directive with an ePrivacy Regulation. Depending on any new provisions this Regulation has, it may have implications for the protection of children online. The EU Strategy also states that in 2021, the European Commission will propose "legislation to tackle child sexual abuse online effectively including by requiring relevant online services providers to detect known child sexual abuse material and require them to report that material to public authorities." The EU has also published a call for proposals for a pilot project to work on the technical infrastructure required to implement child protection mechanisms, such as age verification and parental consent mechanisms.

Two of the countries surveyed have plans to introduce legislation to protect children online. Spain's LPDP requires the government to draft a bill specifically designed to protect the rights of children online, but this has yet to be submitted to Congress. France is currently working on a detailed legal framework and practical advice to protect the rights of minors online and aims to issue its responses to a public consultation in mid-2021. Germany has recently approved an amendment to the Youth Protection Act, which will enter into force on May 1, 2021, and places a burden on providers of internet services aimed at or used by children to establish "adequate and effective structural preventive measures to enable children and adolescents to participate online in a carefree manner." This requires the use of stringent default settings that protect children from a number of issues, such as hate speech, excessive gaming and online tracking, and obligates providers to develop and implement age verification systems and support mechanisms for young audiences. Domestic providers with less than one million users are exempt from the requirements. Internet services that fail to comply with these obligations may be fined up to $60 million.

Denmark, Greece, Portugal, Sweden, Romania, and the UK do not currently have any future plans to further legislate on children's online privacy issues.

European Union

Jenny Gesley
Foreign Law Specialist

Summary

The data protection legal framework in the European Union (EU) currently consists of two main pillars, the Directive on Privacy and

Electronic Communications (ePrivacy Directive) and the General Data Protection Regulation (GDPR). The GDPR contains specific rules governing consent to data processing when "information society services" are offered directly to children. Controllers of data are obligated to make reasonable efforts to verify that consent was given by the holder of parental responsibility.

In addition, the EU Strategy for a More Effective Fight Against Child Sexual Abuse is meant to ensure that existing EU rules are fully implemented and that possible gaps in the current legal framework are addressed, such as the role of online service providers. In September 2020, the European Commission published a proposal for an interim regulation that would temporarily derogate from certain provisions of the e-Privacy Directive to ensure that providers of online communications services can continue their voluntary practices to detect and report child sexual abuse online and remove child sexual abuse material.

The EU's Audiovisual Media Services Directive (AVMSD) obligates video-sharing platforms to take appropriate measures to protect minors from advertisements which may impair their physical, mental, or moral development and prohibits commercial communications for alcoholic beverages aimed specifically at minors and advertisements that cause physical, mental, or moral detriment to minors.

I. Introduction

The protection of personal data and the respect for private life are fundamental rights in the European Union (EU).[1] Personal data is defined as "any information relating to an identified or identifiable natural person (data subject)."[2] The data protection legal framework in the EU currently consists of two main pillars, the Directive on Privacy and Electronic Communications (ePrivacy Directive)[3] and the General Data Protection Regulation (GDPR).[4] The ePrivacy Directive is slated to be replaced by an ePrivacy Regulation; however, the legislative process is still ongoing as the discussions were stalled for several years. On January 5, 2021, the Portuguese Presidency of the

[1] Charter of Fundamental Rights of the European Union (EU Charter) arts. 7, 8, 2012 O.J. (C 326) 391, https://perma.cc/PAX8-4MYJ; Consolidated Version of the Treaty on the Functioning of the European Union (TFEU) art. 16, para. 1, 2016 O.J. (C 202) 1, https://perma.cc/GPB6-64TG.

[2] General Data Protection Regulation (GDPR), art. 4, point (1), 2016 O.J. (L 119) 1, https://perma.cc/7T85- 89ZQ.

[3] Consolidated Version of the Directive on Privacy and Electronic Communications (ePrivacy Directive), 2002 O.J. (L 201) 37, https://perma.cc/YHA5-EFXV.

[4] GDPR, supra note 2.

Council released a new draft version of the proposed ePrivacy Regulation and a new mandate for negotiations was agreed on in February 2021.[5]

A. General Data Protection Regulation

As a regulation, the GDPR is directly applicable in the EU Member States with generally no domestic implementing legislation needed.[6] Processing of personal data[7] according to the GDPR must comply with the principles of lawfulness, fairness, and transparency; purpose limitation; data minimization; accuracy and keeping data up to date; storage limitation; and integrity and confidentiality.[8] Article 6 of the GDPR sets out the conditions under which data processing is considered lawful, with the most common ground being consent given by the data subject.[9]

B. ePrivacy Directive

The aim of the ePrivacy Directive is to ensure an equivalent level of protection of fundamental rights and freedoms (particularly the right to privacy) with respect to data processing in the electronic communications sector and to ensure the free movement of such data.[10] Directives must be transposed into national law and are binding with regard to their goals; the means are up to the Member States.[11] The ePrivacy Directive covers the processing of personal data by traditional telecom providers in public communications networks in the EU and mandates that Member States protect the confidentiality of the

---

[5] ePrivacy Regulation Proposal, COM(2017) 10 final (Jan. 10, 2017), https://perma.cc/N2WU-H2RL; *Legislative Train Schedule. Proposal for a Regulation on Privacy and Electronic Communication*, European Parliament (last updated Mar. 20, 2021), https://perma.cc/XQX9-SUQS.

[6] TFEU, art. 288, para. 2; GDPR, art. 99. Some provisions nonetheless require for their implementation the adoption of measures of application by the Member States—for example, the appointment of a national regulator and administrative sanctions for a violation of the GDPR. The GDPR also contains "opening clauses" that permit diverging national legislation in certain areas—for example, for the processing of special categories of personal data or in the context of employment.

[7] "Processing" means "any operation or set of operations which is performed on personal data or on sets of personal data, whether or not by automated means, such as collection, recording, organisation, structuring, storage, adaptation or alteration, retrieval, consultation, use, disclosure by transmission, dissemination or otherwise making available, alignment or combination, restriction, erasure or destruction." GDPR, art. 4, point (2).

[8] GDPR, art. 5, para. 1. For a more detailed overview, see Jenny Gesley, *Online Privacy Law: European Union* (Law Library of Congress, Dec. 2017), https://perma.cc/D36L-7EH8.

[9] GDPR, art. 6, para. 1(a), art. 7.

[10] ePrivacy Directive, art. 1, para. 1.

[11] TFEU, art. 288, para. 3.

content of electronic communications through national legislation.[12] The proposed ePrivacy Regulation would extend coverage to internet-based voice and messaging services such as WhatsApp, Facebook Messenger, and Skype.[13]

II. Data Protection for Children

A. General Data Protection Regulation

The GDPR contains specific rules governing consent to data processing when "information society services"[14] are offered directly to children.[15] If the child is younger than 16 years, parental consent is needed for the processing to be lawful. Member States may lower the age under which parental consent is needed to 13, and a number of Member States have set the age at 13, 14, or 15.[16] Controllers of data are obligated to make reasonable efforts to verify that consent was given by the holder of parental responsibility.[17] Because children are regarded as particularly vulnerable, any information or communication to a child has to be easily understandable in clear and plain language.[18]

Furthermore, the right to erasure ("right to be forgotten") under the GDPR provides data subjects with the right to require controllers to erase personal data when certain conditions are met.[19] Among other reasons, erasure may be demanded if the personal information has been collected in relation to the offer of information society services directly to a child and consent was given by the child, but he or she was not fully aware of the risks involved by the processing at the time, and later wants to remove such personal data.[20] This right may be exercised even if the data subject is no longer a child.[21]

---

[12] ePrivacy Directive, arts. 3, 5.

[13] ePrivacy Regulation Proposal, art. 18.

[14] "Information society services" are defined as services normally provided for remuneration, at a distance, by electronic means and at the individual request of a recipient of services. See Single Market Transparency Directive, art. 1(b), 2015 O.J. (L 241) 1, https://perma.cc/SQ86-5563.

[15] GDPR, art. 8, para. 1.

[16] Eight Member States opted for 13 years, six for 14 years, and three for 15 years (as of 2020). See SWD(2020) 115 final, at 17 (June 24, 2020), https://perma.cc/5HSH-3S9B.

[17] GDPR, art. 8, para. 2.

[18] Id. art. 12, para. 1, recital 58.

[19] Id. art. 17.

[20] Id. art. 17, para. 1(f), recital 65.

[21] Id. recital 65.

The GDPR calls upon EU Member States, their supervisory authorities, the European Data Protection Board (EDPB), and the European Commission to encourage the drawing up of Codes of Conduct for the proper application of the GDPR.[22] One example mentioned are Codes of Conduct regarding "information provided to, and the protection of, children, and the manner in which the consent of the holders of parental responsibility over children is to be obtained."[23] National accredited competent bodies perform compliance with the Codes of Conduct.[24] Member States' supervisory authorities must raise public awareness of the risks, rules, and safeguards of data processing, and pay special attention to activities addressed directly to children.[25]

B. EU Strategy for a More Effective Fight against Child Sexual Abuse

In addition, the EU Strategy for a More Effective Fight Against Child Sexual Abuse (EU Strategy) includes eight initiatives to put in place a strong legal framework for the protection of children online and offline.[26] The EU Strategy is meant to ensure that existing EU rules are fully implemented, especially the Directive on Combating Sexual Abuse and Exploitation of Children,[27] and that possible gaps in the current legal framework are addressed, such as the role of online service providers. In particular, the EU Strategy states that the European Commission will propose "legislation to tackle child sexual abuse online effectively including by requiring relevant online services providers to detect known child sexual abuse material and require them to report that material to public authorities" in the second quarter of 2021.[28]

In addition, the EU Strategy points out an unintended consequence that resulted from the application of the European Electronic Communications Code (EECC) on December 21, 2020.[29] The EECC made certain online communication services, like webmail or messaging services, subject to the e-Privacy Directive and its rules on confidentiality of communications and conditions for processing of data by expanding the definition of "electronic

---

[22] Id. art. 40.

[23] Id. art. 40, para. 2(g).

[24] Id. art. 41.

[25] Id. art. 57, para. 1(b).

[26] EU Strategy for a More Effective Fight Against Child Sexual Abuse (EU Strategy), COM(2020) 607 final (July 24, 2020), https://perma.cc/SMV6-QU5X.

[27] Directive 2011/93/EU, 2011 O.J. (L 335) 1, https://perma.cc/EM9S-4N4S.

[28] EU Strategy, supra note 26, at 6.

[29] Id. at 4.

communications services."[30] Unlike the GDPR, the ePrivacy Directive does not contain an explicit legal basis for voluntary processing of content or traffic data for the purpose of detecting child sexual abuse online. As a result, providers of online communications services have to discontinue their voluntary practices to detect and report child sexual abuse online and remove child sexual abuse material unless EU Member States adopt specific national legislative measures according to article 15 of the ePrivacy Directive. Article 15 allows Member States to adopt national legislation that limits the scope of the ePrivacy Directive to prevent, investigate, detect, and prosecute criminal offenses, among other reasons.

In September 2020, the European Commission therefore published a proposal for an interim regulation to ensure that providers of online communications services can continue their voluntary practices.[31] The proposed regulation would temporarily derogate from certain provisions of the e-Privacy Directive and would cease to apply in December 2025 at the latest.[32]

The legislative process is still ongoing.[33] However, the voluntary practices must meet GDPR requirements and concerns have been raised with regard to their compliance.[34]

III. Advertisements on Platforms Designed for Children

One of the goals of the EU's Audiovisual Media Services Directive (AVMSD) is to protect children and consumers.[35] Audiovisual media services include

---

[30] European Electronic Communications Code, art. 2 (4), 2018 O.J. (L 321) 36, https://perma.cc/H3TH-6PUN.

[31] Proposal for a Regulation on a Temporary Derogation from Certain Provisions of Directive 2002/58/EC, COM(2020) 568 final (Sept. 10, 2020), https://perma.cc/Z6AB-JXM6.

[32] The proposal would allow a temporary derogation from art. 5, para. 1, and art. 6 of the ePrivacy Directive.

[33] See Procedure File on 2020/0259 (COD), Use of Technologies by Number-independent Interpersonal Communications Service Providers for the Processing of Personal and Other Data for the Purpose of Combatting Child Sexual Abuse Online (Temporary Derogation from Certain Provisions of Directive 2002/58/EC), Legislative Observatory European Parliament, https://perma.cc/N3GU-3T5C.

[34] *Legislative Train Schedule. Proposal for a Regulation on a Temporary Derogation from Certain Provisions of the ePrivacy Directive for the Purpose of Combating Child Sexual Abuse Online*, European Parliament (last updated Mar. 20, 2021), https://perma.cc/BX7Y-4HCB.

[35] Consolidated Version of Audiovisual Media Services Directive (AVMSD), 2010 O.J. (L 95) 1, https://perma.cc/8T3W-SNG3. Original Version of AVMSD, recital 104, 2010 O.J. (L 95) 1, https://perma.cc/JE3P-PNHL.

both traditional TV broadcasts and on- demand audiovisual media services. Since an amendment of the AVMSD in 2018, it also covers video-sharing platforms and audiovisual content shared on certain social media services.[36] The AVMSD is supplemented by a 1998 Recommendation and 2006 Recommendation on the protection of minors and human dignity with a focus on online services.[37] Furthermore, the European Commission has issued a communication that specifies the definition of "video-sharing platform."[38]

Under the AVMSD, video-sharing platforms must take appropriate measures to protect minors from audiovisual commercial communications that may impair their physical, mental, or moral development, whereby the most harmful content must be subject to the strictest access control measures. Such measures are age-verification systems or parental control systems, among others.[39] Furthermore, EU Member States must encourage the adoption of Codes of Conduct for video-sharing platforms to reduce the exposure of children to audiovisual commercial communications for unhealthy foods and beverages.[40]

The AVMSD prohibits audiovisual commercial communications for alcoholic beverages aimed specifically at minors.[41] Member States should encourage the adoption of Codes of Conduct to limit the exposure of children to alcoholic beverage advertisements.[42] Furthermore, advertisements may also not cause physical, mental, or moral detriment to minors, meaning "they shall not directly exhort minors to buy or hire a product or service by exploiting their inexperience or credulity, directly encourage them to persuade their parents or others to purchase the goods or services being advertised, exploit the special trust minors place in parents, teachers or other persons, or unreasonably show minors in dangerous situations."[43]

It is prohibited to process personal data of minors collected or otherwise generated by media service providers and video-sharing platforms to prevent showing harmful content to minors for commercial purposes, such as direct marketing, profiling and behaviorally targeted advertising.[44]

---

[36] AVMSD, art. 1, paras. 1(a), 1(aa).

[37] Council Recommendation 98/560/EC, 1998 O.J. (L 270) 48, https://perma.cc/K55Y-J2DG; Recommendation 2006/952/EC of the European Parliament and of the Council, 2006 O.J. (L 378) 72, https://perma.cc/X8H9- UJ6X.

[38] Communication from the Commission, 2020 O.J. (C 223) 3, https://perma.cc/X6RZ-9YQW.

[39] AVMSD, art. 28b, paras. 1, 3.

[40] Id. art. 28b, paras. 2, 3.

[41] Id. art. 9, para. 1(e).

[42] Id. art. 9, para. 3.

[43] Id. art. 9, para. 1(g).

[44] Id. art. 6a, para. 2, art. 28b, para. 3 at the end.

IV. Future Plans to Protect Children Online

As mentioned above, the European Commission will propose legislation to tackle child sexual abuse online in the second quarter of 2021.[45]

In addition, the EU has published a call for proposals for a pilot project to "demonstrate an interoperable technical infrastructure dedicated to the implementation of child protection mechanisms (such as age verification) and parental consent mechanisms based on relevant EU legislation such as the AVMSD and GDPR."[46]

Denmark

Elin Hofverberg
Foreign Law Specialist

Summary

The right to privacy is constitutionally protected in Denmark. As Denmark is a member of the European Union, the General Data Protection Regulation applies directly. The age for legal consent to data processing is set at 13 years. The Data Protection Authority has issued guidelines providing that the processing of data pertaining to children always warrants an impact assessment.

Advertisements that target children, both offline and online, must be clearly identifiable as advertisements to the child. Such advertisements may not promote violence. Advertisements of tobacco products, including e-cigarettes, targeting children are specifically prohibited. The Consumer Ombudsman has found that sending products to underaged influencers intending that they promote the products online constitutes hidden advertising and is prohibited.

There are no bills regarding children's privacy protection online pending before parliament.

---

[45] See note 28.

[46] European Commission, Pilot Project. Call for Proposals Document (June 15, 2020), https:// perma.cc/A2MP- R7JL.

I. Introduction

The Danish Constitution protects the right to privacy.[47] Denmark is a member of the European Union (EU), and the General Data Protection Regulation (GDPR) is automatically applicable there; implementing legislation was not required.[48] At the time of entry into force of the GDPR, on May 25, 2018, additional rules regarding data protection were enacted in a new Data Protection Act.[49] Denmark has also implemented the ePrivacy Directive.[50] As specified in the Data Protection Act, the Data Protection Authority oversees compliance with the GDPR and the ePrivacy Directive.[51] Thus, the Data Protection Authority may issue fines for violating the GDPR.[52]

The Authority has issued a guide on the issuance of fines in relation to the GDPR.[53] As prescribed in GDPR article 83.1, the fine must be "effective, proportionate and dissuasive."[54] The Data Protection Authority guide explains how the fines must first be determined using a benchmark value, which is then adjusted to reflect "the circumstances the art of the infringements, and the seriousness and duration."[55] Violations regarding the consent of children are considered among the most serious infringements, and the standard bench value will be set to 20% of the maximum fine before issues such as seriousness and duration are considered,[56] which is DKK 15 million (about US$2.4

---

[47] § 72 Grundloven (LOV nr 169 af 05/06/1953) [*The Constitution (ACT no. 169 of 05/06/1953)*], https://perma.cc/62DH-W7W6.

[48] General Data Protection Regulation (GDPR), 2016 O.J. (L 119) 1, https://perma.cc/JG59-NUXN.

[49] Lov om supplerende bestemmelser til forordning om beskyttelse af fysiske personer i forbindelse med behandling af personoplysninger og om fri udveksling af sådanne oplysninger (Databeskyttelsesloven) [*Act on supplementary provisions to the regulation on the protection of natural persons in connection with the processing of personal data and on the free exchange of such information (Data Protection Act)*] (LOV nr 502 af 23/05/2018), https://perma.cc/83RT-CXKU.

[50] Lov om ændring af lov om elektroniske kommunikationsnet og -tjenester, lov om radiofrekvenser og forskellige andre love [*Act to amend the Electronic Communications Networks and Services Act, the Radio Frequencies Act and various other Acts*] (LOV nr 1833 af 08/12/2020), https://perma.cc/T6E9-5JLN, implementing Directive (EU) 2018/1972 of the European Parliament and of the Council of 11 December 2018 establishing the European Electronic Communications Code, 2018 O.J. (L 321, 36) (Consolidated).

[51] § 2 Databeskyttelsesloven [*The Data Protection Act*].

[52] GDPR art. 83; §§ 39-44 Databeskyttelsesloven [*The Data Protection Act*].

[53] Datatilsynet, *BødevejledningUdmåling af bøder til virksomheder* [*Fine guidance on the assessment of fines for companies*] (Jan. 2021), https://perma.cc/ RK48-U54U.

[54] GDPR art. 83.1.

[55] Datatilsynet, *BødevejledningUdmåling af bøder til virksomheder* [*Fine guidance on the assessment of fines for companies*], supra note 7, at 10.

[56] Id. at 6-7.

million).[57] For smaller organizations, the standard bench value for violations against children may be reduced, but not to less than DKK 60,000 (about US$10,000).[58]

II. Data Protection for Children

As provided for in the GDPR, children may consent to data processing in accordance with member state legislation. Under the Data Protection Act, children in Denmark must be at least 13 years old to consent to the processing of their personal data.[59] If the child is not old enough to consent, a parent may consent on the child's behalf.[60]

The Danish Data Protection Authority has issued guidelines regarding the use of personal data from visitors to individual websites.[61] However, these rules do not specifically address children's rights or protections.[62] The Data Protection Authority's guidance on article 35 of the GDPR also does not specifically mention children, but provides guidance pertaining to "vulnerable groups," which includes children.[63] The guidance says the processing of data pertaining to these groups always warrants an impact assessment.[64]

In 2021, the Data Protection Authority issued serious criticism of a firm called Epic Bookings for violating the GDPR by publishing pictures of children on its website without sufficient consent.[65] The Data Protection Authority noted that although the children aged 14 and up had consented to some uses of the pictures, the company used them for other purposes for which the children did not specifically and voluntarily provide consent.[66] In addition,

---

[57] Id. at 8.

[58] Id.

[59] § 6 stk 2 Databeskyttelsesloven [*The Data Protection Act*].

[60] Id. § 6 stk 3.

[61] Dattilsynet, *Vejledning - Behandling af personoplysninger om hjemmesidebesøgende* [*Guidance - Processing of personal data about website visitors*] (Feb. 2020), https://perma.cc/22L4-N3R9.

[62] Id.

[63] Dattilsynet, Datatilsynets liste over de typer af behandlingsaktiviteter, der er underlagt kravet om en konsekvensanalyse vedrørende databeskyttelse jf. databeskyttelsesforordningens artikel 35, stk. 4 [*The Data Protection Authority's list of the types of processing activities that are subject to the requirement for a data protection impact analysis cf. the data protection regulation, article 35, subsection 4*], https://perma.cc/2GYK-VCQW.

[64] Id.

[65] Datatilsynet, Epic Booking's processing of personal data (Mar. 1, 2021), https://perma.cc/5ZQM- ZMDD.

[66] Id.

the Data Protection Authority seriously criticized Epic Bookings for not providing a time limit for how long the pictures would be used, a clear violation of the GDPR.[67]

III. Advertisements on Platforms Designed for Children

Recital 38 of the GDPR provides that the use of personal data of children for marketing purposes requires additional safeguards.[68] Marketing rules in Denmark are based on good practice and custom.[69] Advertisements that directly target children "must be designed with special consideration to the child or youth's natural credulity and lack of experience and critical sense, which means that they are easier to influence and impress."[70] Specifically, all advertisements to minors of tobacco products, including non-tobacco e-cigarettes, are prohibited.[71] Similarly, advertisements targeting children may not promote violence.[72] Per the Consumer Ombudsman's guidance, advertisements online must be identifiable as advertisements, and designed with the youngest audience in mind.[73] In 2020, the Consumer Ombudsman declared that it violated Danish law for a cosmetic company to send products to a 13-year-old social media influencer so that the child would post about the products on the child's social media accounts, as it constituted hidden advertising.[74]

---

67 Id.

68 GDPR recital 38.

69 Lov om markedsføring [*Marketing Act*] (LOV nr 426 af 03/05/2017), https://perma.cc/XK6B-7A2A.

70 Id. § 3.

71 § 11 Lov om markedsføring [*Marketing Act*]; § 2 Bekendtgørelse om forbud mod reklame, synlig anbringelse og fremvisning m.v. af elektroniske cigaretter og genopfyldningsbeholdere med og uden nikotin [*Proclamation on prohibition of advertising, visible placement and display, etc. of electronic cigarettes and refill containers with and without nicotine*] (BEK nr 65 af 15/01/2021), https://perma.cc/CL4Y-T47P.

72 § 11 Lov om markedsføring [*Marketing Act*].

73 Forbrugerombudsmanden, *Gode råd til influenter om skjult reklame* [*Good advice for influencers about hidden advertising*] 6, https://perma.cc/W27N-VBPN; Forbrugerombudsmanden, *Markedsføring over for børn og unge* [*Marketing to children and young people*], https://perma.cc/ 6NSM-CCQ8.

74 Forbrugerombudsmanden, *Ulovligt at bruge barns SoMe-profil til markedsføring* [*Illegal to use child's SoMe profile for marketing*] (June 18, 2020), https://perma.cc/S6PH-D2A5.

IV. Future Plans to Protect Children Online

There are currently no pending proposals in the Danish Parliament to increase the protection of children's privacy protections online.

France

Nicolas Boring
Foreign Law Specialist

Summary

Data protection in France is principally governed by the European Union General Data Protection Regulation and by the domestic Law on Information Technology and Freedoms (*Loi Informatique et Libertés*). Personal data must be processed lawfully and fairly, and must not be used in a manner that is incompatible with the explicit and legitimate purposes for which it was collected. Mishandling personal data in or through a computerized system is punishable under the French Penal Code. Data protection rules are enforced by an independent agency called the National Commission on Information Technology and Freedoms (*Commission nationale de l'informatique et des libertés*), referred to by its French acronym, CNIL. The CNIL also provides advisory opinions to the government and informs the public on data privacy issues.

The Law on Information Technology and Freedoms provides that minors may consent to the processing of their personal data only if they are 15 years old or older. Younger children may consent to the processing of their personal data only if their parents or legal guardians also consent. The processor must write the information and communications regarding the processing of the child's data in terms that are clear, simple, and easily understood by a child. Currently, there do not appear to be any other specific rules regarding data protection for children, but the CNIL is in the process of drafting a more detailed legal framework as well as practical advice to better protect the rights of minors online.

I. Introduction

The French Civil Code provides that everyone has a right to privacy.[75] However, data protection in France is primarily governed by the European

[75] Code civil art. 9, https://perma.cc/UPQ8-MH6K.

Union (EU) General Data Protection Regulation (GDPR), and by the domestic Law on Information Technology and Freedoms (Loi Informatique et Libertés).[76] The latter was originally adopted in 1978, but has been amended many times since. For example, it was amended in 2004 to incorporate provisions from the EU's ePrivacy Directive,[77] and it was amended in 2018 to be consistent with the GDPR and EU Directive 2016/680 on the processing of personal data.[78]

The Law on Information Technology and Freedoms states that information technology "should not infringe upon human identity, human rights, privacy, or public or individual freedoms."[79] Personal data must be processed lawfully and fairly, and data that falls under the GDPR should be processed in a manner that is also transparent for the data subject.[80] Data may not be used in a manner that is incompatible with the explicit and legitimate purposes for which it was collected.[81]

Mishandling personal data in or through a computerized system, whether intentionally or by negligence, is punishable under the French Penal Code.[82] Someone who violates the rules set out in the GDPR or the Law on

---

[76] Loi n° 78-17 du 6 janvier 1978 relative à l'informatique, aux fichiers et aux libertés (as amended) (Loi Informatique et Libertés) [*Law n° 78-17 of January 6, 1978 relating to data processing, files and freedoms (as amended) (Data Protection Act)*], https://perma.cc/ZW2C-R6QN.

[77] Loi n° 2004-801 du 6 août 2004 relative à la protection des personnes physiques à l'égard des traitements de données à caractère personnel et modifiant la loi n° 78-17 du 6 janvier 1978 relative à l'informatique, aux fichiers et aux libertés [*Law No. 2004-801 of August 6, 2004 relating to the protection of individuals with regard to the processing of personal data and amending Law No. 78-17 of January 6, 1978 relating to data processing, files and to freedoms*] (Aug. 6, 2004), https://perma.cc/FPZ7-DBA6.

[78] Loi n° 2018-493 du 20 juin 2018 relative à la protection des données personnelles [*Law n° 2018-493 of June 20, 2018 relating to the protection of personal data*] (June 20, 2018), https://perma.cc/2Y25-G7ZW; Ordonnance n° 2018-1125 du 12 décembre 2018 prise en application de l'article 32 de la loi n° 2018-493 du 20 juin 2018 relative à la protection des données personnelles et portant modification de la loi n° 78-17 du 6 janvier 1978 relative à l'informatique, aux fichiers et aux libertés et diverses dispositions concernant la protection des données à caractère personnel [*Ordinance No. 2018-1125 of December 12, 2018 taken pursuant to Article 32 of Law No. 2018-493 of June 20, 2018 relating to the protection of personal data and amending Law No. 78-17 of 6 January 1978 relating to data processing, files and freedoms and various provisions concerning the protection of personal data*] (Dec. 12, 2018), https://perma.cc/7U58-XB42.

[79] Loi Informatique et Libertés [*Data Protection Act*] art. 1

[80] Id. art. 4.

[81] Id.

[82] Penal Code arts. 226-16 to 226-24, https://perma.cc/UCG5-CHKV.

Information Technology and Freedoms can be sentenced to a fine of up to 300,000 Euros (about US$361,400) and up to five years in jail.[83]

The Law on Information Technology and Freedoms set up the National Commission on Information Technology and Freedoms (Commission nationale de l'informatique et des libertés, CNIL), an independent agency tasked with enforcing regulatory or legislative texts regarding the use of personal data.[84] The CNIL also provides advisory opinions to the government and informs the public about data privacy issues.[85]

II. Data Protection for Children

A. Consent Requirements

In applying article 8 of the GDRP, the Law on Information Technology and Freedoms provides that minors may consent to the processing of their personal data only if they are 15 years old or older.[86] Children under the age of 15 may only consent to the processing of their personal data if their parents or legal guardians also consent to it.[87] The processor must write the information and communications regarding the processing of the child's data in terms that are clear, simple, and easily understood by a child.[88] Similarly, under article 13 of the GDPR, the information to be provided where personal data are collected from a child aged 15 or younger must be clear and easily understood.[89]

B. Data Protection

Beyond these provisions, currently there do not appear to be any specific rules regarding data protection for children. Rather, the same rules that apply to adults would apply to children.

As a general rule, data may not be retained in a manner that allows the data subjects' identification beyond the time necessary to fulfill the purpose for which it was collected.[90] The main exception is that data, even personal information, may be retained for archival purposes, for historical or scientific research, or for statistical purposes. Even within this exception, however, the

---

[83] Id.
[84] Loi Informatique et Libertés [*Data Protection Act*] art. 8.
[85] Id.
[86] Loi Informatique et Libertés [*Data Protection Act*] art. 45.
[87] Id.
[88] Id.
[89] Id. art. 48.
[90] Id. art. 4.

data must be kept in a manner that complies with the GDPR, and it may not be used to make decisions concerning the data subjects.[91] Additionally, data must be kept in a manner that adequately protects personal information from being lost, destroyed, damaged, or used in an illegal or unauthorized manner.[92]

Data that is found to be inaccurate with regard to the purpose for which it was collected should be immediately corrected or erased.[93] Additionally, data subjects have a right to demand that their personal data be erased.[94] Furthermore, the CNIL has the authority to demand that data be rectified or erased if it finds that the GDPR or other legal requirements have not been respected.[95]

C. Official Guidance

There does not yet appear to be official guidance on the specifics of implementing the digital privacy rights of children. However, the CNIL is currently in the process of elaborating a more detailed legal framework as well as practical advice to better protect the rights of minors online.[96] The CNIL organized a public consultation on this topic from April to June 2020, and it is expected to issue its conclusions by the middle of 2021.[97]

D. Advertisements on Platforms Designed for Children

While television advertisements aimed at children are regulated,[98] there does not appear to be any specific legislation or regulation regarding online advertising designed for children.

---

[91] Id.

[92] Id.

[93] Id.

[94] Id. arts. 51, 106.

[95] Id. art. 20.

[96] CNIL, *Droits Numériques des Mineurs: La CNIL Publie les Résultats du Sondage et de la Consultation Publique* [*Digital Rights of Minors: The CNIL Publishes the Results of the Survey and the Public Consultation*] (Jan. 11, 2021), https://perma.cc/AKU7-F6CM.

[97] Id.

[98] Décret n°87-239 du 6 avril 1987 pris pour l'application de l'article 27-I de la loi n° 86-1067 du 30 septembre 1986 relative à la liberté de communication et fixant pour les services privés de radiodiffusion sonore diffusés par voie hertzienne terrestre ou par satellite le régime applicable à la publicité et au parrainage [*Decree No. 87-239 of April 6, 1987 taken for the application of Article 27-I of Law No. 86-1067 of September 30, 1986 relating to freedom of communication and fixing for private sound broadcasting services broadcast terrestrially or by satellite the regime applicable to advertising and sponsorship*] (as amended), https://perma.cc/KE9V-B3DA.

III. Future Plans to Protect Children Online

As mentioned above, the CNIL is currently engaged in a project to provide a more detailed legal framework and guidance regarding children's online privacy. Apart from this project, there currently do not appear to be any other plans on this issue in France.

Germany

Jenny Gesley
Foreign Law Specialist

Summary

The right to informational self-determination and the right to confidentiality and integrity of information technology systems are constitutionally guaranteed in Germany. The data protection legal framework consists of the directly applicable European Union General Data Protection Regulation (GDPR) and the German Federal Data Protection Act, which supplements the GDPR. The GDPR contains special rules for consent to data processing when "information society services" are offered directly to children.

German law prohibits advertisements that directly exhort children to purchase the goods or services marketed or to persuade their parents or other adults to do so, as well as those that exploit their young age or inexperience. In general, advertisements may not harm the physical or mental development of children. Advertisements for alcoholic beverages aimed specifically at minors are prohibited. Service providers must take appropriate measures to reduce the exposure of children to advertisements for unhealthy foods.

An amendment to the Youth Protection Act, which will enter into force on May 1, 2021, will obligate providers of internet services that are aimed at or used by children to set up preventive measures to enable children and adolescents to "participate online in a carefree manner." Such measures are age-appropriate default settings, age-verification systems, and support and complaint mechanisms suitable for a young target audience.

I. Introduction

The right to informational self-determination is constitutionally guaranteed in Germany.[99] Informational self-determination guarantees the right of individuals to decide which personal data they would like to disclose and how such data will be used.[100] In addition, with regard to online protection of personal data, the German Basic Law (Constitution) protects the basic right to confidentiality and integrity of information technology systems ("IT basic right").[101] It ensures "that the data which are created, processed and stored by the information technology system that is covered by its scope of protection remain confidential."[102] Furthermore, article 5, paragraph 2 of the Basic Law requires that legal provisions for the protection of young people be enacted.

The European Union (EU) General Data Protection Regulation (GDPR)[103] is directly applicable in Germany with, generally, no domestic implementing legislation needed.[104] However, the GDPR also contains "opening clauses" that permit derogations for national legislation in certain areas,[105] and it specifically allows EU Member States to incorporate elements of the GDPR into their national law as far as necessary for coherence and comprehensibility.[106] Germany therefore published the amendment of its Federal Data Protection Act (Bundesdatenschutzgesetz, BDSG) in July

---

[99] Grundgesetz für die Bundesrepublik Deutschland [Grundgesetz] [*Basic Law for the Federal Republic of Germany [Basic Law]*] [GG], May 23, 1949, *Bundesgesetzblatt* [*Federal Law Gazette*] [BGBl.] I at 1, as amended, art. 2, para. 1 in conjunction with art. 1, para. 1, https://perma.cc/4JK9-TYXG (original), https://perma.cc/6FCR-JZZP (English translation, updated through Mar. 28, 2019).

[100] Bundesverfassungsgericht [*Federal Constitutional Court*] [BVerfG], Dec. 15, 1983, Entscheidungen des Bundesverfassungsgerichts [*Decisions of the Federal Constitutional Court*] [BVerfGE] 65, 1, para. 147, https://perma.cc/3T5W-GA7A (original), https://perma.cc/B52M-CTSU (English abstract).

[101] GG, art. 2, para. 1 in conjunction with art. 1, para. 1; BVerfG, BVerfGE 120, 274, paras. 166, 201, https://perma.cc/42A4-THNJ (original), https://perma.cc/3U9C-LUDH (English translation).

[102] BVerfG, para. 204.

[103] General Data Protection Regulation (GDPR), 2016 O.J. (L 119) 1, https://perma.cc/7T85-89ZQ.

[104] Consolidated Version of the Treaty on the Functioning of the European Union (TFEU) art. 288, para. 2, 2016 O.J. (C 202) 1, https://perma.cc/GPB6-64TG. Some provisions nonetheless require for their implementation the adoption of application measures by the Member States—for example, the appointment of a national regulator and administrative sanctions for a violation of the GDPR.

[105] GDPR, recitals 10, 19, 52; art. 9, para. 4; art. 88.

[106] Id. recital 8.

2017.[107] It entered into force at the same time as the GDPR started applying in Germany, on May 25, 2018. The ePrivacy Directive of the EU, which aims to ensure an equivalent level of protection of fundamental rights and freedoms (particularly the right to privacy) with respect to data processing in the electronic communications sector, was transposed in the German Telecommunications Act (Telekommunikationsgesetz, TKG).[108]

The new German Federal Data Protection Act focuses on the areas for which the GDPR contains "opening clauses" allowing Member States to initiate more restrictive provisions, as the other areas are governed by the provisions of the GDPR itself.[109] It also has a wider scope than the GDPR; it applies to the processing of personal data by federal and state public authorities and bodies as well as by private bodies.[110]

The processing of personal data,[111] according to the GDPR, must comply with the principles of lawfulness, fairness, and transparency; purpose limitation; data minimization; accuracy and keeping data up to date; storage limitation; and integrity and confidentiality.[112] Article 6 of the GDPR sets out the conditions under which data processing is considered lawful, with the most common ground being consent given by the data subject.[113]

---

107 Bundesdatenschutzgesetz [*Federal Data Protection Act*] [BDSG], June 30, 2017, BGBl. I at 2097, https://perma.cc/74U7-UR8M (original), https://perma.cc/E827-452T (English translation).

108 Telekommunikationsgesetz [*Telecommunications Act*] [TKG], June 22, 2004, BGBl. I at 1190, as amended, https://perma.cc/3JUK- 3BXK. For a detailed overview of the ePrivacy Directive, see the EU survey in this report.

109 The new German Federal Data Protection Act took advantage of the opening clauses related to collection and use of employee data (§ 26), special categories of data (sensitive data) (§ 22), processing of data for research purposes and statistical purposes (§ 27), processing for archiving purposes in the public interest (§ 28), processing for other purposes than the ones for which the personal data have been originally collected (§ 24), restrictions on the investigative power of data protection authorities in cases of professional secrecy (§ 29, para. 3), appointment of data protection officers (§ 38), consumer loans (§ 30), credit reports and scoring (§ 31), sanctions (§§ 41-43), the right of data protection authorities to file an action against a decision of the EU Commission (§ 21), video surveillance (§ 4), and restrictions on some of the data subjects' rights (§§ 32–37).

110 BDSG, § 1; GDPR, recital 19.

111 "Processing" means "any operation or set of operations which is performed on personal data or on sets of personal data, whether or not by automated means, such as collection, recording, organisation, structuring, storage, adaptation or alteration, retrieval, consultation, use, disclosure by transmission, dissemination or otherwise making available, alignment or combination, restriction, erasure or destruction." GDPR, art. 4, point (2).

112 Id. art. 5, para. 1. For a more detailed overview, see Jenny Gesley, *Online Privacy Law: European Union*, Law Library of Congress (Dec. 2017), https://perma.cc/D36L-7EH8.

113 GDPR art. 6, para. 1(a), art. 7.

II. Data Protection for Children

Among other things, the German Federal Data Commissioner is tasked with promoting public awareness and understanding of the risks, rules, safeguards, and rights in relation to the processing of personal data, and must pay special attention to measures addressed specifically to children.[114]

The GDPR contains specific rules governing consent to data processing when "information society services"[115] are offered directly to children.[116] If the child is younger than 16 years, parental consent is needed for the processing to be lawful. Germany did not make use of the option to lower the age of consent. Controllers of data are obligated to make reasonable efforts to verify that consent was given by the holder of parental responsibility.[117] It appears that the German data protection authorities have published no official guidance on how this GDPR requirement should be implemented.

However, a case decided by the German Federal Court of Justice (Bundesgerichtshof, BGH) in 2007 that involved age-verification systems for accessing pornographic websites might provide some insight.[118] The court held that requiring users to enter their national ID or passport number and the zip code of the city where the identity document was issued was insufficient. Entering a name, address, and credit card or bank account information and paying a minor amount in addition was equally insufficient. In the opinion of the Federal Court of Justice, these were not effective entry barriers, because children could easily get ahold of the ID or passport number of an adult and oftentimes had their own bank accounts.[119] As alternative age-verification systems, the court listed ones recommended by the Commission for Youth Media Protection (Kommission für Jugendmedienschutz (KJM),[120] in

---

[114] BDSG § 14, para. 1, no. 2.

[115] "Information society services" are defined as services normally provided for remuneration, at a distance, by electronic means and at the individual request of a recipient of services. See Single Market Transparency Directive, art. 1(b), 2015 O.J. (L 241) 1, https://perma.cc/SQ86-5563.

[116] GDPR art. 8, para. 1.

[117] Id. art. 8, para. 2.

[118] BGH, Oct. 18, 2007, docket no. I ZR 102/05, https://perma.cc/EU64-YUQ4.

[119] Id. para. 30.

[120] Staatsvertrag über den Schutz der Menschenwürde und den Jugendschutz in Rundfunk und Telemedien [Jugendmedienschutz-Staatsvertrag] [*State Treaty on the Protection of Human Dignity and the Protection of Young Persons in Broadcasting and Telemedia [State Treaty on the Protection of Young Persons in the Media]*] [JMStV], Sept. 10-27, 2002, Gesetz-und Verordnungsblatt Bayern [*Law and Ordinance Gazette of Bavaria*] [GVBl. Bayern] 2003 at 147, as amended, § 14, https://perma.cc/86PK-MCM4.

particular a one-time in-person identification, such as PostIdent;[121] an identification with a USB stick and a pin code every time the user logs on; or identification by technical means, such as a webcam or recognition of biometrical features.[122]

III. Advertisements on Platforms Designed for Children

German law provides special rules for advertisements geared towards children. These rules apply on all types of platforms, not just those designed for children. The German Act Against Unfair Competition (Gesetz gegen den unlauteren Wettbewerb, UWG) prohibits unfair commercial practices.[123] Among other things, commercial practices that are always considered unfair and therefore illegal are advertisements that directly exhort children to purchase the goods or services marketed or to persuade their parents or other adults to do so.[124] In addition, there is a prohibition on exploiting their young age or inexperience to cause them to make a transactional decision that they would not have made otherwise (aggressive commercial practices).[125]

The Interstate Treaty on the Protection of Minors in the Media (Jugendmedienschutz-Staatsvertrag, JMStV) contains additional requirements for advertisements geared towards children and adolescents.[126] It implements the requirements of the EU's Audiovisual Media Services Directive (AVMSD).[127] Video-sharing platforms must take appropriate measures to protect minors from offers that may impair their development, such as using age-verification systems or parental control systems.[128]

---

[121] PostIdent is a method of secure personal identification of a person by an employee of the German post office.

[122] BGH, paras. 34, 35. For a list of positively evaluated age-verification systems, see *Technische Mittel*, KJM, https://perma.cc/9Z2N-UBU8. See also Press Release, KJM, *KJM bewertet sechs weitere Altersverifikationssysteme positiv* [*KJM rated six other age verification systems positively*] (Apr. 13, 2021), https://perma.cc/6VPX-7J5D.

[123] Gesetz gegen den unlauteren Wettbewerb [*Unfair Competition Law*] [UWG], Mar. 3, 2010, BGBl. I at 254, as amended, § 3, para. 1, https://perma.cc/EM59-LPC3 (original), https://perma.cc/PBU6-3JRG (English translation, updated through Apr. 18, 2019).

[124] Id. § 3, para. 1 in conjunction with annex, no. 28.

[125] Id. § 4a, para. 1, sentence 1, sentence 2, no. 3 in conjunction with § 4a, para. 2, sentence 1, no. 3, sentence 2.

[126] JMStV, supra note 22.

[127] Consolidated Version of Audiovisual Media Services Directive (AVMSD), 2010 O.J. (L 95) 1, https://perma.cc/8T3W-SNG3.

[128] JMStV § 5a.

In general, advertisements may not physically or mentally harm children and may not:

1. directly exhort minors to buy or hire a product or service by exploiting their inexperience or credulity,
2. directly encourage them to persuade their parents or others to purchase the goods or services being advertised,
3. exploit the special trust minors place in parents, teachers or other persons, or
4. unreasonably show minors in dangerous situations.[129]

Furthermore, advertisements for alcoholic beverages aimed specifically at minors are prohibited, as are those that appeal to minors or show them consuming alcohol.[130] Service providers must take appropriate measures to reduce the exposure of children to advertisements accompanying or included in children's programs, for foods containing nutrients and substances with a nutritional or physiological effect, in particular fat, trans-fatty acids, salt, sodium, and sugars, of which excessive intakes in the overall diet are not recommended.[131]

IV. Future Plans to Protect Children Online

On March 26, 2021, the German Bundesrat, the legislative body through which the German states participate in the legislative process, approved an amendment to the Youth Protection Act that the German Bundestag (parliament) passed on March 5, 2021.[132] The amendment will enter into force on May 1, 2021.[133]

---

[129] Id. § 6, para. 2.

[130] Id. § 6, para. 5.

[131] Id. § 6, para. 7.

[132] Deutscher Bundesrat: Drucksachen und Protokolle [*German Bundesrat: Printed matter and minutes*] [BR-Drs.] 195/21 (Beschluss), https://perma.cc/R46T- HK3Z; Jugendschutzgesetz [*Youth Protection Act*] [JuSchG], July 23, 2002, BGBl. I at 2730, as amended, https://perma.cc/3GHJ-K82X; Zweites Gesetz zur Änderung des Jugendschutzgesetzes [*Second law amending the Youth Protection Act*], Apr. 9, 2021, BGBl. I at 742, https://perma.cc/9KUC- LAGD.

[133] Zweites Gesetz zur Änderung des Jugendschutzgesetzes [*Second law amending the Youth Protection Act*] art. 2.

The explanatory memorandum to the draft act states that the amendment was necessary because of changes in media usage by children and adolescents, and to cover risks that are associated with online interactions.[134] The amendment specifies requirements for advertisements and other content shown to young people. The aims of children and youth protection in the media are protecting minors from content that impairs or is harmful to their development, protecting their personal integrity, and promoting media literacy.[135] Significant risks to their personal integrity may arise from communication and contact functions, purchasing options, gambling-like mechanisms, mechanisms to encourage excessive media usage, disclosure of user data without consent to third parties, and age-inappropriate exhortation of minors to buy a product or service, in particular advertisements for third party services, among others.[136]

The explanatory memorandum states that:

> [T]he media use of children and adolescents is today largely digital, mobile and interactive. They often unconsciously disclose a large amount of sensitive personal data, generate content themselves, are exposed to it and communicate with an almost indefinite group of people, often anonymously. They are potentially endangered in their personal integrity. Phenomena such as sexting, cybergrooming or cyberbullying pose dangers for children and adolescents who can limit their safe participation in digital media. But also phenomena such as the improper collection and use of personal data, the risk of an early and therefore comprehensive creation of an overall picture of children and adolescents (profiling), the promotion of excessive use and the exploitation of the business inexperience of children and adolescents, for example through cost traps, represent real danger[137]

Among other things, the amendment introduces the concept of "provider prevention" to enforce the goals of the law mentioned above. "Provider prevention" means that providers of internet services that are aimed at or used by children and adolescents will be obligated to set up "adequate and effective structural preventive measures to enable children and adolescents to

---

[134] Deutscher Bundestag: Drucksachen und Protokolle [*German Bundestag: Printed matter and minutes*] [BT-Drs.] 19/24909, at 22, https://perma.cc/Q9VF- CYGQ (original), https://perma.cc/X73F-EHVK (English translation).

[135] Zweites Gesetz zur Änderung des Jugendschutzgesetzes [*Second law amending the Youth Protection Act*] art. 1, no. 3, § 10a.

[136] Id. art. 1, no. 3, § 10b, para. 3.

[137] BT-Drs. 19/24909, at 42 (44 in the English version).

participate online in a carefree manner."[138] For example, providers will have to install default settings that protect children and adolescents from mobbing, cyber grooming, self-endangering behavior, excessive gaming, cost traps,[139] hate speech, and tracking.[140] In addition, providers will be obligated to develop and implement adequate protection concepts such as age-appropriate default settings, age-verification systems, and support and complaint mechanisms suitable for their young target audience.[141] Noncompliance with service provider obligations carries administrative fines of up to 50 million euros (about US$60 million).[142] Service provider with less than one million users in Germany will be exempt from these requirements.[143] The obligations apply to domestic and foreign service providers.[144]

Greece

Kayahan Cantekin
Foreign Law Specialist

Summary

The Constitution of Greece guarantees the "right to participate in the Information Society" and the right to protection of personal data against unauthorized collection, processing, and use. The Greek data protection framework consists of the European Union General Data Protection Regulation (GDPR) and the domestic implementation of relevant EU legislation. In accordance with the GDPR, Greece has opted to set the age of consent to data processing at 15 years. Greek law transposes the EU Audiovisual Media Services Directive's general restrictions concerning

138 Zweites Gesetz zur Änderung des Jugendschutzgesetzes [*Second law amending the Youth Protection Act*] art. 1, no. 19, § 24a.

139 Such as "loot boxes" in online games.

140 BT-Drs. 19/24909, at 21.

141 Zweites Gesetz zur Änderung des Jugendschutzgesetzes [*Second law amending the Youth Protection Act*] art. 1, no. 19, § 24a, para. 2.

142 Id. art. 1, no. 23 in conjunction with Gesetz über Ordnungswidrigkeiten [*Administrative Offenses Act*] [OWiG], Feb. 19, 1987, BGBl. I at 602, as amended, § 30, para. 2, sentence 3, https://perma.cc/S2H6-6SA2 (original), https://perma.cc/4NUK-AASY (English translation, updated through June 21, 2019).

143 Zweites Gesetz zur Änderung des Jugendschutzgesetzes [*Second law amending the Youth Protection Act*] art. 1, no. 19, § 24a, para. 3.

144 Id. art. 1, no. 19, § 24a, para. 4.

advertisements directed to minors, including those applicable to video-sharing platform services. The Greek advertising industry has adopted the Greek Code of Advertising-Communications (EKD-E), which is administered by the industry self-regulation organization, the Greek Advertising Self-Regulation Council. The EKD-E provides for certain rules and principles governing the format and content of advertisements directed to children and teenagers. There are presently no reports of future plans to amend the current framework regarding protection of the personal data of minors in Greek law.

I. Introduction

The Greek Constitution enshrines the right of all persons to information and guarantees "the right to participate in the Information Society."[145] Additionally, the Constitution requires the state to facilitate the access to electronically transmitted information and the "production, exchange and diffusion" of such information, subject to the constitutional guarantees of privacy of the home, privacy of correspondence, and the protection of personal data.[146] The right to protection against unauthorized collection, processing, and use of personal data is specifically guaranteed in article 9A of the Constitution. The Constitution also mandates the protection of childhood and youth in the state's regulation of radio and television.[147]

The European Union's (EU) General Data Protection Regulation (GDPR)[148] is directly applicable in Greece.[149] Certain measures provided by the GDPR require additional statutory implementation at the national level, and the GDPR allows the adoption into national law certain specifications or restrictions provided in the Regulation as necessary for coherence or for making them comprehensible.[150] Accordingly, Law No. 4624/2019 was enacted to implement the GDPR, together with Directive (EU) 2016/680,[151]

---

[145] Constitution of the Greece (as revised by the parliamentary resolution of Nov. 25, 2019 of the IXth revisionary parliament) art. 5A(1), https://perma.cc/GUM8-V6KD.
[146] Id. arts. 9, 19, and 9A, respectively.
[147] Id. art. 15(2).
[148] General Data Protection Regulation (GDPR) 2016 O.J. (L 119) 1, https://perma.cc/7T85-89ZQ. For an overview of the EU legislation and an explanation of terms such as "information society services," and "data processing," see the EU survey in this report.
[149] Consolidated Version of the Treaty on the Functioning of the European Union (TFEU) art. 288, para. 2, 2016 O.J. (C 202) 1, https://perma.cc/GPB6-64TG.
[150] GDPR recital 8.
[151] 2016 O.J. (L119) 89, https://perma.cc/AN84-RLDN (consolidated version).

in Greek law.[152] The law entered into force with its publication in the Government Gazette on August 29, 2019.[153] The other major legislation of the Greek data privacy framework is Law No. 3471/2006, which transposes the EU's Directive 2002/58/EC (ePrivacy Directive).[154]

II. Data Protection for Children

In accordance with article 8 of the GDPR, Law No. 4626/2019 provides that minors that have reached the age of 15 may give consent to the processing of their personal data for lawful purposes when "information society services" are provided directly to them.[155] Any processing of personal data of minors younger than 15 years requires the consent of the minor's legal representative.[156] Law No. 4624/2019 also requires data controllers to use clear and concise wording in communications with minors about their rights as data subjects.[157]

The abovementioned rules are the only ones in the Greek data protection framework that specifically address the protection of minors' personal data in the provision of information society services.[158]

III. Advertisements on Platforms Designed for Children

Law No. 4779/2021 transposes the EU's Audiovisual Media Services Directive into Greek law, including its requirements for the protection of minors from certain types and methods of advertising on television and video-sharing platforms. The law generally prohibits commercial communications

[152] Law No. 4624/2019 (E.K.E.D. 2019, A:137), https://perma.cc/BQG8-8ZRK.

[153] Id. art. 87.

[154] Consolidated Version of the Directive on Privacy and Electronic Communications (ePrivacy Directive), 2002 O.J. (L 201) 37, https://perma.cc/YHA5-EFXV.

[155] Law No. 4624/2019, art. 21(1). The Greek limit is one year younger than the GDPR default of 16 years of age. The GDPR allows Member States to set a younger age of consent, provided that it is not below 13 years. GDPR art. 8(1).

[156] Law No. 4624/2019, art. 21(2).

[157] Id. art. 57(1) (implementing art. 12(1) of Directive 2016/680).

[158] An exception is Decision No. 112/2012 of the Greek Data Protection Authority, providing guidelines for the use of geolocation services for the tracking of vulnerable individuals and minors, available at https://perma.cc/RTS5-V2ND (in Greek). See Vassilios Kourtis, *Data Protection in the Internet: Greece*, in D. Moura Vicente, S. de Vasconcelos Casimiro (eds.), *Data Protection in the Internet* (2020), 220.

that (a) directly exhort minors to buy or hire a product or service by exploiting their inexperience or credulity, (b) encourage them to persuade their parents or others to purchase the goods or services being advertised, (c) exploit the special trust minors place in parents, teachers or other persons, or (d) unreasonably show minors in dangerous situations.[159] Commercial communications for alcoholic beverages specifically directed to minors are also prohibited.[160]

Additionally, video-sharing platforms must take appropriate measures to protect minors from programs, user-generated videos and audiovisual commercial communications that may impair their physical, mental or moral development.[161] To protect minors, harmful content on video-sharing platforms such as gratuitous violence and pornography must be subject to strict access- control measures, such as age verification and parental control systems.[162] When video-sharing service providers obtain the personal data of minors through age-verification and parental control systems, it may not be processed for commercial purposes, such as direct marketing profiling and behavioral advertising.[163] Such providers are required to submit information related to the age-verification and parental control systems they implement to the National Broadcasting Council.[164] The law also "encourages" video-sharing service providers to take measures to prevent minors from excessive consumption of food and beverages that are not appropriate for them through the adoption of industry codes of conduct or general terms and conditions preventing the presentation of such foods and beverages.[165]

Law No. 2863/2000 mandates actors in the advertising industry to jointly adopt a code of conduct governing commercial communications in electronic media.[166] The self-regulation organization of the Greek advertising industry—the Greek Advertising Self-Regulation Council (Συμβούλιο Ελέγχου Επικοινωνίας (ΣΕΕ) [SEE])—administers the Greek Code of Advertising-Communications (Ελληνικου Κωδικα Διαφημισησ-Επικοινωνιασ (ΕΚΔ-

---

159 Law No. 4779/2021 (E.K.E.D. 2021, A:27), art. 14(5) (transposing art. 9 of Directive (EU) 2010/13), https://perma.cc/42VN-2TUK.

160 Id. art. 14(4).

161 Id. art. 14(4).

162 Id. arts. 32(6) and 9(1).

163 Id. art. 32(7).

164 Id. art. 32(6)(f),(h) and (10)(e).

165 Id. art. 32(4).

166 Εθνικό Συμβούλιο Ραδιοτηλεόρασης και άλλες αρχές και όργανα του τομέα παροχής ραδιοτηλεοπτικών υπηρεσιών [*(Law on) the National Broadcasting Council and other authorities and bodies in the field of broadcasting*], Law No. 2863/2000 (E.K.E.D. 2000, A:262), art. 9(1), https://perma.cc/J7NX-7UMM.

E)[EKD-E](2007)).[167] The EKD-E is based on the International Chamber of Commerce's *ICC Advertising and Marketing Communications Code*,[168] and includes various rules and principles regarding the appropriate form and content of commercial communications directed to minors.[169]

IV. Future Plans to Protect Children Online

Currently there appears to be no significant future plans or legislative efforts reported in public sources regarding rulemaking in the matter of the protection of personal data of minors.

Portugal

Eduardo Soares
Senior Foreign Law Specialist

Summary

The protection of children's personal data in Portugal relies on the European Union's General Data Protection Regulation, which was implemented in the country's domestic legislation in 2019. Portugal has yet to enact specific regulations to control the type of advertising that can be shown on platforms designed for children. However, the Advertising Code of 1990 regulates advertisements involving or designed for children.

I. Introduction

To implement the European Union's General Data Protection Regulation (GDPR)[170] into its domestic legislation, Portugal enacted Law No. 58 of

---

[167] EKD-E is available at https://perma.cc/9PZL-MF5S (in Greek).

[168] The 2018 edition of the ICC Code is available at https://perma.cc/R2Y2-F7XH.

[169] E.g., EKD-E, arts. 18, D7, and Annex II. The EKD-E, like the ICC Code on which it is based, differentiates between children (aged under 14 years) and teenagers (14-18), and includes more protective rules for the former class.

[170] Regulation (EU) 2016/679 of the European Parliament and of the Council of 27 April 2016 on the Protection of Natural Persons with regard to the Processing of Personal Data and on

August 8, 2019.[171] Law No. 58 applies to the processing of personal data carried out in the national territory, regardless of the public or private nature of the controller or the subcontractor, even if it is carried out in compliance with legal obligations or in pursuit of missions of public interest, applying all the exclusions provided for in article 2 of the GDPR.[172] Under the GDPR, the processing of personal data must comply with the principles of lawfulness, fairness, and transparency; limitation of purpose; data minimization; accuracy; storage limitation; and integrity and confidentiality.[173]

Law No. 58 was approved on June 14, 2019, promulgated on July 26, 2019, published on the Official Gazette on August 8, 2019, and entered into force on the following day of its publication.[174]

II. Data Protection for Children

Law No. 58 of August 8, 2019, establishes that under the terms of article 8 of the GDPR, children's personal data can only be processed based on the consent provided for in article 6(1)(a) of the GDPR and related to the direct offer of information society services when they are 13 years old.[175] If the child is under the age of 13, treatment is only lawful if consent is given by the child's legal representatives, preferably using secure authentication means.[176]

According to article 6(1)(a) of the GDPR, processing must be lawful only if and to the extent that the data subject has given consent to the processing of his or her personal data for one or more specific purposes.[177]

The conditions for consent are set forth in article 7 of the GDPR, which include:

1. Where processing is based on consent, the controller must be able to demonstrate that the data subject has consented to processing of his or her personal data.

---

the Free Movement of Such Data, and Repealing Directive 95/46/EC (General Data Protection Regulation, GDPR), 2016 O.J. (L 119) 1, https://perma.cc/4HPB-DXKW.

[171] Law No. 58/2019, of August 8, art. 1, https://perma.cc/6DCB-V76G.

[172] Id. art. 2(1).

[173] GDPR art. 5.

[174] Law No. 58/2019, of August 8, art. 68.

[175] Id. art. 16(1).

[176] Id. art. 16(2).

[177] GDPR art. 6(1)(a).

2. If the data subject's consent is given in the context of a written declaration, which also concerns other matters, the request for consent must be presented in a manner that is clearly distinguishable from the other matters, in an intelligible and easily accessible form, using clear and plain language. Any part of such a declaration which constitutes an infringement of the GDPR must not be binding.
3. The data subject shall have the right to withdraw his or her consent at any time. The withdrawal of consent must not affect the lawfulness of processing based on consent before its withdrawal. Prior to giving consent, the data subject must be informed thereof. It must be as easy to withdraw as to give consent.
4. When assessing whether consent is freely given, utmost account must be taken of whether, inter alia, the performance of a contract, including the provision of a service, is conditional on consent to the processing of personal data that is not necessary for the performance of that contract.[178]

Article 8(1) of the GDPR sets the conditions applicable to child's consent in relation to information society services. Where article 6(1)(a) of the GDPR applies in relation to the offer of information society services directly to a child, the processing of the personal data of a child must be lawful where the child is at least 16 years old (or a lower consent age if opted for by a Member State, such as 13 in Portugal). Where the child is below the age of 16 years (below 13 in Portugal), such processing must be lawful only if and to the extent that consent is given or authorized by the holder of parental responsibility over the child.[179] The controller must make reasonable efforts to verify in such cases that consent is given or authorized by the holder of parental responsibility over the child, taking into consideration available technology.[180] Article 8(1) of the GDPR does not affect the general contract law of Member States such as the rules on the validity, formation or effect of a contract in relation to a child.[181]

Although article 40 of the GDPR encourages member states to draw codes of conduct intended to contribute to the proper application of the regulation, it seems that Portugal has yet to produce a specific code of practice on standards

---

[178] Id. art. 7.
[179] Id. art. 8(1).
[180] Id. art. 8(2).
[181] Id. art. 8(3).

of age appropriate design of relevant information society services likely to be accessed by children.[182]

III. Advertisements on Platforms Designed for Children

On October 23, 1990, Decree-Law No. 330 approved the Advertising Code, which applies to any form of advertising, regardless of the medium used for its dissemination.[183] According to article 3(1) of the Code, advertising is broadly defined as any form of communication made by entities of a public or private nature, within the scope of a commercial, industrial, artisanal or liberal professional activity, with the direct or indirect purpose of promoting the sale or alienation of any goods or services, or the promotion of ideas, principles, initiatives or institutions.[184]

Advertising especially directed at minors must always take into account their psychological vulnerability, abstaining, from:

a) Directly inciting minors, exploiting their inexperience or credulity, to purchase a certain good or service;
b) Directly encouraging minors to persuade their parents or third parties to buy the products or services in question;
c) Containing elements liable to endanger their physical or moral integrity, as well as their health or safety, namely through pornography scenes or inciting violence;
d) Exploiting the special trust that minors place in their parents, guardians or teachers.[185]

Minors can only be major players in advertising messages in which there is a direct relationship between them and the product or service advertised.[186]

Advertising for alcoholic beverages is not allowed to specifically address minors or introduce them to the consumption of such drinks.[187]

---

[182] Id. art. 40.
[183] Código da Publicidade, Decreto-Lei No. 330/90, 23 de Outubro [*Advertising Code, Decree-Law No. 330/90, October 23*], art. 1, https://perma.cc/ 9T75-MDKP.
[184] Id. art. 3(1).
[185] Id. art. 14(1).
[186] Id. art. 14(2).
[187] Id. art. 17(1)(a).

Commercial communications and advertising of any events in which minors participate, namely sporting, cultural, recreational or other activities, must not display or implicitly or explicitly mention any brand of alcoholic beverages.[188] In the places where these events are held, alcoholic beverage brands cannot be displayed or in any way advertised.[189]

Advertising is prohibited for alcoholic beverages, tobacco, or any kind of pornographic material, in educational establishments, as well as in any publications, programs, or activities especially aimed at minors.[190]

Advertising on websites, social networks, or mobile apps for foods and beverages of high energy value or high salt, sugar, or fat content addressed to minors under 16 years of age are prohibited.[191]

Gambling and betting advertising must be carried out in a socially responsible manner, respecting, in particular, the protection of minors as well as other vulnerable and at-risk groups. It must not, for example, suggest it is easy to obtain a win, or encourage excessive gambling or betting.[192]

It is strictly prohibited to advertise games and bets that target or use minors in the message.[193] Advertising of games and betting within or near schools or other places for children under the age of six is expressly prohibited.[194] It is also strictly forbidden to advertise games and bets near schools or other places intended for minors.[195]

Violations of the Advertising Code may be remedied by fines or an order for precautionary measures to suspend, terminate or prohibit such advertising, regardless of fault or proof of loss.[196]

IV. Future Plans to Protect Children Online

Our research did not reveal any future plans in Portugal for further legislation or regulations to protect children's privacy online.

---

[188] Id. art. 17(5).
[189] Id. art. 17(6).
[190] Id. art. 20.
[191] Id. art. 20-A(3)(d).
[192] Id. art. 21(1).
[193] Id. art. 21(2).
[194] Id. art. 21(3).
[195] Id. art. 21(4).
[196] Id. art. 41(1).

Romania

Georgiana Grozescu
Legal Research Fellow

Summary

As a European Union Member State, the provisions of the General Data Protection Regulation (GDPR) apply directly to Romania. To comply with the regulation, the Romanian Government has amended more than 1,500 laws and regulations that could involve the processing of personal data.

The GDPR's implementing legislation created the institutional framework for its application. The National Supervisory Authority for the Processing of Personal Data is designated as the national regulator tasked with monitoring compliance with the regulation and applying sanctions and corrective measures to public authorities or private data operators that violate its provisions.

In Romania, when "information society services" are offered directly to children, consent must be obtained from the holder of parental responsibility before processing the personal data of a child under 16 years of age. Data controllers must make reasonable efforts to verify that consent was given by the holder of parental responsibility, but Romania has not yet issued any national guidelines for the implementation of these provisions.

General legislation concerning advertising provides for restrictions and prohibitions on products that may be advertised to children, including alcohol, tobacco, drugs or pornography. Audiovisual commercial communications, regardless of the type and duration, must comply with the principles for minors' protection. Audiovisual programs that may seriously impair the physical, mental or moral development of minors can be aired only if a conditional access system restricts their viewing. The personal data of children may be processed on a large scale for advertising, marketing and publicity activities through automatic means of regular monitoring or recording of behavior, but the data controllers doing so must conduct a data protection impact assessment first.

I. Introduction

Because Romania is a European Union (EU) Member State, the provisions of the EU's General Data Protection Regulation (GDPR)[197] are directly applicable. Some provisions, however, require the adoption of measures of application by the Member States for their implementation.

To comply with the regulation, the Romanian Government has amended more than 1,500 laws and regulations that could involve the processing of personal data.[198] This report details only legislation that is most relevant for that purpose.

Romania has passed Law no. 190/2018, which entered into force on July 31, 2018.[199]. It designates the National Supervisory Authority for the Processing of Personal Data (NSA)[200] as the national regulator tasked with monitoring compliance with the regulation and applying sanctions and corrective measures to public authorities or private data operators that violate its provisions.[201]

It details the conditions for processing certain data (genetic data, biometric data, health data, national identification number, and personal data in the context of employment) and sets out reprimands and fines as sanctions for violation of the GDPR's provisions.[202]

---

[197] General Data Protection Regulation (GDPR), 2016 O.J. (L 119) 1, https://perma.cc/7T85-89ZQ.

[198] See, e.g., Law no. 209/2019 concerning payment services, Law no. 95/2006 concerning health reform, Law no. 127/2019 concerning public pensions, and Law no. 211/2004 concerning crime victims.

[199] Legea nr. 190/2018 din 18 iulie 2018 privind măsuri de punere în aplicare a Regulamentului (UE) 2016/679 al Parlamentului European şi al Consiliului din 27 aprilie 2016 privind protecţia persoanelor fizice în ceea ce priveşte prelucrarea datelor cu caracter personal şi privind libera circulaţie a acestor date şi de abrogare a Directivei 95/46/CE (Regulamentul general privind protecţia datelor) [*Law no. 190/2018 on Implementing Measures to Regulation (EU) 2016/679 of the European Parliament and of the Council of 27 April 2016 on the Protection of Natural Persons with Regard to the Processing of Personal Data and on the Free Movement of Such Data and Repealing Directive 95/46/EC (General Data Protection Regulation)*], M.Of. [*Official Bulletin*] pt. I, no. 651, July 26, 2018, https://perma.cc/XJ92-V68A. The law establishes the measures needed to implement, at the national level in particular, the provisions of articles 6(2), 9(4), 37-39, 42, 43, 83(7), 85, and 87- 89 of the regulation.

[200] The authority had already been established in 2005.

[201] Law no.190/2018, arts. 13, 14.

[202] Id. arts. 12, 15.

Law No. 129/2018,[203] which entered into force on June 24, 2018,[204] integrates into the powers of the NSA those created by GDPR for national regulators and details the procedure for monitoring compliance, processing complaints, and sanctioning violations, as well as judicial remedies.[205] It repeals Law No. 677/2001 on the Protection of Individuals Regarding the Processing of Personal Data and the Free Movement of Such Data,[206] and it states that all references to Law no. 677/2001 must be construed as references to the GDPR and to the law for its implementation.[207]

The NSA subsequently passed Decision No. 174/2018.[208] Under article 35(1), (7) of the GDPR, when a type of processing, in particular one using new technologies, is likely to result in a high risk to the rights and freedoms of natural persons, the data controller or operator must first carry out an assessment of the impact of the envisaged processing operations on the protection of personal data.[209] The decision details a list of situations in which data controllers must carry out a data protection impact assessment, such as video surveillance and processing on a large scale of special categories of data.[210]

---

[203] Legea nr. 129/2018 din 15 iunie 2018 pentru modificarea şi completarea Legii nr. 102/2005 privind înfiinţarea, organizarea şi funcţionarea Autorităţii Naţionale de Supraveghere a Prelucrării Datelor cu Caracter Personal, precum şi pentru abrogarea Legii nr. 677/2001 pentru protecţia persoanelor cu privire la prelucrarea datelor cu caracter personal şi libera circulaţie a acestor date [*Law No. 129 of the 15th of June 2018 on Amending and Supplementing Law no. 102/2005 on Organisation and Functioning of the National Supervisory Authority for Personal Data Processing, as well as on Repealing Law no. 677/2001 on the Protection of Individuals with Regard to the Processing of Personal Data and the Free Movement of Such Data*], art. VIII (1), M.Of. [*Official Bulletin*] no. 503, June 19, 2018, https://perma.cc/5G3K-2NNY. The law creates the institutional framework necessary to apply in Romania provisions of articles 51-55, 57-59, 62, 68, 77, 79, 80, and 82-84 of Regulation (EU) 2016/679 of the European Parliament and of the Council on the Protection of Natural Persons with Regard to the Processing of Personal Data and on the Free Movement of Such Data and Repealing Directive 95/46/EC.

[204] Id. art. VIII(2).

[205] Id. art. I.11.

[206] Lege nr. 677/2001 pentru protecţia persoanelor cu privire la prelucrarea datelor cu caracter personal şi libera circulaţie a acestor date [*Law no. 677/2001 for the protection of individuals regarding the processing of personal data and the free movement of such data*], M.Of. [*Official Bulletin*] pt. I, no. 790, Dec. 12, 2001, https://perma.cc/9ZN5-D47F.

[207] Law nr. 129/2018, art. V.

[208] Decizia nr. 174/2018 din 18 octombrie 2018 privind lista operaţiunilor pentru care este obligatorie realizarea evaluării impactului asupra protecţiei datelor cu caracter personal [*Decision No. 174/2018 on the List of Processing Operations that Are Subject to the Requirement for a Data Protection Impact Assessment*], M.Of. [*Official Bulletin*] pt. I, no. 919, Oct. 31, 2018, https://perma.cc/W22V-YCTG.

[209] Id. pmbl.

[210] Id. art. 1.

II. Data Protection for Children

Under Law 272/2004 on Protection and Promotion of the Rights of the Child,[211] children have the right to have their public image and personal, private, and family life protected.[212] Any action that may affect that right is prohibited.[213]

Under the GDPR, when "information society services" are offered directly to a child under 16 years of age, consent by the holder of parental responsibility is needed for data processing to be lawful.[214] Member States may lower the age to 13,[215] but Romania has not done so. According to the Civil Code, consent by the holder of parental responsibility (who may be a parent or guardian) is usually required for any contract involving a child under 18 years old.[216] However, under the code, any processing of personal data, by automated or manual means, must observe the GDPR.[217] Consequently, consent by the holder of parental responsibility is mandatory only for processing the personal data of children under 16.

Data controllers must make reasonable efforts to verify that consent was given by the holder of parental responsibility.[218] Because children are regarded as particularly vulnerable, any information or communication to a child has to be easily understandable in clear and plain language.[219] Romania has not yet issued any national guidelines for the implementation of these provisions. The NSA website contains a reference to the Guidelines 05/2020 on consent under Regulation 2016/679 issued by the European Data Protection Board.[220] Under these guidelines, what is reasonable, both in terms of verifying that a user is old enough to provide their own consent, and in terms of verifying that a person providing consent on behalf of a child is the holder of parental responsibility, may depend upon the risks inherent in the processing as well as

---

[211] Lege nr. 272/2004 privind protecția și promovarea drepturilor copilului [*Law 272/2004 on Protection and Promotion of the Rights of the Child*], M.Of. [*Official Bulletin*] pt. I, no. 159, Mar. 5, 2014, https://perma.cc/89L8-YXE9.

[212] Id. art. 27(1).

[213] Id. art. 27(2).

[214] GDPR art. 8(1).

[215] Id.

[216] Legea nr. 287/2009 privind Codul Civil al României [*Law no. 287/2009 regarding the Civil Code of Romania*] (republished), arts. 38-43, M.Of. [*Official Bulletin*] pt. I, n. 505, July 15, 2011, https://perma.cc/QG3A-QNZQ.

[217] Id. art. 77.

[218] GDPR art. 8(2).

[219] Id. art. 12(1), recital 58.

[220] European Data Protection Board, Guidelines 05/2020 on Consent Under Regulation 2016/679, May 4, 2020, https://perma.cc/B52J-RYDP.

the available technology.[221] In low-risk cases, verification of parental responsibility via email may be sufficient.[222] Conversely, in high-risk cases, it may be appropriate to ask for more proof, so that the controller is able to verify and retain the information under article 7(1) of the GDPR.[223] Trusted third-party verification services may offer solutions that minimize the amount of personal data the controller has to process itself.[224] The guidelines also offer some examples.[225]

Under Romanian law, data controllers who process the personal data of children on a large scale through automatic means of regular monitoring or recording of behavior, including for advertising, marketing and publicity activities, must perform and submit a data protection impact assessment.[226]

The GDPR calls on EU Member States and their supervisory authorities to encourage the drafting of codes of conduct for the proper application of the regulation.[227] According to the latest available data, the NSA has neither drafted nor approved such a code yet.[228]

The NSA is empowered to investigate violations of GDPR provisions of its own accord or upon a complaint by a person whose rights have been infringed.[229] If the NSA finds a violation, it may apply corrective measures such as compelling the data controller or processor to comply with the requests of the data subject for the exercise of the subject's rights or informing the data subjectabout a personal data breach,[230] rectifying or deleting personal data, restricting processing, or withdrawing certification.[231] The NSA may apply a warning, a reprimand, or a fine.[232] The application of the fine is made under

---

221 Id. at 28.

222 Id.

223 Id.

224 Id.

225 Id.

226 Decision no. 174/2018 on the List of Processing Operations that Are Subject to the Requirement for a Data Protection Impact Assessment, art. 1(1)(d).

227 GDPR, art. 40.

228 In 2019, the NSA received for approval 11 draft codes of conduct issued by professional organizations concerning banking, insurance services, credit services, private pensions, bailiffs, notary publics and gambling. According to its Annual 2019 Report, NSA did not approve any codes, https://perma.cc/G6HH-7B33 (in Romanian).

229 Legea nr. 102/2005 privind înfiinţarea, organizarea şi funcţionarea Autorităţii Naţionale de Supraveghere a Prelucrării Datelor cu Caracter Personal [*Law no. 102/2005 regarding the establishment, organization and functioning of the National Supervisory Authority for the Processing of Personal Data*], ch. IV, M.Of. [*Official Bulletin*] pt. I, no. 947, Nov. 9, 2018, https://perma.cc/MU2L- P7WT.

230 Id. art. 16.

231 Id.

232 Id. art. 15.

the conditions of GDPR's article 83.[233] The NSA may order the publication by the data controller or processor or of any corrective measures applied, with the costs incurred by the controller or processor.[234] In case of noncompliance with the measures ordered, tacit or express refusal to provide all the information and documents requested during the investigation procedure, or refusal to submit to the investigation, the NSA may order, by decision, the application of a cumulative fine of up to 3,000 Lei (about US$738) for each day of delay, calculated from the date established by the decision.[235]

III. Advertisement on Platforms Designed for Children

Under Law 148/2000 on Advertising, publications that are mainly designed for children are not allowed to display ads for tobacco or alcohol products.[236] Advertising for alcohol or tobacco products is not allowed to target children or depict children using such products.[237] Products and services destined for children are not allowed to display advertising containing elements that may adversely affect children (physically, morally, intellectually or psychologically); indirectly encourages children to buy products or services, taking advantage of their lack of experience; adversely affects the relationship between children and their parents or teachers; or unreasonably depicts children in dangerous situations.[238] Advertising of drugs or related substances is generally prohibited.[239] Only medications that are available over the counter can be advertised.[240] Violation of these provisions is punishable by a fine.[241]

The Romanian Council for Advertising, a professional organization for self-regulation in advertising, has issued the Code of Practice in Commercial Communications. It states that internet websites dedicated to products or services that are not recommended to children under a certain age must take

[233] Id.
[234] Id.
[235] Id. art. 18(2).
[236] Legea nr. 148/2000 privind publicitatea [*Law no. 148/2000 on advertising*], art. 12, M.Of. [*Official Bulletin*] pt. I, no. 359, Aug. 7, 2000, https://perma.cc/MUB6- WXXQ.
[237] Id. art. 13(1), (2).
[238] Id. art. 16.
[239] Id. art. 14.
[240] Id. art. 17.
[241] Id. art. 23.

measures to limit the access of underage children.[242] The code also contains rules concerning the advertising of toys, food, and beverages to children.

Traditional audiovisual media services are covered by the Audiovisual Code adopted by the National Audiovisual Council of Romania. Under this code, audiovisual media service providers must respect the principle of the best interest of the child.[243] Child have the right to the protection of their public image and their intimate, private, and family life.[244] Audiovisual commercial communications, regardless of type and duration, must comply with the principles for minors' protection.[245] Commercial communication of erotic phone calls as well as of products and services with a sexual purpose are forbidden.[246] Broadcasting any kind of commercial communication or promotional material for pornographic products is forbidden.[247]

Audiovisual programs that could seriously impair the physical, mental, or moral development of minors can be aired only if a conditional access system restricts their viewing.[248] If an appropriate conditional access device is lacking, such programs can only be broadcast during the time period allowed for such content according to its age classification.[249] During video-on-demand audiovisual media services, programs that might impair the physical, mental, or moral development of minors can be made available only on condition that access restriction measures are provided for by means of a parental control system, so that minors cannot normally see or hear such programs.[250] Broadcasters cannot air studio audiovisual programs or live programs where people smoke, drink alcoholic beverages, or behave in an obscene way during the time period between 6 a.m. and 8 p.m.[251] Programs are classified according to strict criteria.[252] Audiovisual programs providing gambling services must comply with minors' protection conditions.[253]

---

[242] Code of Practice in Commercial Communication art. 23.7 (Romanian Council Advert. 2021), https://perma.cc/3MFK-7P72.

[243] Decizia nr. 220/2011 privind Codul de reglementare a conținutului audiovizual [*Decision no. 220/2011 regarding the Audiovisual Content Regulation Code*] art. 2, M.Of. [*Official Bulletin*], pt. I, no. 174, Mar. 11, 2011, https://perma.cc/W8PW-9SJT.

[244] Id. art. 3(1).

[245] Id. art. 93.

[246] Id. art. 96(1).

[247] Id. art. 96(3).

[248] Id. art. 12(1).

[249] Id, art. 12(2).

[250] Id. art. 13.

[251] Id. art. 15.

[252] Id. arts. 19-21.

[253] Id. art. 89(3).

Gambling cannot be included in programs addressed to children, and they cannot be encouraged to take part in gambling, either.[254]

The same rules apply to on-demand audiovisual media services, according to Decision No. 320/2012 Concerning On-Demand Audiovisual Services.[255] However, this decision does not apply to websites that allow video sharing by individual private users, such as YouTube, Google, or Vimeo, or to internet search engines.[256]

The only restriction on processing the personal data of children is stipulated by Decision 174/2018. Data controllers that process the personal data of children on a large scale through automatic means of systematic monitoring or recording of behavior, including for advertising, marketing and publicity activities, must conduct a data protection impact assessment.[257] A data controller that does not observe these provisions is liable for a fine.[258] The NSA can apply corrective measures as well.

IV. Future Plans to Protect Children Online

No future plans to protect children's privacy online were identified.

Spain

Graciela Rodriguez-Ferrand
Senior Foreign Law Specialist

Summary

The Law on the Protection of Personal Data and Guarantee of Digital Rights implements the EU General Data Protection Regulation, providing the legal framework on data privacy protection. Data protection rights are exercised by parents or legal representatives of

---

[254] Id. art. 89(4).

[255] Decizia nr. 320/2012 privind furnizarea serviciilor media audiovizuale la cerere [*Decision no. 320/2012 regarding the provision of on-demand audiovisual media services*], M.Of. [*Official Bulletin*] pt. I, no. 434, June 30, 2012, https://perma.cc/U53T-T6D6.

[256] Id. art. 2(3)(b), (f).

[257] Id. art. 1(d).

[258] GDPR, art. 83(4)(a); Law no. 190, art. 12.

minors younger than 14 years of age, including the required consent for the processing of their personal data in cases required by law. Minors are also protected from inappropriate advertising online, with specific restrictions applicable to tobacco products and gambling. The data protection agency provides guidelines for minors, parents, and teachers on best practices to prevent breaches of privacy and exposure to inappropriate content.

I. Introduction

In Spain, the EU General Data Protection Regulation (GDPR)[259] and Organic Law 3/2018 of December 5, 2018, on the Protection of Personal Data and Guarantee of Digital Rights (Ley Orgánica 3/2018 de Protección de Datos Personales y Garantía de los Derechos Digitales; LPDP)[260] constitute the legal framework applicable on privacy and data protection.

In implementing the GDPR, the LPDP aims at protecting the intimacy, privacy, and integrity of the individual, in compliance with article 18.4 of the Spanish Constitution, which provides that, to guarantee the honor and personal and family privacy of citizens and the full exercise of their rights, the use of information technology will be limited by law.[261]

The Agencia Espanola de Protección de Datos (AEPD) is the enforcement authority in charge of the protection of personal data in Spain.[262]

The LPDP applies to personal data as defined in the GDPR, being any information in text, image, or audio form that allows the identification of a person.[263] It regulates the obligations of the individual in any data transfer process to guarantee the security of the exchange.[264] Some data isconsidered to be of low risk, such as a person's name or email address, while other data is considered of higher risk because of its sensitive character, such as data

---

[259] Regulation (EU) 2016/679 of the European Parliament and of the Council of 27 April 2016 on the Protection of Natural Persons with Regard to the Processing of Personal Data and on the Free Movement of Such Data, and Repealing Directive 95/46/EC (General Data Protection Regulation) (GDPR), 2016 O.J. (L119), https://perma.cc/VX6F-5JTL.

[260] Ley Orgánica 3/2018 de Protección de Datos Personales y Garantía de los Derechos Digitales (LPDP), Boletin Oficial del Estado (B.O.E.) [*Organic Law 3/2018 on the Protection of Personal Data and Guarantee of Digital Rights (LPDP), Official State Gazette (B.O.E.)*] Dec. 6, 2018, https://perma.cc/7P49-UFAK.

[261] Id. art. 1; Constitución Espanola [*Spanish constitution*] (CE) BOE Dec. 29, 1978, art. 18.4, https://perma.cc/N4WK-4D9U.

[262] LPDP art. 44.

[263] GDPR art. 4; LPDP art. 2.

[264] Id. art. 12.

related to a person's religion or personal health.[265] The processing of sensitive data requires the free, informed, specific, and unequivocal consent of the affected person.[266] Furthermore, the processing of personal data must be limited to that which is necessary for its intended purpose.[267]

The LPDP also provides for the protection of personal data on the internet.[268] In this regard, it implements the right to be forgotten and the right of portability, as well as mandating that consent be obtained in order to collect and use personal information.[269]

The LPDP also requires that the AEPD be notified of security breaches affecting protected personal data within a maximum period of 72 hours.[270]

According to the GDPR and the LPDP, the processing of personal data must be based on the principles of legality; trustworthiness; transparency; restrictive purpose in order to safeguard individual's vital and essential interests; accuracy; and data minimization.[271]

II. Data Protection for Children

Under the LPDP, minors and adults have the same personal data protection rights, as follows:

- Right of access, being the right to contact and obtain information from those responsible for the treatment of personal data regarding the way in which one's personal data is treated;
- Right to rectification, in order to have inaccurate personal data corrected;
- Right to be forgotten, being the right to request personal data be erased in specific circumstances, such as when it is no longer necessary, or if it was obtained without consent, etc.;
- Right to limitation of treatment, being the right to request the suspension of personal data treatment in certain situations, such as

---

265 Id. art. 9.
266 Id. art. 6.
267 Id. art. 8.
268 Id. arts. 70-86.
269 Id. arts. 80-87 and 93.
270 Id. art. 22.3.
271 GDPR art. 5; LPDP arts. 4-10.

when the data processed is being challenged in terms of its accuracy or legality;

- Right of portability, requiring that, in case of automated treatment, personal data has to be structured in a format that allows it to be transferred to another data controller; and
- Right to object to the treatment of personal data in certain situations, such as when the data is used for marketing purposes.[272]

Parents and legal representatives with parental authority over minors may exercise these rights on behalf of those under 14 years of age. Those older than 14 years of age may exercise the rights by themselves.[273] Therefore, minors 14 years of age or older may give consent for the processing of their personal data, unless a law specifically requires the consent of parents or guardians.[274] Minors younger than 14 years of age may only consent to the processing of their personal data upon their parent or guardian's consent.[275]

According to the LPDP, parents, guardians, or legal representatives "will ensure that minors make a balanced and responsible use of digital devices and the services of the information society in order to guarantee the adequate development of their personality and preserve their dignity and fundamental rights."[276]

Under the LPDP, the use or dissemination of images or personal information of minors in social networks, which may imply an illegitimate interference in their fundamental rights, will be subject to the intervention of the Public Prosecutor's Office, which will establish precautionary measures and protection provided for under the Organic Law 1/1996 on the Protection of Minors.[277]

The LPDP provides that the education system will guarantee the full insertion of students in the digital society. It will provide students with instruction to enable responsible consumption and critical and safe use of digital media, respecting and protecting personal data privacy.[278]

Educational institutions and any natural or legal persons that carry out activities in which minors participate are required to guarantee the protection

---

[272] LPDP arts. 12-18.
[273] Id.
[274] Id. art. 7.
[275] Id.
[276] Id. art. 84.1.
[277] Id. art. 84.2; Ley 1/1996 Orgánica de Protección del Menor [*Organic Protection of Minors*], BOE Jan. 17, 1996, https://perma.cc/7LD6-2X7F.
[278] LPDP art. 83.1.

of the best interests of the minor and their fundamental rights, especially the right to the protection of personal data, in the publication or dissemination of their personal information through information society services.[279]

The AEPD provides guidelines for parents, teachers, and children in order to protect them from breaches of privacy and exposure to inappropriate content on the internet.[280]

In addition, the Law on Services of the Society of Information and Electronic Commerce provides that public administrations will promote voluntary codes of conduct, through coordination and consultation with corporations, associations, or commercial, professional, and consumer organizations.[281] These codes will take into account the protection of minors, establishment of common criteria agreed by the industry for the classification and labeling of content, and the adherence of the providers to them.[282] The codes of conduct must be accessible electronically and translated into other official languages of the European Union.[283]

The LPDP includes infractions that are designated as minor, serious, and very serious.[284] These are subject to monetary penalties, warnings, and disciplinary sanctions.[285]

III. Advertisements on Platforms Designed for Children

The General Law on Advertising provides that advertising aimed at minors that encourages them to buy a good or a service, exploiting their inexperience or ingenuity, or providing misleading or dangerous information regarding products and its safety, is illegal.[286]

---

[279] Id. art. 92.

[280] AEPD, *Nota Técnica de Protección del Menor en Internet – Evita el Contenido Inapropiado Preservando su Privacidad* [*Technical Note on the Protection of Minors on the Internet – Avoid Inappropriate Content Preserving their Privacy*] (Apr. 2020), https://perma.cc/G3NZ-FG2N.

[281] Ley 34/2002 de Servicios de la Sociedad de la Información y de Comercio Electrónico [*Law 34/2002 on Services of the Information Society and Electronic Commerce*], BOE July 12, 2002, art. 18, https://perma.cc/4EGH-FMUA.

[282] Id.

[283] Id.

[284] LPDP arts. 70-74.

[285] Cuales son las Sanciones por Incumplir el RGPD? [*What are the sanctions for breaching the GDPR?*], *Egida* (Apr. 6, 2020), https://perma.cc/ 7CFP-ZSFL.

[286] Ley 34/1988, General de Publicidad [*Law 34/1988, General Advertising*], BOE Nov. 15, 1988, art. 3.b, https://perma.cc/VL7J-W79F.

The Law on Sanitary Measures against Smoking and Regulating the Sale, Supply, Consumption and Advertising of Tobacco Products prohibits any kind of advertising, promotion, or sponsorship of tobacco products in all media and supports, including vending machines and information society services, with limited exceptions.[287] One of the exceptions to the prohibition is publications that contain advertising of tobacco products that are edited or printed in countries that are not part of the European Union. However, this exception does not apply if the publication is primarily aimed at minors.[288]

The broadcast of programs or images in which the presenters, collaborators, or guests appear to be smoking, and the mentioning or display of brands, trade names, logos, or other identifying signs or associations with tobacco products is also prohibited in any media format, including information society services.[289]

Gambling operators may not direct advertising directly or indirectly to minors, or persuade or incite gambling to minors through advertising.[290] Commercial communications are specifically prohibited when they present gambling as a sign of maturity or indicative of the passage to adulthood, or where they are disseminated or placed in media, programs, applications, web pages, or digital content (specifically or together with links to web pages) aimed mainly at minors.[291] Commercial communications must include a warning that minors may not participate in gambling activities, such as "no minors," "18+," or similar.[292]

IV. Future Plans to Protect Children Online

The LPDP provided that, within one year of its entry into force, the government will draft a bill specifically aimed at guaranteeing the rights of minors in the face of the impact of the internet, in order to guarantee their

---

287 Ley 28/2005, de Medidas Sanitarias Frente al Tabaquismo y Reguladora de la Venta, el Suministro, el Consumo y la Publicidad de los Productos del Tabaco [*Law 28/2005, on Sanitary Measures Against Smoking and Regulating the Sale, Supply, Consumption and Advertising of Tobacco Products*], BOE Dec. 27, 2005, art. 9.1.b, https://perma.cc/252A-2RGT.

288 Id. art. 9.1.c.

289 Id. art. 9.3.

290 Real Decreto 958/2020, de Comunicaciones Comerciales de las Actividades de Juego [*Royal Decree 958/2020, on Commercial Communications of Gambling Activities*], BOE Nov. 4, 2020, art. 11.1, https://perma.cc/ULP4-K9HJ.

291 Id. art. 11.2.

292 Id. art. 11.3.

safety and fight against discrimination and violence that is exerted on them through new technologies.[293] It appears that such a bill has not yet been submitted to the Congress.

Sweden

Elin Hofverberg
Foreign Law Specialist

Summary

The right to privacy and the protection against unlawful processing of personal data are protected in Sweden. As Sweden is a member of the European Union, the General Data Protection Regulation (GDPR) applies directly. The legal age to consent to the processing of personal information in Sweden is 13 years.

The Swedish Authority for Privacy Protection oversees compliance with the GDPR. It fined the City of Stockholm School Board for violating the GDPR when it stored student personal data in its digital attendance system.

Sweden prohibits the direct targeting of children in advertising, specifically prohibiting games from using advertisements aimed at children and requiring strict age requirements for games with adult advertising. The self-regulatory Swedish Advertising Ombudsman monitors compliance with advertising standards.

There are currently no bills pending in parliament concerning the protection of children's data online. A motion to increase fines for GDPR violations has been presented to the Constitutional Committee for further review.

I. Introduction

The right to privacy and the right to be protected against the unlawful compilation of personal data are protected in the Swedish Constitution.[294] The right to protection of one's personal data is established by European Union

---

[293] LPDP, Dispocisión Adicional Diecinueve [*Additional Provision Nineteen*].

[294] 2 ch. 6 § 2st Regeringsformen [*The form of government*] (RF) (SF 1974:152), https://perma.cc/3DU4-FBWQ.

(EU) law in the General Data Protection Regulation (GDPR).[295] Although the GDPR is directly applicable in Sweden as of May 25, 2018, when the regulation entered into force, the GDPR has been codified in Swedish law through the Law on Additional Provisions to the EU Data Protection Regulation,[296] and the Regulation on Additional Rules to the EU Data Protection Regulation.[297] The law and regulation do not extend the protections otherwise found in the GDPR.

Sweden has also implemented the EU e-Privacy Directive[298] in the Act on Electronic Communications, which among other things restricts the use of location data and regulates when user consent is required for the collection or storage of data.[299]

The Swedish Authority for Privacy Protection (formerly the Swedish Data Protection Authority) is responsible for enforcing the GDPR.[300] Under the GDPR, the maximum monetary sanction that may be issued for not complying with an order from the Authority following a GDPR violation 4% of worldwide revenue.[301] Sweden has capped certain violations at SEK 5 million (about US $600,000) (for violations of article 83.4) and SEK 10 million (about US $1.2 million) (for violations of articles 83.5 and 83.6).[302]

---

[295] General Data Protection Regulation (GDPR), 2016 O.J. (L 119) 1, https://perma.cc/JG59-NUXN.

[296] Lag med kompletterande bestämmelser till EU:s dataskyddsförordning [*Act with supplementary provisions to the EU data protection regulation*] (SFS 2018:218), https://perma.cc/MB2K-7KDT. Prop. 2017/18:, https://perma.cc/R2GW-GYCZ. SOU 2017:39, Ny dataskyddslag Kompletterande bestämmelser till EU:s dataskyddsförordning [*New data protection law Supplementary regulations to the EU's data protection regulation*], https://perma.cc/T84S-868Y.

[297] Förordning med kompletterande bestämmelser till EU:s dataskyddsförordning [*Regulation with supplementary provisions to the EU data protection regulation]* (SFS 2018:219), https://perma.cc/CA75-FXLH.

[298] Consolidated Version of the Directive on Privacy and Electronic Communications (ePrivacy Directive), 2002 O.J. (L 201) 37, https://perma.cc/YHA5-EFXV.

[299] Lag om elektronisk kommunikation [*Electronic Communications Act*] (LEK) (SFS 2003:389), https://perma.cc/3H9W-88VW.

[300] 3 § Förordning (2018:219) med kompletterande bestämmelser till EU:s dataskyddsförordning; 6 kap. Lag med kompletterande bestämmelser till EU:s dataskyddsförordning [*Regulation (2018:219) with supplementary provisions to the EU data protection regulation; 6 ch. Act with supplementary provisions to the EU's data protection regulation*]. Currently the agency is called Integritetsskyddsmyndigheten (IMY) (Swedish Authority for Privacy Protection), formerly known as Datainspektektionen (Swedish Data Protection Authority).

[301] GDPR art. 83.6.

[302] 6 kap. 2 § Lag med kompletterande bestämmelser till EU:s dataskyddsförordning [*6 ch. § 2 Act with supplementary provisions to the EU's data protection regulation*].

Sweden follows the EU's guidelines for administrative fines under the GDPR.[303]

II. Data Protection for Children

In accordance with Swedish law and the GDPR, children aged 13 and up can provide consent to allow data processing.[304] Processing of data on children not yet 13 years old requires the consent of their legal guardian.[305]

In 2020, the Swedish Authority for Privacy Protection fined the City of Stockholm's Board of Education SEK 4 million (about US$476,000) for violating the GDPR when processing and storing personal data of underaged students.[306]

Several agencies have also issued guidance pertaining to children's use of the internet and social media. For example, the Child Ombudsman, the Swedish Authority for Privacy Protection, and the State Media Council have together issued a guide titled "Children and Youths' Rights on Digital Platforms."[307] The guide, which targets platform providers, recommends among other things that nudge techniques (design features to influence user behavior) not be used except to promote the highest protection for personal data available, and that websites design their age verification methods to prevent children from providing an incorrect older age.[308] The guide is expressly inspired by the United Kingdom Information Commissioner's Office's code, Age Appropriate Design: A Code of Practice for Online Services, but does not have legal status.[309]

---

303 Article 29 Data Protection Working Party, *Guidelines on the Application and Setting of Administrative Fines for the Purposes of the Regulation 2016/679* (Oct. 3, 2017), https://perma.cc/E92X-JMJ6.

304 2 kap. 4 § Lag med kompletterande bestämmelser till EU:s dataskyddsförordning [*2 ch. § 4 Act with supplementary provisions to the EU's data protection regulation*].

305 Id.

306 *Serious Deficiencies in the Stockholm Online School Platform*, IMY (Nov. 24, 2020), https://perma.cc/UW6T- BRF2. Case available in Swedish at Datainspektionen, Diarienr. DI-2019-7024, https://perma.cc/6JYA-DSST.

307 Barnombudsmannen, *Datainspektionen, Statens medieråd, Barns och Ungas Rättigheter på Digitala Plattformar* [*The Children's Ombudsman, the Data Inspectorate, the Swedish Media Council, Children's and Young People's Rights on Digital Platforms*] (2020), https://perma.cc/58HL-62YT.

308 Id. at 43.

309 Id. at 9. For more on the UK code, see the UK country survey in this report.

In addition, the State Media Council has published guidance on how parents can protect their children's personal data online.[310] It recommends that parents should:

- Talk to their child about privacy and content online.
- Think about what pictures [they] share of [their] children.

With the help of technology, it is possible to strengthen the protection of one's privacy in several different ways:

- In smartphones, it is possible to review what so-called rights different apps have and turn off access to, for example, address book or location positioning.
- On social media, it is often possible to decide what contacts that may see what you upload, or at least the opportunity to choose between making your account public or private.
- By choosing secure passwords and keeping your login details to yourself, you reduce the risk of hacked accounts. (See the text on why passwords are important.)
- By screenshot images and messages sent and shared online, it is possible to gather evidence of violations and threats, prior to a possible report to the company providing the service or to the police.
- Report any privacy breaches that you perceive as criminal to the police.[311]

III. Advertisements on Platforms Designed for Children

Under Swedish law, all advertisements must comply with good practice and custom.[312] In practice, this means that all advertisements that target children are prohibited. For example, advertisements targeting children expressly may not be part of games, including online games.[313] In addition, the International Chamber of Commerce Code on Advertisement and Communication restricts

---

310 *Hur Skyddar Jag Mitt Barns Digitala Integritet?* [*How Do I Protect My Child's Digital Privacy?*], Statens Medieråd, https://perma.cc/PZ2S-HFEK.

311 Id.

312 5 § Marknadsföringslag [*Marketing Law*](SFS 2008:486), https://perma.cc/H5R7-EEB2.

313 15 kap. 1 § Spellagen [15 ch. § 1 Gambling Act] (SFS 2018:1138), https://perma.cc/6PHC-6FA6.

all advertisements that target children.[314] Game providers must also clearly state age requirements.[315]

In addition, the Swedish Consumer Agency (Konsumentverket) has issued guidance for advertisements on blogs and in social media.[316] The guidance states that it must be clear when content is an advertisement, and that advertisements may never directly encourage children to purchase a product.[317] IAB Sweden, the national affiliate of the industry organization the Interactive Advertising Bureau, has issued specific industry guidelines for different use of advertisements, including for online influencers,[318] gaming,[319] and online video.[320]

Violations against advertisement law and custom is enforced by the Swedish Advertising Ombudsman (Reklamombudsmannen).[321] Rekalmombudsmannen is an industry self-regulation enforcement body that facilitates compliance by Swedish companies with meeting industry guidelines on advertisements.[322] Reklamombudsmannen is part of the EU network European Advertising Standards Alliance (EASA).[323] In 2018, Reklamombudsmannens opinionsnämnd found that an advertisement for educational services by the company Albert in Snapchat violated the ICC rules for advertisements, as it directly encouraged children to convince their parents to sign up for the service.[324]

---

[314] ICC:s regler for marknadsföring och kommukation [*ICC's rules for marketing and communication*], https://perma.cc/A7KT-WAWU.

[315] 14 kap. 3 § Spellagen [*14 ch. § 3 Gambling Act*].

[316] Konsumentverket, *Vägledning Marknadsföring i Sociala Medier* [*The Swedish Consumer Agency, Guidance on Marketing in Social Media*], https://perma.cc/G85N-GMB5.

[317] Id. at 4-5.

[318] IAB Sweden, *Standards & Guidelines Influencer Marketing* (Jan. 31, 2019), https://perma.cc/7G28-GCYL.

[319] IAB Sweden, *Gaming, Gamers & Esport* (Feb. 5, 2021), https://perma.cc/HLT9-6UFC.

[320] IAB Sweden, *Standards & Guidelines Online Video* (June 19, 2019), https://perma.cc/SNQ4-EQ73.

[321] *Vanliga frågor*, Reklamombudsmannen [*Frequently asked questions, the Advertising Ombudsman*], https://perma.cc/NS4R-EEAQ.

[322] *Vanliga frågor*, Reklamombudsmannen [*Frequently asked questions, the Advertising Ombudsman*], https://perma.cc/NS4R-EEAQ.

[323] *Homepage*, The European Advertising Standards Alliance (EASA), https://perma.cc/K2MK-DFHU.

[324] Rekalmomubdsmannens opinionsnämnd [The Advertising Ombudsman's opinion board], Beslut Ärende 1801-12, May 16, 2018, https://perma.cc/3Q2V- QC9K.

IV. Future Plans to Protect Children Online

There are currently no bills pending in parliament regarding children's privacy online.

The Liberals (Liberalerna), which holds 19 out of 169 seats in parliament, have submitted a motion that Sweden increase the monetary fine for violations against data protection rules.[325] The motion has been assigned to the Constitutional Committee (Konstitutionsutskottet) for review and is not expected to be voted on in the near future.

United Kingdom

Clare Feikert-Ahalt
Senior Foreign Law Specialist

Summary

The UK has taken measures to provide children with special protections over the collection and use of their personal data they generate online. In September 2020, pursuant to a mandate in the Data Protection Act 2018, the Information Minister introduced a Code of Practice, titled the *Age Appropriate Design: A Code of Practice for Online Services*. The Code is comprised of 15 design standards for online services with special safeguards to protect children. The Code notes the difficulties of parents in exercising control over the use of their children's personal data, and places responsibility on Information Society Services (ISSs) to ensure age-appropriate use of personal data, respecting children's rights, and making decisions in children's best interests.

The Code has a 12-month transition period, providing service providers whose online sites or services include child users with time to redesign their webpages. The Information Commissioner's Office will oversee the implementation of the Code and has the power to take action to ensure it is complied with, including levying significant fines.

---

[325] Motion 2020/21:1520, Skydda människors privatliv vid datainsamling, av Helena Gellerman och Robert Hannah (båda L) [*Protecting people's privacy in data collection, by Helena Gellerman and Robert Hannah (both L)*], https://perma.cc/BPK7-SHGX.

The UK has also implemented additional requirements for marketers utilizing online advertisements to ensure children are protected from those that are not age appropriate. An advertising code requires marketers to take care over the placement and content of any ads. Online behavioral advertisements are regulated by several overlapping laws, including the General Data Protection Regulation, the Privacy and Electronic Communications Regulations, the Committee of Advertising Practice Code, and the Age-Appropriate Design Code.

I. Introduction

The UK incorporated the European Union's General Data Protection Regulation (GDPR)[326] into its national law through the Data Protection Act 2018 (the DPA) on May 23, 2018.[327] The DPA regulates how personal information may be processed, "requiring personal data to be processed lawfully and fairly, on the basis of the data subject's consent or another specified basis."[328] There are six lawful bases for processing personal data: where an individual has given valid consent to data processing for a specific purpose; if the processing is necessary for contractual purposes; to enable compliance with a legal obligation; if it is necessary to protect someone's life; to perform a task in the public interest; or if the processing is necessary for the official functions of the processor and there is not a good, overriding reason to protect the personal data.[329]

The DPA requires that any data collected should be limited in scope, necessary for the reasons it is processed, accurate, and kept up to date. It also requires providers of online services, which it calls Internet Society Services (ISSs), to adopt a risk-based approach when "using people's data, based on certain key principles, rights and obligations."[330]

---

[326] General Data Protection Regulation (GDPR), Regulation (EU) 2016/679, https://perma.cc/CQ9F-AYNN. When the UK left the EU, it incorporated all EU law as it existed on December 31, 2020, into a new body of domestic law known as "retained EU legislation." References to the GDPR throughout this report refer to the Regulations incorporated in the domestic law of the UK.

[327] Data Protection Act 2018, c. 12, https://perma.cc/39Y3-H34A.

[328] Id. § 2(1)(a).

[329] Information Commissioner's Office, *Age Appropriate Design: A Code of Practice for Online Services* Annex C (ver. 2.1.114, Sept. 2, 2020), https://perma.cc/376E-YMNX.

[330] Id. at 10.

Any personal data collected must be stored in a manner that enables the identification of the data subject and held for no longer than necessary. Personal data must be processed in a way that ensures the security of the data and protects against unauthorized processing, accidental loss, destruction, or damage. The DPA places a duty on the data controller to ensure the principles of the DPA are complied with, and to demonstrate how this compliance is achieved.[331] It also provides for regulatory oversight of its provisions and enforcement mechanisms to ensure it is implemented properly.

The GDPR requires Member States to protect children's data and must take extra care to ensure their interests are protected.[332] Recital 38 of the GDPR provides:

> Children merit specific protection with regard to their personal data, as they may be less aware of the risks, consequences and safeguards concerned and their rights in relation to the processing of personal data. Such specific protection should, in particular, apply to the use of personal data of children for the purposes of marketing or creating personality or user profiles and the collection of personal data with regard to children when using services offered directly to a child.[333]

The DPA requires the Information Commissioner's Office (ICO), the independent body set up to uphold information rights,[334] to publish four Codes to supplement the implementation of the GDPR: a children's code, a data-sharing code, a direct marketing code and a data protection and journalism code.[335] This report provides an overview of the recently introduced Children's Code, titled the *Age Appropriate Design: A Code of Practice for Online Services* (the Code).[336]

The DPA defines age-appropriate design as "the design of services so that they are appropriate for use by, and meet the development needs of, children."[337] The Code is comprised of 15 design standards, the first of which is to make the best interests of children a primary consideration.[338] While acknowledging that parents form a key role in protecting children, it notes the

---

[331] Data Protection Act 2018, pt. 2, ch. 2.
[332] GDPR art. 8.
[333] Id. recital 38
[334] *Who We Are*, ICO, https://ico.org.uk/about-the-ico/.
[335] Data Protection Act 2018 §§ 121-124.
[336] ICO, *Age Appropriate Design: A Code of Practice for Online Services*, supra note 4.
[337] Data Protection Act 2018 § 123.
[338] ICO, *Age Appropriate Design: A Code of Practice for Online Services*, supra note 4, at 24.

difficulties faced by parents in making informed choices or exercising control over how Information Society Services (ISSs) use children's data. The Code places responsibility on the ISS to "take responsibility for ensuring that the way their services use personal data is appropriate to the child's age, takes account of their best interests, and respects their rights; as well as supporting parents or older children in making choices (where appropriate) in the child's best interests."[339] This will require many ISSs to rework their sites to meet the standards in the Code; there will be "noticeable changes to the designs of websites that are accessed by children," with many ISSs having to put in substantial redesign work to comply with the Code.[340]

II. Data Protection for Children

The ICO estimates that one in five internet users in the UK is under the age of 18 and considers they are using an internet that is "not designed for them."[341] Section 123 of the DPA required the ICO to produce "a code of practice which contains such guidance as the Commissioner considers appropriate on standards of age-appropriate design of relevant information society services which are likely to be accessed by children."[342] Such services include not only those designed to be accessed by children, but also those where it is more probable than not a child will access it. This is a broad test, and the ICO notes:

> In practice, whether your service is likely to be accessed by children or not is likely to depend on: the nature and content of the service and whether that has particular appeal for children; and the way in which the service is accessed and any measures you put in place to prevent children gaining access.[343]

The ICO states that a common sense approach should be taken when determining these factors and recommends that ISSs that do not choose to implement the Code after determining their service is not likely to be accessed by children should clearly document the reasons for this decision.[344]

---

[339] Id. at 10.
[340] Gareth Oldale, 5 Data Protection and Privacy Predictions for 2021, *Privacy & Data Protection* 5 (Jan.-Feb. 2021) (available on Lexis-Nexis by subscription).
[341] ICO, *Age Appropriate Design: A Code of Practice for Online Services*, supra note 4, at 3.
[342] Data Protection Act 2018 § 123.
[343] ICO, *Age Appropriate Design: A Code of Practice for Online Services*, supra note 4, at 17.
[344] Id.

In drafting the Code, the ICO was required to consider that children have different needs at different ages,[345] along with the UK's obligations under the United Nations Convention on the Rights of the Child (UNCRC):[346]

> In particular, this code aims to ensure that online services use children's data in ways that support the rights of the child to: freedom of expression; freedom of thought, conscience and religion; freedom of association; privacy; access information from the media (with appropriate protection from information and material injurious to their well-being); play and engage in recreational activities appropriate to their age; and protection from economic, sexual or other forms of exploitation.[347]

The Code applies to online services based in the UK, or those based outside the UK that have a branch, office or other establishment that processes personal data in the course of activities in the UK. The Code also applies to an ISS that is based outside the UK if it offers services to users in the UK or monitors the behavior of users in the UK.[348]

A. Age Appropriate Design Code

The Code entered into force on September 2, 2020, and has a 12 month transition period, which is the maximum time allowed under the DPA.[349] The term ISS is defined broadly to include most online services.[350] ISSs will be required to comply with the provisions of the Code on September 2, 2021.[351] The Code is a statutory code of practice and the courts and tribunals must take its provisions into account when it is relevant in any proceedings before them.

The Code sets out 15 cumulative, interlinked standards of design, detailing how the principles, rights and obligations provided for in the DPA apply to children. "Child" is defined as anyone under 18 years of age.[352] Its coverage includes the use of inferred data, which is information inferred from

---

[345] ICO, *Age Appropriate Design: A Code of Practice for Online Services*, supra note 4, Annex B.
[346] Data Protection Act 2018 § 123(4). See also ICO, *Age Appropriate Design: A Code of Practice for Online Services*, supra note 4, at 6.
[347] ICO, *Age Appropriate Design: A Code of Practice for Online Services*, supra note 4, at 10.
[348] Id. at 18.
[349] Department for Digital, Culture, Media & Sport, *Explanatory Memorandum to the Age Appropriate Design Code 2020*, at ¶ 7.6 (June 2020), https://perma.cc/CD4K-XQ86.
[350] ICO, *Age Appropriate Design: A Code of Practice for Online Services*, supra note 4, at 15-16.
[351] Id. at 9.
[352] Id. at 91.

online behavior or inferred from other information, and data collected directly from children.[353]

The Code aims,

> ... to support compliance with the DPA and general principles of the General Data Protection Regulation ("the GDPR") to ensure online services appropriately safeguard children's personal data. The Code supports compliance with those general principles by setting out specific protections services need to build in when designing online services likely to be accessed by children. In particular, the Code sets out practical measures and safeguards to ensure processing under the GDPR can be considered 'fair' in the context of online risks to children.[354]

The Code is,

> ... not intended as technical standards, but as a set of technology-neutral design principles and practical privacy features. The focus is on providing [benchmark] default settings which ensure that children have the best possible access to online services whilst minimising data collection and use, by default.[355]

Instead, the Code,

> ... sets out practical measures and safeguards to ensure processing under the GDPR can be considered 'fair' in the context of online risks to children, and will help you comply with [Articles 5, 6, 12-20, 22, 25 and 35].[356]

The Code aims to help organizations providing online services to children by "translat[ing] the GDPR requirements into design standards for online services, and tak[ing] into account the UNCRC that recognises the special safeguards children need in all aspects of their life."[357]

To meet the Code, ISSs must design their services in a way that complies with the GDPR, which makes it clear that children's personal data requires specific protections, as children are likely to have a lower level of

---

353 Id. at 11.

354 *Explanatory Memorandum to the Age Appropriate Design Code 2020*, supra note 24, ¶ 7.1.

355 Id. ¶ 7.2.

356 ICO, *Age Appropriate Design: A Code of Practice for Online Services*, supra note 4, at 11.

357 *The Information Commissioner's Office (ICO) Age Appropriate Design Code*, Gov.uk (Feb. 10, 2021), https://perma.cc/74JQ-YN6G.

understanding of the risks of the processing of their data."[358] The Code incorporates a key principle from article 3 of the UNCRC, that the best interests of the child shall be a primary consideration in actions concerning them. This principle should be specifically considered by ISSs when they design online services.[359]

B. Definition of Relevant ISS

As noted above, the Code applies to ISSs that "provide online products or services . . . that process personal data and are likely to be accessed by children in the UK. It is not only for services aimedat children."[360] "Relevant ISS" is defined in the Code as "any service normally provided for remuneration, at a distance, by electronic means and at the individual request of a recipient of services."[361] The definition is broad and covers those that receive funding for the service, even if it not provided by the end user, such as through advertising. It encompasses search engines, social media platforms, online messaging services, content streaming services, news websites, retail websites, etc.[362]

The ICO has stated "[e]ssentially this [definition] means that most online services [are an] ISS."[363] Websites provided for preventative and health services, such as counselling or health screening, are exempt from the definition,[364] but general health, fitness and wellbeing services or apps are included. Websites provided by public authorities are not considered to be a relevant ISS as these types of services are typically not for commercial purposes. Websites that provide information about "real world" businesses, without allowing the purchase of goods or services online, also fall outside the scope of the Code.[365]

C. The 15 Standards

The 15 standards are considered to be flexible and do not ban or prescribe content. Instead, the standards aim for organizations to have an "age appropriate design reflecting a risk-based approach. The focus is on providing default settings which ensures that children have the best possible access to

---

358 Oldale, supra note 15.

359 ICO, *Age Appropriate Design: A Code of Practice for Online Services*, supra note 4, at 24.

360 Id. at 9.

361 Id. at 16.

362 The ICO has provided a flow chart to help ISSs determine whether or not their sites fall within the Code, at id. Annex A.

363 Id. at 16.

364 Data Protection Act 2018 § 123(7).

365 ICO, *Age Appropriate Design: A Code of Practice for Online Services*, supra note 4, at 16.

online services whilst minimising data collection and use, by default."[366] The 15 standards are described below.

1. Best Interests of the Child

Standard 1 provides that the best interests of the child should be a primary consideration in the design and development of online services that are likely to be accessed by a child.[367] This fulfils the obligation the ICO has to regard to the UNCRC when drafting the Code.[368] Notably the ICO provides the following instructions to ISSs:

In particular you should consider how, in your use of personal data, you can:

- Keep [children] safe from exploitation risks, including the risks of commercial or sexual exploitation and sexual abuse;
- Protect and support their health and wellbeing;
- Protect and support their physical, psychological and emotional development;
- Protect and support their need to develop their own views and identity;
- Protect and support their right to freedom of association and play;
- Support the needs of children with disabilities in line with your obligations under the relevant equality legislation for england, scotland, wales and northern ireland;
- Recognise the role of parents in protecting and promoting the best interests of the child and support them in this task; and
- Recognise the evolving capacity of the child to form their own view, and give due weight to that view.[369]

2. Data Protection Impact Assessments

ISSs must undertake a data protection impact assessment (DPIA) to "assess and mitigate risks to the rights and freedoms of children who are likely to access [the] service, which arise from your data processing."[370] When conducting the DPIA, the ISS must consider the different ages, capacities and

[366] ICO, *Age Appropriate Design: A Code of Practice for Online Services*, supra note 4, at 16.
[367] Id. at 10. See also *Protecting Children's Digital Privacy with the Age Appropriate Design Code*, Children's Commissioner (Sept. 2, 2020), https://perma.cc/EU83-CTFH.
[368] ICO, *Age Appropriate Design: A Code of Practice for Online Services*, supra note 4, at 24.
[369] Id. at 25.
[370] Id. at 27. A template ISS can use to record DPIAs is contained in Annex D of the Code.

developmental needs of child users. DPIAs have been described as "a key part of controller's accountability obligations and must be carried out before undertaking any processing that is likely to result in a high risk to the rights and freedoms of individuals."[371]

The ICO has stated that any processing conducted by online services will likely pose a high risk to children's rights and freedoms, and the DPIAs should specifically focus on these issues and assess and document the ISS's compliance with the Code. ISSs should regularly review DPIAs' and update them when necessary.

3. Age Appropriate Application

Standard 3 requires ISSs to take steps to establish the age of any users. It directs ISSs to use,

> . . . a risk-based approach to recognising the age of individual users and ensure you effectively apply the standards in this code to child users. Either establish age with a level of certainty that is appropriate to the risks to the rights and freedoms of children that arise from your data processing, or apply the standards in this code to all your users instead.[372]

The Code does not provide measures that ISSs should take to establish a user's age. It recommends that the method the ISS selects should "be appropriate to the risks . . . that arise from its data processing."[373] Methods that the ICO have suggested include:

- A self-declaration in low-risk processing situations;
- The use of artificial intelligence to analyze how a user interacts with the webpage, although as this involves a level of data processing, this must comply with the requirements contained in the DPA;
- A third-party verification service; or
- By confirmation from existing account holders; or through other technical measures.[374]

---

[371] Emma Erskine-Fox, *Understanding the ICO's Age Appropriate Design Code*, Privacy & Data Protection 4 (Apr.- May 2020) (available on LexisNexis by subscription).

[372] ICO, *Age Appropriate Design: A Code of Practice for Online Services*, supra note 4, at 7.

[373] ICO, *ICO Answer to the Call for Submissions of the UNSRP* 8, https://perma.cc/EM5M-6T6S.

[374] ICO, *Age Appropriate Design: A Code of Practice for Online Services*, supra note 4, at 34.

The ICO advises that if an ISS cannot ascertain the age of the users of their service with any certainty on a level "that is appropriate to the risks to children arising from [its] data processing,"[375] the standards in the Code should be applied to all users. This ensures that any data obtained from children receive the correct processing protections.

4. Transparency

Standard 4 requires an ISS to be clear, honest and open about what users should expect when using its online services. It states that privacy information and other terms, policies and community standards provided to users "must be concise, prominent and in clear language suited to the age of the child."[376] It requires that in the event that a new use of personal data is activated, an additional, specific explanation known as a "just in time notice" should be provided to the user at that point in time. Depending upon the age of the child and the risks in processing, the notice should also direct them to speak with an adult and not proceed if they are unsure. In cases where the ISS wishes the notices to be "legally robust," explanations at the level appropriate for the correct age and developmental stage of the child user should be provided alongside more detailed information.

To help ensure transparency, information presented to child users should be done in a user- friendly manner and designed to appeal to the age of the child accessing the service, such as through cartoons, graphics, video and audio content, or other interactive content that attracts and interests the child user.[377] Full privacy information for parents should be provided alongside the information presented to children aged 12 and under.[378]

5. Detrimental Use of Data

Standard 5 notes that children's personal data should not be used "in ways that have been shown to be detrimental to their wellbeing, or that go against industry codes of practice, other regulatory provisions or Government advice."[379] To meet this standard, ISSs should ensure they are aware of, and in compliance with, any standards or codes of practice within their particular industries or sectors, along with government advice relating to the welfare of

---

375 Id. at 35.
376 Id. at 7.
377 Id. at 19.
378 Id.
379 Id. at 7.

children regarding online or digital services.[380] In any case where the "use of personal data is clearly, or has been shown to be, detrimental to children's physical or mental wellbeing, this should be avoided."[381]

6. Policies and Community Standards

Standard 6 requires ISSs to not just state, but uphold and actively enforce, any published terms, policies and community standards.[382] For example, if personal data is collected from children to join or access services and the service does not do what claimed to do, the collection of personal data would be unlawful. In order to meet this standard, an ISS at a minimum should only use personal data collected in accordance with the privacy policy and uphold any policies or terms.[383]

7. Default Settings

The ICO notes that children typically accept the default standards offered to them and rarely change them. Taking this into account, standard 7 requires ISSs to have the default setting as "high privacy." This requirement can be waived if the ISS can "demonstrate a compelling reason for a different default setting, taking account of the best interests of the child."[384] Thus, ISSs should only collect personal data required to provide each element of their online service and should not allow users' personal data to be visible to other users.[385]

8. Data Minimization

Standard 8 requires ISSs to collect only the minimum amount of personal data needed to deliver each individual element of the service when a child user is knowingly and actively using the service. Any data collected should be retained for the shortest amount of time required. Standard 8 notes that children should be provided with clear information and separate choices over each individual element of the service they wish to use. Personal data collected from children should not be "bundled," as doing so means the ISS is "effectively collecting personal data for different purposes."[386]

---

[380] Id. at 44.
[381] Erskine-Fox, supra note 46.
[382] ICO, *Age Appropriate Design: A Code of Practice for Online Services*, supra note 4, at 47.
[383] Id.
[384] Id. at 61.
[385] Id.
[386] Id.

9. Data Sharing

Any personal data collected from children should not be disclosed or made visible to third parties unless there is a compelling reason for doing so and the best interests of the child have been considered. Standard 9 notes that any settings that permit general or unlimited sharing of a child's personal data will typically not be in compliance with the Code.

The standard provides several examples of compelling reasons to share data, including to prevent child sexual exploitation, or to prevent or detect crimes against children. It specifically states that selling personal data collected from children for commercial reuse "is unlikely to amount to a compelling reason for data sharing."[387]

ISSs should further refrain from sharing children's personal data if they can,

> ... reasonably foresee that the sharing could result in third parties using personal data in a manner detrimental to the child. Providers should obtain assurances from any recipients about the use of personal data and should carry out due diligence on recipients' data protection practices.[388]

10. Geolocation

Standard 10 requires that geolocation capabilities, meaning the capability to obtain data that reveals the geographical location of a user's device, should be turned off by default.

The standard notes the potential for abuse of such data and its significance in relation to the physical safety of children. It also notes the potential for use of such data to "fail to respect the child's rights under the UNCRC to privacy, freedom of association, and freedom from economic exploitation, irrespective of threats to their physical safety."[389]

In cases where there is a compelling reason for geolocation data to be turned on, an obvious sign must be provided to child user that such tracking is active and must be return to the default off setting at the end of each session. Any geolocation data that is processed also falls within the definition of location data within the Privacy and Electronic Communications Regulations

---

[387] Id.

[388] Erskine-Fox, supra note 46.

[389] ICO, *Age Appropriate Design: A Code of Practice for Online Services*, supra note 4.

(PECR),[390] and additional requirements must be met when processing such data.[391]

11. Parental Controls

Standard 11 requires ISSs that provide parental controls, which are tools that enable parents to limit or monitor their child's online activity or track their location, to make it clear to child users that such controls are in place and to notify them if they are being tracked or monitored.[392] The information provided should vary according to the child's age, for example for children under the age of nine, the information could take the form of a video or audio explaining what controls are in place and why.[393]

12. Profiling

Profiling is defined in the GDPR as:

> Any form of automated processing of personal data consisting of the use of personal data to evaluate certain aspects relating to a natural person, in particular to analyse or predict aspects concerning that natural person's performance at work, economic situation, health, personal preferences, interests, reliability, behaviour location or movements.[394]

Profiles are generated based on a user's online activity and are specifically mentioned in Recital 38 of the GDPR as an area in which children should receive specific protection. Standard 12 notes that, while profiling must be off by default, it is permissible to profile a user if consent has been obtained and privacy settings are in place.

Cookies are regulated by the PECR, which requires ISSs to inform users that cookies are being used, what they do, and why. ISSs must obtain a person's consent to store a cookie on their device.[395] The use of cookies also falls under this standard 12 if they are used for the purposes of profiling. Thus, the regulations contained in the PECR must be followed for the placement of

---

[390] Privacy and Electronic Communications (EC Directive) Regulations 2003, SI 2003/2426, https://perma.cc/4PFG-FXVT.

[391] See also *Location Data*, ICO, https://perma.cc/RG3Q-XNJH.

[392] ICO, *Age Appropriate Design: A Code of Practice for Online Services*, supra note 4, at 61.

[393] Id.

[394] GDPR art. 4(4).

[395] Privacy and Electronic Communications (EC Directive) Regulations 2003, reg. 6. See also *What are the Rules on Cookies and Similar Technologies?*, ICO, https://perma.cc/SPW5-ZXZL.

cookies, and the GDPR and the code must be followed "for the underlying processing of personal data (profiling) that the cookie supports or enables."[396]

Profiling used for behavioral advertising to fund a service that is not part of the core service the child is accessing must have a privacy setting. In cases where cookies are essential to the provision of core services, the privacy setting will not be appropriate and, provided the ISS has a lawful basis for the profiling, consent will not be required for the cookie.[397] Cookies used to profile users in order to comply with the implied age verification requirements of the GDPR or to apply the standards of the Code are considered to be essential and, provided the information is only used for these purposes, no consent is required for the cookie.

Cookies that are not essential to the service the child is accessing, or for optional, non-core services, should be subject to a privacy setting that allows the child to control the processing of their personal data, and that provides a lawful basis for any processing connected with data provided by the cookie. In this situation, if there is a lawful basis for the underlying processing, consent for the use of the cookie is not required, "as the child is specifically requesting to access part of [the ISS's] service and the cookie is strictly necessary for this purpose."[398]

In cases where profiling is lawful, the ISS is responsible for implementing measures to ensure the profiling does not suggest content inappropriate to the child user. The standards note that the ISSshould test their algorithms to assess whether the methods implemented are effective.[399] The Code states:

> If you are using children's personal data to automatically recommend content to them based on their past usage/browsing history then you have a responsibility for the recommendations you make. This applies even if the content itself is user generated. In data protection terms, you have a greater responsibility in this situation than if the child were to pro-actively search out such content themselves. This is because it is your processing of the personal data that serves the content to the child. Data protection law doesn't make you responsible for third party content but it does make you responsible for the content you serve to children who use your service, based on your use of their personal data.

---

[396] ICO, *Age Appropriate Design: A Code of Practice for Online Services*, supra note 4, at 66.
[397] Id.
[398] Id.
[399] Id. at 69.

Your general approach should be that if the content you promote or the behaviours your features encourage are obviously detrimental, or are recognised as harmful to the child, in one context (eg marketing rules, film classification, advice from official Government sources such as Chief Medical Officers' advice, PEGI ratings) then you should assume that the same type of content or behaviour is harmful in other contexts as well. Where evidence is inconclusive you should apply the same precautionary principle.[400]

13. Nudge Techniques

Standard 13 requires ISS providers to refrain from using nudge techniques—design features which lead or encourage users to follow the designer's preferred paths in the user's decision making—to:

1. Encourage children to provide personal data that is not necessary for the services they are using,
2. Obtain additional unnecessary personal data from children, or
3. Encourage them to turn off or otherwise weaken the default privacy protections.[401]

The Code notes that nudge techniques may be used for pro-privacy decisions, or to promote health and wellbeing.[402]

14. Connected Toys and Devices

Children's toys and devices that collect personal data and send it to a network connection—such as a fitness band, talking teddy bear or "hub" device—are of particular concern to the ICO. Standard 14 requires these devices to carry clear packaging and product leaflet or instructions that describes how personal data collected by the device is processed. This information should be made available to individuals prior to purchasing or setting up the device. The Code recommends that should a "just in time" notice be warranted, it should be communicated using audio messages, or by only allowing the default settings to be changed through an app that provides more information.[403]

If the seller of the product uses a third party to connect the device to the internet, the third party's responsibilities depend upon whether they process the data on the seller's behalf, or if they are a data controller. The Code notes

400 Id.
401 Id. at 72.
402 Id.
403 Id. at 78.

that sellers using a third party are still required to comply with the obligations contained in the GDPR as well as the Code and must ensure that the third parties they use do so also.[404]

15. Online Tools

Standard 15 of the Code requires ISSs to "[p]rovide prominent and accessible tools to help children exercise their data protection rights and report concerns."[405] The rights relevant to this standard are contained in Articles 15-22 of the GDPR and include the right to be informed, the right of access, the right to rectification, the right to erasure, the right to restrict processing, the right to data portability, the right to object, and rights regarding automated decision making and profiling.[406]

Standard 15 requires tools to be prominently displayed, age appropriate, and easy to use. A mechanism should be in place to allow the child user to indicate whether the request or complaint is urgent and why, along with a method to prioritize such requests or complaints. When the user submits a request or complaint to the ISS, a mechanism for tracking the progress of any request or complaint should be provided, along with information about the timelines for responding to requests.[407]

D. Enforcement and Penalties

The ICO states in the Code that data protection relating to children is a one of its regulatory priorities[408] and that it,

> ... consider[s] that the public interest in protecting children online is a significant factor weighing in the balance when considering the type of regulatory action. This means that where see harm or potential harm to children we will likely take more severe action against a company than would be the case for other types of personal data.[409]

The Code is not legally binding; however, section 127 of the DPA requires the ICO to take the Code into account when determining if an ISS has complied

---

[404] Id.

[405] Id. at 80.

[406] *Guide to the General Data Protection Regulation (GDPR): Individual Rights*, ICO, https://perma.cc/8UC8-S6NX.

[407] ICO, *Age Appropriate Design: A Code of Practice for Online Services*, supra note 4, at 83.

[408] Id. at 88.

[409] Id. at 90.

with the data protection obligations contained in the GDPR or PECR.[410] The ICO has stated that how ISSs conform to the code will "be a key measure of [their] compliance with data protection laws."[411] The ICO has stated that while it will assess any conformity to the Code with the headline standards, the Code as a whole is provided to help ISSs understand how they can implement each standard properly.[412] The ICO will monitor compliance with the Code through a series of measures including using intelligence gathering, auditing and assessment powers, and reviewing complaints.[413] ICO has stated that it will encourage conformance with the standards and will "focus[] on organisations and individuals suspected of repeated or willful misconduct or serious failure to comply with the law."[414] The ICO states:

> Where we find issues we take fair, proportionate and timely regulatory action with a view to guaranteeing that individuals' information rights are properly protected. We will take account of the size and resources of the organisation concerned, the availability of technological solutions in the marketplace and the risks to children that are inherent in the processing. We will take a proportionate and responsible approach, focusing on areas with the potential for most harm and selecting the most suitable regulatory tool.[415]

The Code notes that an ISS failing to comply with its provisions "may find it difficult to demonstrate compliance with the law and . . . may invite regulatory action."[416]

The ICO has a number of tools it can utilize to take action against organizations that fail to comply with the Code, such as issuing warnings, reprimands, stop now orders and fines of up to £17.5 million (approximately US$25 million), or 4% of a company's global turnover.[417] It has stated that the efforts an ISS has made to conform with the Code will be considered, and those that have clearly documented their approach will be more likely to be provided with time to comply. The ICO will be more likely to take formal action towards an ISS that has not taken steps to comply with the Code and has "evidence or constructive knowledge that children are likely to access [its]

---

410 Data Protection Act 2018 § 127.
411 Id. at 88.
412 Id. at 13.
413 Id. at 89.
414 ICO, *Age Appropriate Design: A Code of Practice for Online Services*, supra note 4, at 89.
415 Id.
416 Id. at 11.
417 Id.

service[s], and clear evidence of significant risk arising from the use of children's data."[418]

E. Review of the Code

The ICO must keep the Code under review. If it determines any amendments to the Code are necessary, it is under a duty to consult the Secretary of State and other appropriate parties. In addition to the duty to keep the Code under review, the ICO has stated it will review the Code a year after it comes into force to assess whether it is meeting its aims.[419]

F. Reaction to the Code

The ICO held a six-month consultation period to solicit public views on the Code.[420] Respondents to the consultation who had favorable views considered the Code was an opportunity to protect children's privacy and improve "expectations and norms for children online." Others expressed concern that the Code was too restrictive and would increase costs and discourage innovation, and that verifying the age of a child and obtaining parental consent would pose a challenge, especially in light of the international aspect of the internet.[421] Some ISS expressed concern,

> ... that the Code could reach beyond the ICO's regulatory remit for data protection, and could result in regulatory overlap, duplication or potential inconsistency and could overburden services which are already heavily regulated.[422]

III. Advertisements on Platforms Designed for Children

A. Advertising Codes

In the UK, non-broadcast advertising is industry self-regulated by the Advertising Standards Authority (ASA), which enforces advertising codes.[423] The Committee of Advertising Practice (CAP) is responsible for publishing

---

[418] Id.

[419] *Explanatory Memorandum to the Age Appropriate Design Code 2020*, supra note 24, ¶ 13.

[420] ICO, *Consultation on Age Appropriate Design: A Code of Practice for Online Services* (2019), https://perma.cc/AX8J-X23H.

[421] *Explanatory Memorandum to the Age Appropriate Design Code 2020*, supra note 24, ¶ 9.

[422] Id. ¶ 9.8.

[423] House of Commons Library, *Advertising to Children* 7(Briefing Paper #8198, Mar. 2021), https://perma.cc/D6J8-WTWR.

these codes.[424] In 2011, the role of the ASA was extended to "cover marketing communications on companies' own websites and in other third-party space under their control, such as on social networking sites."[425] This extension was done with the aim of protecting children, defined in the CAP Code as those under the age of 16 years old,[426] online.[427]

In 2017, additional guidance was provided to ensure that advertisements targeted at users under the age of 12 can be easily identified as such.[428]

The ASA "advise[s] marketers to check the audience profiles of any media they plan to advertise in, online and offline, in order to satisfy themselves that they are not at risk of targeting the wrong age groups."[429] The ASA has further stated:

> The [CAP] Code has an impact on where advertisements can be placed and the ASA has issued guidance on the placement of advertisements. There should be no ads that are age- restricted either in or around media that is obviously directed to the protected age category. This rule applied regardless of the method of targeting this ad. The rules have three key implications for different approaches to ad placement:
>
> - No age-restricted ads should appear in or around media obviously directed at the protected age category irrespective of the method of targeting.
> - Where marketing communications are directed at audiences based on data held by the marketer, media platform and/or other third party, targeting measures must be utilized to prevent the likelihood of those in the relevant protected age category from receiving them.
> - In one-to-many media [an area where the audience cannot be determined from a simple assessment], marketers must not place ads where children or children and young people are likely to make up more than 25% of the audience.

The CAP Code does not specify the type of data marketers should use to ascertain these percentages, but advises them to use data to show that over

---

424 Id.

425 Id. at 6.

426 Committee of Advertising Practice, *The CAP Code* Rule 5 (12th ed.), https://perma.cc/XM4J-NTUB.

427 House of Commons Library, *Advertising to Children*, supra note 98, at 19.

428 Committee of Advertising Practice, *Recognition of Advertising: Online Marketing to Children Under 12: Advertising Guidance*, https://perma.cc/U35T-BL6Q.

429 *Making Advertising to Children 'Child's Play'*, ASA (Nov. 26, 2020), https://perma.cc/5944-UF3P.

75% of the audience is not within the protect age range.[430] The ASA has stated that it expects marketers to use all the tools available to them, including interest-based targeting and linked external data, to ensure that ads are targeted to age-appropriate users, noting that advertisers should factor in that children may misreport their age.[431]

In addition to general rules relating to advertisements, the CAP Code contains restrictions that specifically apply to children. Sexualized imagery of anyone who looks younger than 18 years of age is prohibited;[432] any advertisement that will result in a child's physical, mental or moral harm, such as frightening imagery that in a medium likely to be seen by children, is prohibited;[433] portraying children taking part in unsafe activities is prohibited; and advertisements for age restricted products, such as alcoholic drinks, gambling products, lotteries, electronic cigarettes and dieting products or services should not be displayed, or designed to appeal to, persons under16 or under 18, depending upon the product.[434] CAP recently published additional guidance on age-restricted ads online that restrict children under the age of 16 years from being targeted with marketing communications for food or soft drinks that are high in fat, salt or sugar and from any that advertise the lottery.[435]

B. Behavioral Advertising

The ICO has stated that it acknowledges the importance of the revenue created by advertisements to the media industry and that the risks posed by behavioral advertising are lowered when advertisers apply the ASA codes.[436] The current law governing online behavioral advertising is contained in overlapping areas, including the GDPR, the PECR, the Code and the CAP Code. The ASA regulates online behavioral advertising; it requires businesses to disclose when they are collecting and using information for this purpose and to provide users the ability to opt out from providing information for this purpose. While the CAP Code regulates online behavioral advertising, it does not require user

---

[430] CAP, Media Placement Restrictions: Protecting Children and Young People: Advertising Guidance 6, https://perma.cc/HVT9-KYNR.

[431] Children: Targeting, *ASA* (Aug. 1, 2018), https://perma.cc/T2MZ-Z9J4.

[432] Committee of Advertising Practice, *The CAP Code*, supra note 101, Rule 4.8.

[433] Id. Rule 5.1.

[434] Id. See also Committee of Advertising Practice, *Age-Restricted Ads Online: Advertising Guidance* 3, https://perma.cc/6QFL-YCT6.

[435] *Children: Targeting*, ASA, supra note 106.

[436] *Explanatory Memorandum to the Age Appropriate Design Code 2020*, supra note 24, ¶ 9.8.

consent for businesses or organizations to place a cookie on a browser.[437] This area falls within the remit of the ICO and the laws contained in the GDPR and PECR, discussed in part II.C.12 above. For children, standard 12 of the Code, discussed above, further requires profiling to be turned off by default for child users, or if the age of the user cannot be established, turned off for all users.[438]

C. Enforcement

If the CAP Code is breached, the ASA has a number of tools at its disposal. It can issue an alert advising its members and media to withhold services, including access to advertising space; withdraw or withhold trading privileges, such as bulk mail discounts; requiring repeat or serious offenders to have their marketing reviewed prior to publication; and impose digital sanctions, such as the removal of a company's advertisements if it links to a page with non-compliant marketing materials.[439]

The tools available to the ICO for enforcement are detailed in part II.D above.

IV. Future Plans to Protect Children's Online Privacy

There is currently no additional legislation or policy that the government is considering to protect children's online privacy.

---

[437] What We Cover, *ASA*, https://perma.cc/T2MZ-Z9J4.

[438] *Explanatory Memorandum to the Age Appropriate Design Code 2020*, supra note 24, ¶ 10.

[439] House of Commons Library, *Advertising to Children*, supra note 98, at 16.

Chapter 3

Social Media: Tips for Foster Parents and Caregivers*

U.S. Department of Health and Human Services

While social media has changed the way the world communicates, it has also created privacy and safety concerns. This chapter briefly discusses the benefits of social media for children and youth in foster care and provides tips for parents and caregivers who want to help them use social media safely. It also provides advice for foster parents on how to responsibly use your own social media accounts.

Helping Children and Youth Use Social Media Responsibly

Social media has become a standard tool for communication and self-expression. For children and youth in foster care, it can also create normalcy by helping them connect with others in their communities and maintain relationships with friends and caregivers from previous living situations. However, children and youth in care may be particularly vulnerable to inappropriate contact, cyberbullying, or child predators when using social media, and networks and private messages may aid in communication with adults or family members who are "off limits."

Prohibiting the use of social media can be harmful to children and youth and is often unrealistic, given the widespread accessibility of computers, mobile devices, and the internet. Instead, foster parents should provide

* This is an edited, reformatted and augmented version of Children's Bureau/ACYF/ACF/HHS publication, dated October 2022.

In: Keeping Our Children Safe Online
Editor: Joyce B. Dew
ISBN: 979-8-88697-659-5

guidance and boundaries to help them use social media safely and responsibly. Here are some tips to help foster parents and caregivers guide social media use for the children and youth in their care.

Understand How Children and Youth Use Social Media

- *Discuss social media with children and youth.* Ask the children or youth in your care how they use social media and private messaging apps and get an understanding of why it's important to them. Share and discuss Child Welfare Information Gateway's Social Media: Tips for Youth in Foster Care[1].
- *Learn about social media apps.* New social media tools are released frequently and children and youth are often quick to adopt them. Keep abreast of current technology and best practices for the most popular social media apps that young people of various age groups are using today. (See the Popular Teen Apps Parents and Teachers Need to Know[2] section of the Smart Social website.)
- *Be aware of online gaming risks.* Online games can be unsafe, as players often interact with others on gaming platforms. Be aware of the kind of games your child or youth plays and discuss the risks. Let them know that they should avoid posting pictures of themselves or giving personal information while playing online games, and that they can come to you if they are being harassed or bullied. (Learn more at Internet Matters' Online Gaming Advice Hub[3].)
- *Understand their language.* Children and youth may use slang, hashtags, and emoji in their online communications. Understand that young people communicate in a language different from yours. (See Smart Social's Teen Slang, Emojis, & Hashtags Parents Need to Know [The Ultimate List][4] to learn more.)

---

[1] https://www.childwelfare.gov/pubs/smtips-youth/.
[2] https://smartsocial.com/app-guide-parents-teachers.
[3] https://www.internetmatters.org/resources/online-gaming-advice/.
[4] https://smartsocial.com/teen-slang-emojis-hashtags-list.

Set and Reinforce Social Media Guidelines

- *Talk with your child's caseworker.* Familiarize yourself with your child welfare agency's social media policies. Ask about safety needs and concerns that may affect your child's use of social media and whether they have had issues with social media use in the past.
- *Set house rules.* Set social media rules early and, when possible, in collaboration with children and youth. Ensure that these rules align with agency guidelines and foster youth rights and be prepared to answer questions why the rules exist. (Find sample media agreements for different age groups on the Family Contracts & Pledges[5] section of the Connect Safely website.)
- *Coordinate with your child or youth's birth relatives.* Setting up new social media accounts and establishing usage rules might require consent or input from a young person's birth family. Approach your caseworker first for guidance and collaborate with birth relatives when appropriate. (For more information, see Information Gateway's Partnering With Birth Parents to Promote Reunification[6].)
- *Be prepared to deal with mistakes.* When a child or youth slips up and doesn't follow guidelines, approach the situation as a teachable moment and calmly work together on what to do next.

Help Safeguard Child and Youth Privacy

- *Teach children and youth about keeping their personal information private.* Advise children and youth in foster care not to reveal their full name, address, school name, phone number, or other identifying information on social media, and caution them against posting photos that reveal these types of details (e.g., school logos and mascots). (Find internet privacy lessons for a range of age groups at Common Sense Education's 23 Great Lesson Plans for Internet Safety[7].)
- *Set strict privacy settings.* Use privacy settings to help children and youth limit who can find them online, which posts or photos are visible, and who has contact permissions. (For information on privacy

[5] https://www.connectsafely.org/contracts/.
[6] https://www.childwelfare.gov/pubs/factsheets-families-partnerships/.
[7] https://www.commonsense.org/education/articles/23-great-lesson-plans-for-internet-safety.

settings for various apps, see the Social Media Privacy Guides[8] section of the Internet Matters website.)

- *Conduct searches.* Every so often, search a child or youth's name and address to see what information or tagged photos are publicly available.

Address Risky or Harmful Social Media Activities

- *Explain the need to avoid explicit content.* Make sure youth understand that online, not everyone is who they say they are. Advise youth to avoid sharing intimate photos and messaging about sex online, regardless of their relationship with a person. (Read more about protecting youth with "Tips for Dealing with Teen Sexting"[9] by Connect Safely.)
- *Discuss cyberbullying.* Warn children and youth not to send, forward, or respond to mean or embarrassing messages or pictures. Help youth document, block, and report bullying if needed. (To learn more, see "Parent's Guide to Cyberbullying"[10] by Connect Safely.)
- *Check in on your child or youth's mental health.* Social media can trigger negative feelings, such as anxiety or depression. From time to time, ask children and youth if they ever see things on social media that upset them, and encourage them to limit their use to social media spaces where they feel supported. (See Common Sense Media's "How to Help Teens Manage the Effects of Social Media on Their Mental Health"[11] to learn more.)
- *Monitor use.* Place computers in a shared area and keep track of mobile device use. Know what type of social media your children and youth use and the amount of time they are spending on social media apps. Consider asking them for passwords and permission to let a trusted adult connect with them on their social media pages. However, try to balance monitoring with respecting their privacy. Installing an online monitoring program can help you watch for inappropriate use.

---

[8] https://www.internetmatters.org/parental-controls/social-media/.
[9] https://www.connectsafely.org/tips-for-dealing-with-teen-sexting/.
[10] https://www.connectsafely.org/cyberbullying/.
[11] https://www.commonsensemedia.org/articles/how-to-help-teens-manage-the-effects-of-social-media-on-their-mental-health.

(For more information, see the Guide to Monitoring Apps[12] section of the Internet Matters website.)

- *Watch for activity on risky sites.* Be aware of risky apps that have inappropriate or unmoderated content and set boundaries with children and youth if you notice them using these apps. (For a list of risky apps, see the Popular Teen Apps Parents and Teachers Need to Know[13] section of the Smart Social website.)
- *Keep lines of communication open.* Encourage children and youth to let you know if an exchange makes them uncomfortable, if someone is sending them inappropriate photos, or if anyone asks to meet them in person. Appreciate their participation in their online communities and show interest in their friends. (To learn more, see "How to Connect with Your Teen about Smart & Safe Media Use"[14] by the American Academy of Pediatrics.)

Using Social Media Responsibly as a Foster Parent or Caregiver

You may wish to use social media for support and to share information with other foster parents and caregivers. If permitted by the agency, you can also use social networks to keep in touch with your child' birth relatives. Here are some tips for using social media responsibly when you are caring for a foster child or youth.

- *Talk with your caseworker about agency policies.* Ask about guidelines for your social media communication with your child or youth's birth relatives, other foster parents and caregivers, and child welfare agency staff. Find out whether there are specific considerations for the children or youth in your care.
- *Get permission from the agency and your child or youth before posting family pictures that include children in care.* Agencies might have guidelines around posting photos, such as concealing identifying

---

[12] https://www.internetmatters.org/resources/monitoring-apps-parents-guide/.

[13] https://smartsocial.com/app-guide-parents-teachers.

[14] https://www.healthychildren.org/English/family-life/Media/Pages/Points-to-Make-With-Your-Teen-About-Media.aspx.

information with emojis or other editing features. It's important to ensure that photos do not create privacy or safety risks.

- *Avoid searching for a child or youth's birth relatives.* When you connect with birth relatives online, you might expose yourself to information that raises concerns or complicates your dynamic. Caseworkers likely can't respond to information found on social media, so it's best to avoid birth relatives' pages.
- *Protect privacy and confidentiality.* Do not identify a child or youth as a foster child or post their full name or address on a social media network. Never discuss case information in an online forum. (Learn more at "How to Protect My Foster Child on Social Media"[15] on the Embrella website.)
- *Be aware that photos may reveal a child or youth's location.* Some smartphone photos and network services (such as the location features on Facebook and Instagram) provide GPS information. Learn how to manage location services on your smartphone or turn them off completely. (See more information about these settings at "How to Limit Location Tracking on Your Phone"[16] by Consumer Reports.)
- *Think before you post.* Be sensitive to how messages may be interpreted by others, including your child or youth's birth relatives and agency staff.

For additional resources on social media safety in foster care arrangements, see the Social Media Safety[17] section of the Information Gateway website.

Suggested Citation

Child Welfare Information Gateway. (2022). *Social media: Tips for foster parents and caregivers.* U.S. Department of Health and Human Services, Administration for Children and Families, Children's Bureau[18].

---

[15] http://foster-adoptive-kinship-family-services-nj.org/how-to-protect-my-foster-child-on-social-media/.

[16] https://www.consumerreports.org/privacy/how-to-turn-off-location-services-on-your-smartphone-a8219252827/.

[17] https://www.childwelfare.gov/topics/management/workforce/socialmedia/safety/.

[18] https://www.childwelfare.gov/pubs/smtips-parent/.

Index

A

B

D

E

I

L

M

N

O

P

Q

R

S

T